ALEXANDER HAMILTON

ALEXANDER HAMILTON

America's Forgotten Founder

Joseph A. Murray

Algora Publishing
New York

© 2007 by Algora Publishing.
All Rights Reserved
www.algora.com

No portion of this book (beyond what is permitted by
Sections 107 or 108 of the United States Copyright Act of 1976)
may be reproduced by any process, stored in a retrieval system,
or transmitted in any form, or by any means, without the
express written permission of the publisher.
ISBN-13: 978-0-87586-500-3 (trade paper)
ISBN-13: 978-0-87586-501-0 (hard cover)
ISBN-13: 978-0-87586-502-7 (ebook)

Library of Congress Cataloging-in-Publication Data —

Murray, Joseph A., 1935-
Alexander Hamilton : America's forgotten founder / Joseph A. Murray.
    p. cm.
Includes bibliographical references and index.
    ISBN 978-0-87586-500-3 (soft: alk. paper) — ISBN 978-0-87586-501-0 (hard: alk.
paper) — ISBN 978-0-87586-502-7 (ebook: alk. paper) 1. Hamilton, Alexander, 1757-1804.
2. Hamilton, Alexander, 1757-1804—Influence. 3. Statesmen—United States—Biography.
4. United States—Politics and government—1783-1809. I. Title.

    E302.6.H2M88 2007
    973.4092—dc22
    [B]
                        2006036901

Front Cover:
Alexander Hamilton by John Trumbull © Archivo Iconografico, S.A./CORBIS
Date Created: 1806

Printed in the United States

To my wife, JoAnn, without whose understanding, support and tolerance this book could not have been written.

TABLE OF CONTENTS

Preface

Alexander Hamilton lived in the most challenging period of American history, when its institutions were being formed and its direction was being determined. He produced a legacy of the strongest government and national economy in the world. Born on a remote island in the West Indies, Hamilton entered America when he was not yet sixteen years of age, at a time when the colonies were torn by political unrest over their oppressive treatment at the hands of the British Parliament.

In three years, while Hamilton was acquiring an education, the political unrest with Great Britain transitioned into a crisis that finally ignited at Lexington and Concord. With his education interrupted by the Revolution, Hamilton involved himself in the struggle for independence by joining New York's militia as a captain of artillery. He had the good fortune to be offered a position on the staff of General Washington, which began a relationship that was to have a lasting and beneficial effect on the formation and development of the United States government. Hamilton continued his education in stolen moments during the Revolution by reading the works of classical writers on politics, law and economic principles. He distinguished himself during the war, both on the field of battle and in his administrative role as Washington's chief aide-de-camp. In this latter position Hamilton became acquainted with many of the important military and political leaders of the period, establishing relationships that would be enhanced over the years.

This book contains a brief coverage of the important events of the era including the Revolution, the struggle to forge a viable nation under the the Articles of Confederation, the difficulties of the Constitutional Convention and ratification process and the development of the republican form of government under the new Constitution. Alexander Hamilton was ubiquitous in all of these events and he exerted a defining influence in the development of the new government. Although he had very little formal education, his reading of Pufendorf, Locke, Montesquieu, Grotius and Blackstone provided him with an understanding of the history and theory of politics and of the law which equipped him to write the major part of the *Federalist Papers*, that widely accepted and lasting guide to understanding the Constitution. The writings of Adam Smith and David Hume aided his own genius in the formation of national fiscal policies that gave stability and respectability to the emerging government.

At the conclusion of the revolution, self-styled patriots (encouraged by the state of New York) were taking retribution against the Tories by seizing their properties and businesses. Hamilton argued against the practice, even defending Tories in lawsuits, recognizing that the wealth and skills possessed by the Tories would be invaluable in the reconstruction of the country. He argued that if America were to grow large and strong it would have to be done through the labor of immigrants and that the country had to demonstrate to the world that it was strong enough to grow and to flourish while tolerating internal opposition.

Hamilton was among those who feared that the loose union of states under the Confederation would not survive as a political entity and would forever be an enticement to foreign intervention; he strongly promoted the Philadelphia Convention, the creation of a new Constitution and the formation of strong central government. As Secretary of the Treasury, Hamilton believed that a strong financial system was essential, first to gain international respect and, second, to encourage a vigorous American economy. He based his financial plan on the consolidation of the national debt and the adoption of a system of revenue collection to service and retire that debt. The national bank that was chartered under his aegis was the keystone to his financial plan, serving to stabilize the country's monetary system, to liquidate the national debt through individual investments and to serve as the transactional institution for handling the government's monies. At the direction of Congress, Hamilton set the standards for the formation of the national mint.

Hamilton was subject to the frailties of his humanity and paid a severe price for his human weaknesses. He engaged in an extra-marital affair with a woman who, in collusion with her husband, had set out to destroy him politically. He and his family had to endure the torment of having this affair made public, years after its termination. When confronted with a public accusation of this indiscretion he did not attempt to deny it or to cover it up, but acknowledged his wrongdoing; he also exposed the political calumny of his opponents who had engineered the scandal.

One of Hamilton's weaknesses was his low threshold of tolerance for personal affronts or attacks on his character. While Secretary of the Treasury, Hamilton experienced many attacks on his plan for national financial recovery by the Jeffersonian Republicans, who viewed America as having its greatest national potential as an agrarian society, where ultimate sovereignty rested in the individual states. The differing views of Hamiltonian Federalists and Jeffersonian Republicans were to persist, grow rancorous and eventually threaten the survival of the country in the Civil War. Thomas Jefferson and his supporters saw in the complexities of Hamilton's financial plan ideal opportunities for their own political gain by pandering to their constituents — who generally were men unschooled in such arcane financial details. Hamilton did not possess the politician's knack for tactfully handling disputes with political opponents. He formed opinions carefully but, once they were formed, he was blunt in expressing his disapproval of political opponents or their positions. His opposition to the defects and tactics of one of these opponents, Aaron Burr, eventually led to the pistol duel that ended Hamilton's life.

CHAPTER 1. HAMILTON'S YOUTH

Alexander Hamilton was born into an illegitimate union on the remote Leeward Island of Nevis in the West Indies in January 11, 1757. Christopher Columbus first discovered the island in 1493 on his second voyage to the New World. Columbus listed it as being uninhabited. He mistook a cloud hanging over the extinct volcanic crater as snow and named the island Las Nieves, that is "snow," in Spanish.[1] Taken from the Spanish by the British, the island was first settled in 1628 by French Huguenots seeking refuge from the Catholic Louis XIV.[2]

The settlements in the West Indies were originally established as colonies of England, France, Spain, The Netherlands and Denmark, primarily for their potential agricultural production. During the 1640s it was discovered that the climate on many of the islands in the "Caribees" was ideally suited for the growing of sugar cane. Starter plants were imported from Brazil and the West Indies rapidly took on a new importance in the world, supplying the needed sweetener for the newly discovered treats of chocolate, tea and coffee.

Sugar plantations offered a new bonanza where a grower conceivably could become wealthy within the period of a few years — provided the weather and warring rivalries between colonizing nations permitted, and if

1 Randall, Willard S., *Alexander Hamilton — A Life*, Harper-Collins, New York, 2003, 10
2 Dunn, R. S., *Sugar & Slaves — The Rise of the Planter Class in the English East Indies 1624-1713*, University of North Carolina Press, 1972, Chapel Hill, xiii

the essential labor was available. The backbreaking labor involved in sugar farming, the often-hostile weather, and insect-borne diseases prompted the plantation owners to seek a plentiful supply of cheap, expendable labor. The importation of great numbers of slaves from the Guinea coast of Africa solved this labor problem and large numbers of English and French planters realized their ambition of acquiring incredible wealth. Many others fell prey to the weather, poor management, insufficient initial capital and the near constant clash with armed invaders. Drought was a serious problem to sugar growing. Tropical storms and hurricanes were feared above all else. In the islands an afternoon storm would often deluge one plantation and completely miss a neighboring one.[3] A hurricane often decimated a plantation, taking all of the crops, the buildings, the presses, families, slaves and animals. Few sugar planters were able to recover from such devastation. If the plantation owner had made his fortune before the destruction of a hurricane, he would often sell out and move back to England; otherwise, a hurricane meant financial ruin.

Success in establishing a sugar plantation required a large investment. The largest single capital expense was the purchase of slaves, one slave being required for each acre of cane production. The tropical heat, hard work and the ravages of tropical fever limited the expected lifetime of slaves to a few years, a fact which necessitated planned replacement. Those who entered the sugar growing enterprise with a small investment, hoping to grow through the re-investment of each year's profits, soon encountered unforeseen expenses that could only be met by incurring onerous mortgages. Eventually their indebtedness grew beyond any possibility of repayment and they lost their plantations.

The opportunity for sudden riches, the social debasement of the slave trade, and the need for legitimate supply and support businesses to support sugar production, attracted both the savory and unsavory to the West Indies. The furious rush to riches, the despair of failure, the freedom of the bold and raw culture of the islands magnified the strengths and weaknesses of many who came to this new world.

Records on the life of Alexander's father, James Hamilton, are scanty. He migrated to the West Indies from Scotland, where he had been born as the fourth son of Alexander and Elizabeth Hamilton in about 1718. Alexander

---

3 Flexner, James, *The Young Hamilton*, Little, Brown & Co., Boston, 1978, 11

reigned over the lesser branch of the ducal family of Hamilton. They resided in Stevenson Parish in the county Ayreshire. The family home, named *The Grange*, stood on a lowlands estate suitable for raising sheep. The elder Alexander owned considerable income property. His wife, the former Elizabeth Pollock, brought with her a dowry of some £41,000 when they married.[4]

That James was the fourth son of the family effectively disqualified him from any share in the family fortunes, as his elder brothers would have inherited all of the considerable family fortune through the British laws of primogeniture. It was usual in such families for later sons to be provided secure futures through an arranged career in church, government or in the military. Proper marriage into well-to-do families without male heirs was another avenue to protect the younger sons of affluent families.[5] History is silent on the reason James was not afforded any of these opportunities in life. Whether from lack of talent or ambition, James made little of his life and drifted to the West Indies in search of easy riches in the sugar growing business. He does not appear to have been a man gifted in learned skills, native intelligence or grit; once in the islands he seems to have drifted from one menial employment to another until finally he became overwhelmed by the reality of the life he had made and he descended into drink.

Hamilton's mother was born Rachael Fawcett, the daughter of physician John Fawcett in 1730. Rachael's sister, Ann, had been born about 1714. Rachael and Ann were the only survivors of seven children born to this couple. John managed a successful sugar plantation on Nevis. The family's time was split between the plantation, where they maintained a work force of scores of slaves, and the capital city of Charlestown, where they owned a fine stone house overlooking the sea. The Fawcett home was not to be a happy one. John was considerably older than Mary and whether for this or other unknown reasons the marriage was very contentious. In 1741 when Rachael was barely eleven years old, her mother won an *Agreement of Separate Maintenance*. Since Mary had brought a dowry into the marriage, in this settlement she was entitled to a one-third share of her husband's net worth. She agreed to receive an annual income of some £53 plus her share of her husband's real estate and slaves. The older daughter, Ann, had married a successful planter, James Lytton, while Rachael was still a small child. Rachael and James

4 Flexner, *The Young Hamilton*, 16
5 Ibid., 17

Lytton originally had a plantation on the island of Nevis; that was destroyed by a hurricane and they moved to the Danish possession of St. Croix. Therefore, when Mary Fawcett obtained her legal separation from John Fawcett, she and her younger daughter moved to St. Croix and lived with the Lyttons. Barely four years later, in 1745, John Fawcett died and willed his entire estate to his daughter Rachael. His older daughter, Ann, was not mentioned in the will, presumably because she was comfortably settled in her marriage. Since Rachael was, at this time, only sixteen years of age, her mother controlled her bequest and used it in a vain effort to attract another husband for herself. Being still a minor, Rachael was a liability to her mother's matrimonial efforts. To remove this obstacle to her own happiness, Mary concentrated in seeking to arrange a comfortable marriage for her daughter.[6]

Thus at an early age Rachael was pushed by her mother into marrying Johann Michael Levien, a sometimes merchant and would-be plantation owner ne'er-do-well. Within his first year as a sugar planter Levien had failed and the plantation was sold at auction. In an attempt to avoid regression to the role of shopkeeper he purchased a cotton plantation that was only half the acreage of the sugar plantation. His efforts at managing a cotton plantation, which had the dubious name of *Contentment,* met the same disappointing end as did his sugar enterprise. At *Contentment* the Leviens' only surviving child, Peter, was born in 1746. From there Levien descended through a series of less promising occupations. Rachael had entered the marriage to Levien, twenty-two years her senior, with a substantial inheritance from her father. In a very short time Levien managed to squander this money. With each debt-driven demotion he slid into smaller houses, dropped rungs on the social ladder and became more and more impoverished. These difficulties added nothing to an already strained marriage. Frustrated by his own financial failures, he began to abuse his wife.

Eventually Rachael left him. Levien retaliated by having her jailed in Christiansted, charging that she had abandoned her wifely duties. According to the precepts of Danish law at the time, in order for Levien to place Rachael in jail he had to charge that she had been "twice guilty of adultery" and that he no longer lived with her. After she had been jailed for some time, Levien had her released, hoping that she would return to his home and "that every-

---

6 Ramsing, H. V. *Birth and Parenting of Alexander Hamilton*, Lidskript, Copenhagen, 1939 (S. Vahl, translator), 3

thing would change for the better and that she, as a wedded wife, would change her unholy way of life and as is meet and proper live with him."[7] Instead, Rachael went off to Nevis to live with her mother, never to see her firstborn son, Peter, again.

When Rachael returned to Nevis in 1750 she met and began an intimate relationship with James Hamilton. During their fifteen-year union James and Rachael had two sons, James and Alexander, two years younger. A church record from October 1758, on the Danish island of St. Eustatius, when young Alexander was less than two years of age, shows that "John Hamilton and his wife Rachael Hamilton" stood as godparents of an infant's baptism. In this instance at least they were passing themselves off as a properly married couple.[8]

In early 1759, Rachael's legitimate husband, John Michael Levien, filed divorce proceedings in the matrimonial court on St. Croix. The official charging document reiterated Levien's conduct of some nine years earlier where he had Rachael imprisoned for marital infidelity. It went on to state that, rather than use that opportunity to reform her lifestyle, she had "shown herself to be shameless, rude and ungodly" and had "completely forgotten her duty and let her husband and child alone and instead gave herself up to whoring with everyone" and that she had had several illegitimate children from her whoredom. Rachael was summoned to St. Croix to answer these charges. An examination was to be made of her evidence along with that of other witnesses. These specific charges were never refuted because Rachael, if she received notice of the summons at all, must have reasoned that she was likely not to fare well in such an examination and may indeed have suffered an extended prison sentence. It was more prudent to ignore the summons and not contest the charges. Given her failure to present herself to the court for examination, it was ruled that her silence proved the case against her. The marriage was dissolved. Rachael was allowed "no rights whatsoever as wife to either [Levien's] person or means," Neither Rachael nor her illegitimate children would have any claim to Levien's possessions. He was free to re-marry if he chose — but Rachael was not.[9]

Unable by law to marry, Rachael and James continued to live together and to jointly raise their sons Alexander and James. Although her two sons

7 Randall, *Alexander Hamilton — A Life*, 14
8 Ibid., 17
9 Ibid., 19

were not eligible for public education because of the illegitimacy of their birth, Rachael did send Alexander to a Hebrew school on Nevis when he was five years old. He had earlier learned to read and write in French at home and he learned some Hebrew at the school, and could recite the Decalogue in Hebrew.

In his later years Hamilton wrote of his life in this contentious family, "It's a dog's life when two dissonant tempers meet."[10] Alexander's father finally abandoned the family when the younger Hamilton boy was eight years old. They never met again, although they did correspond intermittently through the years until James' death at age eighty-one in 1799. As late as 1783, Alexander wrote to his brother, "What has become of our father? It is an age since I have heard from him. Perhaps, alas! He is no more and I shall not have the pleasing opportunity of contributing to render the close of his life more happy than the progress of it."[11]

After being abandoned on St. Croix by James Hamilton, Rachael determined to make a better life for herself and her two sons than they had endured under James' support. She established a store in Christiansted where she sold provisions and other supplies to plantations on St. Croix. She obtained her merchandise from the island shippers of Dipnall (her landlord), and from Beckman & Cruger. Alexander worked in his mother's store and clerked for the firm of Beckman & Cruger, starting from the age of about eight. Alexander's brother James seems to have been apprenticed out to a carpenter, Thomas McNobeny, who taught him the trade he pursued his entire life.[12] Alexander was more interested in the business his mother was conducting and in his employer's shipping firm. He eagerly learned all he could of accounting practices and the way the businesses were run. Between her store and the income from hiring out at least three slaves, Rachael was successful in providing better for the family than James had done.

In February 1768, when Alexander was eleven years old, Rachael took ill of a fever and died. James and Peter Lytton, the husband and son of Rachael's sister, Ann, took custody of the boys.[13] Since Rachael died in testate her property was gathered, inventoried and auctioned off. James Lytton told the pro-

10 Flexner, *The Young Hamilton*, 21
11 Syrett (ed.), *Papers of Alexander Hamilton*, Vol. III, Columbia University Press, New York, 1962, 617
12 Ramsing, *The Birth and Parentage of Alexander Hamilton*, 29
13 Flexner, *The Young Hamilton*, 32

bate judge that the boys' ages in 1768 were fifteen and thirteen years of ages, respectively. This testimony would place Alexander's birth in the year 1755. In later life Alexander stated he had been born in 1757. Whatever the source of this inconsistency, it is assumed both statements were made in good faith and that it is more likely that Alexander would have known his correct age than might a remote uncle by marriage.

Rachael possessed some thirty-four books that were auctioned along with the rest of her possessions. Peter Lytton bought these books and gave them to Alexander. It is likely that they formed the bulk of his education to that point. The titles of these books are unknown although from some of Hamilton's early writing it has been conjectured that the works of Pope and Machiavelli were included.[14]

It is speculated that, upon the death of Rachael, James went to live with his master carpenter. Alexander was cared for by the family of his boyhood friend, Edward Stevens. Edward's father, Thomas Stevens, was a partner in a mercantile trading company on St. Croix. Alexander had full employment in the Beckman & Cruger trading company and found no further opportunity for formalized education while in the West Indies. Certainly the library of thirty-four books that he received from his mother's estate through the largesse of his cousin, Peter Lytton, formed his early education.

While at the Stevens's and with the help of his older friend, Edward (Ned), Hamilton delved into mathematics and chemistry. Together the boys dreamed of becoming physicians. In later years Hamilton told his children that the experience he gained through his clerical apprenticeship at Cruger's firm formed the most substantial part of his education. His daily experiences in overseeing the loading and unloading of ships, the selling of goods and taking orders for goods to be purchased, as well as in observing business practices from his high stool in the countinghouse, he learned to be at ease with financial matters and interactions with peers, subordinates and superiors.

Hamilton's job as apprentice clerk required him to know the island of St. Croix intimately, to know its population, its crops and harvesting schedules and the material needs of the population. He needed to understand the dynamics of the slave industry; how many slaves were engaged in sugar production, what food and clothing needs they had, and how many might be expected to perish from the grueling labor, the oppressive heat, the fever and

14 Mitchell, Broadus, *Alexander Hamilton — Youth to Maturity*, Macmillan, New York, 1962, 17

the harsh discipline. He needed to learn where the material needs of the island could be obtained, what ships plied those routes, which ships' captains
could be relied upon and which had their own less reliable agendas. He had
to understand the politics that affected shipping — what international con-
flicts might deter free shipping and between which ports. It was important
to understand where piracy was a threat and whether it made more business sense to avoid those areas or to equip their ships for self-defense. If the
decision was to equip the merchant vessels against piracy, that decision had
to be predicated on the knowledge that the cost of the munitions could be
amortized by increased prices. Hamilton threw himself into these learning
experiences with enthusiasm. In the countinghouse he learned the practiced
accounting procedures, the rules of credit, the strategies of the most profitable buying and the tactics for minimizing risk. These learning experiences
awakened and challenged his native genius. His quick learning and innova-
tive applications of the principles he was taught made a striking impression
on his employer, Nicholas Cruger, and on the many merchants, ship captains
and influential customers with whom he came in contact.

As an apprentice clerk Hamilton participated in the slave trade. He assisted Cruger in determining the quantity of replacement slaves that would
be needed on the sugar plantations and cotton fields of St. Croix. When the
captives were brought in for auction Hamilton observed their condition; as
a rule they were much the worse for the rough voyage, poorly fed and in despair. Before being placed for auction they would be rubbed down with oil
to make them appear sleek and fit. In 1772, at the age of fifteen, Hamilton was
assigned to assist in the sale of a shipload of some 250 slaves from Africa's
Gold Coast consigned to the Cruger Trading Company. Cruger himself had
described this particular cargo of slaves as "very indifferent indeed, sickly
and thin." At auction they brought an average price of £30, as recorded by
Hamilton.[15] He noted this was less than would be paid for one good mule
from the Spanish Main. Hamilton reluctantly participated in this unseemly
aspect of his employer's business. He learned to function with and around
the wealthy planters who purchased the slaves. On St. Croix, he observed
the gulf between the opulent lifestyle of the planters and the dismal life of
the slaves who produced the wealth. He developed a sense of moral repug-

15 Flexner, *The Young Hamilton*, 38 — 39

nance of the institution of slavery and in later life he was an outspoken opponent of slavery.[16]

Hamilton's close friendship with Edward Stevens had buoyed him up during four tragic years in Alexander's life. The generosity of the Stevens family provided Alexander with a more stable home life than he had ever before experienced. Ned left St. Croix nearly a year after Hamilton's mother's death and traveled some fifteen hundred miles to New York to attend preparatory school prior to entering pre-medical schooling at King's College there. That their friendship was both deep and meaningful is evidenced in Stevens' reminiscence in later life, when he recalled their parting, saying that they renewed "those vows of eternal friendship which we have so often mutually exchanged."[17]

Late in the year 1769 Hamilton received a letter from young Stevens advising him of a visit home which Ned was planning. In a reply dated November 11, 1769, Hamilton shared his view of his own current position and of his aspirations for grander opportunities, "though [I] doubt whether I shall be present or not, for to confess my weakness, Ned, my ambitions are [so] prevalent that I contemn [sic] the groveling and condition of a clerk or the like, to which my fortune, etc., condemns me, and would willingly risk my life, though not my character, to exalt my station."[18] It can only be speculated whether he was feeling a bit envious of his friend's opportunity to study abroad or had some sense that he too would find an opportunity to break out of the small island world.

Alexander's clerical stock in Cruger's counting house increased in the years following Rachael's death. By August of 1771 evidence exists in the firm's records of business letters in his handwriting. In mid-October of that year Cruger took ill and had to travel to New York for medical treatment where he remained until March of 1772. During the five months of Cruger's absence, Hamilton, though barely fifteen, conducted the business of the trading company. Nicholas Cruger had joined in limited partnership with two other men for the building of a trading vessel they named *Thunderbolt*. At the time that Cruger fell ill he had not as yet seen this new ship. It made its first visit to St. Croix about a month after Nicholas left for New York. Hamilton received cargo shipped to St. Croix from New York; made disposition

16 Randall, *Alexander Hamilton, - A Life*, 25 - 26
17 Syrett, *Papers of Alexander Hamilton*, Vol. I, 369
18 Ibid., 4

of the cargo as to what was to debark at St. Croix and what was to be assigned to another business in Curacao. He made arrangements for shipping the island exports of sugar, muscovado and rum. He instructed the ship's captain as to the cargo he would acquire according to the projected needs of the plantation owners. Ample evidence exists that Hamilton did a credible and profitable job of conducting the business of the trading company in Cruger's absence.

Hamilton wrote a letter to the *Thunderbolt's* captain, Capt. William Newton, directing him to obtain an urgently needed supply of mules from the Spanish Main. Hamilton ordered, "I desire you will proceed immediately to Curacao." Instructions were specific regarding the need to make three trips between the Spanish Main and St. Croix to obtain the quantity of mules necessary for the sugar harvest. Newton was directed to proceed to the Spanish Main, purchase the best quality of mules and to bring "as many as your vessel can conveniently contain.... Remember you are to make three trips this season and unless you are very diligent, you will be too late as our crops will be early in."[19]

While awaiting the *Thunderbolt's* return, Hamilton picked up the reins of the rest of the business of the Cruger Trading Company. Conducting unfinished business and initiating new transactions, he drafted a memorandum to his employer to keep him fully informed. He reported that he had had a bout of illness himself but was back on the job. He had "sold about 30 bbls of flour and Collected a little more money from different people."[20] He gave the bad news as well as the good: "Your Philadelphia flour [presumably that previously ordered by Nicholas] is ... of a most swarthy complexion and withal very untractable; the Bakers complain that they cannot by any means get it to rise." He goes on to note that he observed a kind of worm about the surface of the flour and concluded that the flour was quite old when it was shipped. On his own authority he marked the price of the stale flour down so that he could sell it without his employer taking a loss.[21]

His main focus was on the *Thunderbolt* and whether Capt. Newton would obtain the quantities of mules necessary for cane harvest, lest Cruger's reputation for reliability suffer under his management. The *Thunderbolt* had sailed

19 Syrett, *Papers of Alexander Hamilton*, Vol. I 14; Hamilton, John C. (ed.), *The Works of Alexander Hamilton*, John Trow, Printer, New York, 1850, Vol. I, 3
20 Syrett, *Papers of Alexander Hamilton*, Vol. I, 11 - 12
21 Ibid., 11

in mid-November. Finally on January 29, 1772 she docked once more at St. Croix. To Hamilton's great dismay what he found on board were forty-one near skeletons of mules. Hamilton's report states,

> A worse parcel of mules never was seen. She took in at first forty-eight and lost seven on the passage. I got all that were able to walk to pasture in number thirty-three. The other eight could hardly stand for two minutes together, and in spite of the greatest care, four of them are now in limbo....[22]

The late delivery was a result of light winds that slowed the ship on its way. Capt. Newton was reminded of the importance of completing two additional voyages for mules; Hamilton gave him specific instructions concerning the amount of feed to procure against the event of continued calm seas. On this second voyage Capt. Newton came back with fifty mules in such good condition that they brought a top price of £36 per head on the average. Since there was not time enough for a third trip for more mules, the *Thunderbolt* was loaded with a cargo of sugar and cotton bound for New York.[23]

Hamilton also discharged the company lawyer for misusing company funds. When Cruger returned to the business in March 1772 he wrote to Hans Buus, the attorney subsequently retained by Alexander Hamilton, to say that he approved of Hamilton's action to place all legal matters into his hands. He was openly critical of the discharged attorney, Mr. Hassells, "who I am confident has been very neglectful in them, and trifled away a good deal of money to no purpose."[24]

Following the loss of both parents, Hamilton benefited from the positive influence of both his employer, Nicholas Cruger, and another man on St. Croix, the Presbyterian minister Dr. Hugh Knox. In the summer of 1771 Knox had been offered the post of pastor of the Presbyterian Church on St. Croix, where he met the young Hamilton. Knox preached a brand of religious fundamentalism that must have resonated in Hamilton's mind that was so inherently geared to structured and well-ordered reasoning. The library that Knox brought with him offered Hamilton broad new vistas of ideas and knowledge. Finally, here was a man of significant intellect, a source of answers, and ready to engage in intellectual pursuits. Knox's friendship awak-

---

22 Ibid., 27
23 Mitchell, *Alexander Hamilton — Youth to Maturity*, 26 - 27
24 Flexner, *The Young Hamilton*, 44

ened in Hamilton a religious fervor, stimulated his intellectual development and gave direction to his powers of expression.

At this time Hamilton was fifteen years old. Cruger and Knox were both teachers and counselors to Hamilton and they were impressed by his quick learning and by the genius displayed in his application of any new knowledge.

In late summer of 1772 a powerful hurricane struck St. Croix. It battered the island for six hours; tides rose fourteen feet above their normal range and all of the ships in the harbor were torn from their moorings and tossed up on the shore. The crops of the island were entirely destroyed. At a public meeting Rev. Knox gave a sermon and charged the people to take the storm as God's testimony against the lax morals prevalent on the island.[25]

Hamilton went home and summarized his impressions of the storm and his emotional and spiritual reaction to it in a letter to his father. Prior to sending the letter, he asked Hugh Knox to read it. Impressed, Knox made a copy and, with Hamilton's reluctant permission, offered it to the Royal Danish–American Gazette, where it appeared on October 3.

> It began about dusk, at North and raged very violently till ten o'clock. Then ensued a sudden and unexpected interval, which lasted about an hour. Meanwhile the wind was shifting round to the South West point, from whence it returned with redoubled fury and continued so 'til near three o'clock in the morning. Good God! What horror and destruction. Its impossible for me to describe or you to form any idea of it. It seemed as if a total dissolution of nature was taking place. The roaring of the sea and wind, fiery meteors flying about it in the air, the prodigious glare of almost perpetual lightening, the crash of the falling houses, and the ear-piercing shrieks of the distressed, were sufficient to strike astonishment into Angels.[26]

The letter went on to describe the storm's destruction in terms of God's vengeance and man's impotence against it. Surely an adolescent who thinks and writes on such a level, thought Knox, should not spend his life as a countinghouse clerk. Knox circulated the letter among the wealthy and influential on the island and solicited their sponsorship to send Hamilton to America for a proper education. Perhaps he would study medicine and return to tend to the ills of St. Croix; perhaps he would study scripture and return to tend to the spiritual needs of the island. Nicholas Cruger and his business associate Cornelius Kortwright together agreed to consign four annual "cargoes of

25 Ibid., 48
26 Syrett, *The Papers of Alexander Hamilton*, Vol. I, 35

West India produce" which would be sold by Kortwright and Company of New York and "appropriated to the support of Hamilton."[27]

Hamilton eagerly grabbed the opportunity. This was the chance he had dreamed of; the one he told his friend, Ned, about — thinking it was only a "castle in the air." He was determined to make the most of this "preferment."

Knox provided Hamilton with letters of introduction to his close friends in New York as well as in neighboring New Jersey. Never did Hamilton express a wish to again see the West Indies of his birth, although he continued an intermittent correspondence with his father, his brother and Hugh Knox throughout his life.

Hamilton arrived in New York at the very end of October. Armed with his letters of introduction from Knox, Hamilton prepared to present himself at the countinghouse of Kortwright and Company, the assigned executor of Hamilton's educational funding from his St. Croix sponsors. The managing partner of the firm, Lawrence Kortwright, received him and subsequently introduced Alexander to another partner, Hugh Mulligan, an Irish immigrant. The season was late for Hamilton's most immediate need, education, and Mulligan's brother Hercules was designated to expedite Hamilton's entry into a suitable school.

While Hamilton was in New York he lived as a guest in Hercules' Water Street home. Mulligan took several days to show Hamilton the sights and landmarks of the city that had a population of 20,000 — comparable to the population of the entire island of St. Croix — meanwhile regaling him with tales of his own politics and his experiences.

A stronghold of loyal Tory politics, the colony of New York was sharply divided on the question of the British Parliament's right to tax the colonies in the aftermath of the French and Indian War. In addition, Parliament had demanded that the colonies construct barracks to house British regulars at taxpayers' expense. Though the soldiers were there supposedly for the defense of the colonies, the only defense needed on the seacoast was against British domination. The New York Assembly had voted down Parliament's demand for taxes to construct Fort George to house British troops. A citizen's group calling themselves Sons of Liberty protested against Britain and influenced the colonial legislature to deny British demands. In a con-

---

27 Mitchell, *Alexander Hamilton — Youth to Maturity*, 34

tinuation of the highhanded treatment of the rights and prerogatives of the colony, Parliament dissolved the New York Assembly and required the election of new delegates who would be favorable to the British demands. This new Assembly did accede to Parliament's demands. Hercules Mulligan and the Sons of Liberty renewed their protests by constructing a Liberty Pole on New York's Bowling Green as a rallying site for protests against imperial Parliamentary legislation. On January 17, 1770 the British troops surprised the Sons of Liberty and attempted to topple the pole by exploding gunpowder at its base. This attempt failed due to the iron casing that sheathed the Liberty Pole; the British vented their frustration by attacking Montagne's Tavern on the West Side waterfront, the headquarters of another group of freedom fighters calling themselves the Liberty Boys. Two more British attempts were required to fell the Liberty Pole and then they cut it into pieces and stacked them in front of Montagne's Tavern. The melee that followed has been named the Battle of Golden Hill. A combined force of Sons of Liberty, sailors armed with swords, and laborers wielding clubs attacked British soldiers, who defended themselves with bayonets. This was the first armed clash of the American Revolution.[28] This story, related by Hercules Mulligan, was Hamilton's introduction to the rising contentions between Great Britain and her American colonies.

Included in Rev. Knox's introductory letters were two addressed to leading Presbyterian clergy in New York, Drs. John Rodgers and John Mason. Hercules took Alexander to meet both men. Hamilton's sponsors on St. Croix strongly promoted him for an education at the Presbyterian school of the College of New Jersey (later to be named Princeton University) and no one could be more influential in bringing this about than John Rodgers. However, in discussions with Hamilton, Dr. Rodgers came to doubt that Alexander could pass the rigorous mathematics and language requirements of this school. It was suggested that Hamilton devote himself to a year's hard study at a preparatory school in Elizabethtown, New Jersey (the town name has since been shortened to Elizabeth).

Mulligan escorted Hamilton to Elizabethtown, across the bay from Manhattan. The description of Elizabethtown given by a Swedish traveler some

---

28 Champagne, R., *Alexander McDougall and the American Revolution in New York*, Union College Press, Schenectady, 1975, 24 - 25

ten years prior to Hamilton's arrival there gives the impression of an idyllic pastoral setting.

> Elizabeth-town is a small town, about twenty English miles from New Brunswick: we arrived there immediately after sun setting. Its houses are mostly scattered, but well built, and generally of boards, with a roof of shingles, and walls covered with the same. A little rivulet passes through the town from west to east; it is almost reduced to nothing when the water ebbs away, but with the full tide they can bring up small yachts. Here were two fine churches, each of which made a much better appearance than any one in Philadelphia. That belonging to the people of the Church of England was built of bricks, had a steeple with bells, and a balustrade round it, from which there was a prospect of the country. The meetinghouse of the Presbyterians was built of wood but had both a steeple and bells, and was, like the other houses covered with shingles. The town house made likewise a good appearance, and had a spire with a bell. The banks of the river were red, from the reddish limestone; both in and about the town were many gardens and orchards, and it might truly be said that Elizabeth-town was situated in a garden; the ground hereabouts being even and well cultivated.[29]

Once in Elizabethtown, Hamilton met and presented Knox's letters of introduction to two of the more prominent men of that village, William Livingston and Elias Boudinot. They befriended Hamilton during his nine months of study at the Academy, gave him access to their homes and libraries, and exerted great influence on the development of his academic and political thinking, and continued to be beneficial throughout Hamilton's career.

William Livingston was a member of a large land-holding New York aristocratic family. He was a lawyer, having graduating from Yale. His successful and lucrative law practice in New York combined with his inherited wealth and the large real estate holdings of his wife provided them a most comfortable life. Following a stressful political loss Livingston had recently given up his law practice in New York for the bucolic life in Elizabethtown where he could devote more time to his polemical writings and to New Jersey politics. He was to become that state's first governor following the Declaration of Independence, succeeding the Tory governor of that state, William Franklin. When Hamilton arrived on the scene Livingston was in the process of constructing a mansion, which he later named *Liberty Hall*. While construction was in progress he and his wife lived with their eight children in the village. The ages of the children ranged from six years older than Hamilton to four years younger. They accepted Alexander into their circle and provided him with a sense of family life during his stay in Elizabethtown. He enjoyed a

---

29 Kalm, Peter, *Travels in North America*, Vol. 1, Wm. Eyres, Washington, 1770, 232-234

flirtatious relationship with several of the Livingston daughters, one of who may have introduced him to their cousin, Elizabeth Schuyler, whom Hamilton would later court and marry. Sarah Livingston married John Jay, a prominent New York attorney who became a major driving force in the formation of the Federalist government system some years after the War for Independence. He would be appointed by George Washington to be the first Chief Justice of the Supreme Court and was a lifelong friend and close collaborator of Hamilton's.[30]

Elias Boudinot, also a successful lawyer, would become the President of the Continental Congress. The Boudinots lived with their children in a mansion named Boxwood Hall. The doors of Boxwood Hall were laid open to Hamilton where he lived for much of the time he attended Elizabethtown Academy. Hamilton's early thoughts and instruction in a republican form of government were learned within the walls of Liberty Hall and Boxwood Hall.[31]

The Elizabethtown Academy was housed in a large two-story wooden building situated near the Presbyterian Church. It prepared boys principally for the seminary of the College of New Jersey (Princeton College). The Academy advocated the teaching of both theoretical and practical aspects of mathematics, as well as Latin, Greek and elocution. The headmaster, a man named Francis Barber, was a recent graduate of the College of New Jersey. Barely six years senior to Hamilton, he was also a graduate of the Elizabethtown Academy. Through Barber's tutoring Hamilton learned sufficient Greek to pass the oral entrance examinations at both the College of New Jersey and at King's College (later Columbia) in New York.[32] Later, during the Revolution, and principally due to Hamilton's sponsorship, Barber commanded a unit during the battle of Yorktown. Barber's men, under his pupil's leadership, stormed a British redoubt and their success contributed to the defeat of General Cornwallis' forces and the virtual end of the Revolution

During his attendance at the Elizabethtown Academy Hamilton was permitted a course of independent study. He requested tutoring from the faculty as needed and presented himself for examination when he felt prepared. Hamilton was observed to study until midnight and was also seen in the early morning walking in the town or sitting in the cemetery practicing

---

30 Flexner, *The Young Hamilton*, 55 - 56
31 Ibid.
32 Mitchell, *Alexander Hamilton, Youth to Maturity*, 42 - 3

for an oral recitation. Hamilton applied himself to his studies with a single-minded focus that would become his signature approach to work. Within nine months he was ready to apply for admission to any of the better colleges in the colonies.

He also found time to engage in the heated politics of the day. When he came to America, Hamilton had a respectful, if naïve, regard for British government. At first he viewed the protest over taxes as petty and inconsequential. He listened to Livingston, Boudinot, and their friends, John Jay and Lord Sterling, discuss with rising concern the refusal of Parliament to hear or to ameliorate the political differences that distressed the colonies. As Benjamin Franklin had pointed out to the House of Commons in 1766 in discussions regarding the Stamp Act, Americans considered themselves as much British subjects as anyone living in England. They simply wanted the respect, recognition and treatment afforded to British subjects living on the British Isles, specifically the right to legislate, adjudicate and levy taxes for themselves, through representatives that the colonists themselves selected. They claimed these rights were in strict accordance with the conditions of their original charters.

The history of the relationship between the British government and the colonies had been contentious regarding self-government and the degree of autonomy to be granted to the colonies for developing their economy. Prior to the Paris Treaty of 1763 ending the French and Indian War, the rural life of the colonies had been made hellish by French-incited Indian attacks. The colonists had looked to England for military assistance to remove this impediment to their stability and growth. With the cessation of hostilities with the French and the Indians, the colonists felt more secure in their westward expansion across the Appalachian Mountains. The act of carving settlements out of the wilderness of the eastern section of America had made the colonists a strong, hardy and independent-minded people.

Already the seeds of dissension existed between the colonies and England. Strong objections had already been raised from all over America against the quartering of British troops in the colonies, along with questions of colonial autonomy in judicial matters and issues of free press and speech. The haughty British perspective of superiority considered the colonists as a dependent populace inherently inferior to native-born Englishmen. This was vividly illustrated in General Braddock's ill planned and fatally executed excursion into the interior of Pennsylvania during the French and Indian War that was intended to put a stop to the harassment of rural colonial expansion. In this military exercise British regulars were combined with groups of colonial militia. But the British regulars refused to acknowledge any authority of the militia officers, even though it was abundantly clear that the militia were more experienced in fighting in the close confines of the western Pennsylvanian forests where guerrilla tactics were effective. The British army ignored the experience, advice and combat tactics of the colonial militia, and that was disastrous in this decisive battle.

At the close of the French and Indian War a gradual change developed in the attitude between England and America. England's economic plan was generally to regulate the international commerce of its colonies in the interests of Britain. Parliament had enacted a series of measures that dictated the conditions for imports into the colonies, exports from America to other countries, and intra-colonial trade. Foreign ships were excluded from trading in the colonies and from participating in trade between the colonies. Only British citizens could act as merchants in the colonies. Strict limitations were placed on colonial exports of sugar, cotton, tobacco, wool and indigo. These products could only be shipped to ports in England, Ireland and British owned islands. But during the French and Indian War the attention of the British was focused on that campaign and colonial trade was left to pursue its own interests, resulting in some widespread abuses of British regulations.

While the navigation and trade laws had existed for some time, the British had not been in a position to enforce them for a number of years. During the reign of the Stuarts internal affairs had consumed the full attention of the British government. Later the hostile influence of France, both in Europe and in America, had diverted attention from commercial control over the colonies. This had permitted the colonies to pursue their own avenues to commercial development. They traded freely with French, Spanish and Dutch interests. In a legal sense this forbidden trade could be considered smuggling; but since it had operated freely for so many years the colonies had come to view those trade practices as their right.[33]

The English had their own perspective with regard to realizing revenue from the colonies. The governmental budget of England had increased three-

33 Stokes, Isaac, *Iconography of Manhattan Island — 1498-1909,* Arno Press, New York, 303

fold since Braddock's defeat in 1755. The principal source of revenue was the land tax, but costs were rising much faster than the landowners' capability to pay. Under Charles Townshend, England developed a renewed focus on the control of colonial commerce. This policy included a strict enforcement of existing trade and navigation acts; the establishment of a series of taxes on the colonies; and, as a parliamentary prerogative, the payment of salaries of colonial officers, thereby removing any dependence they might feel on colonial legislatures.[34]

To enforce these objectives, warships were sent to America to put stop the smuggling that was so commonplace. British captains were empowered as customhouse officers and were rewarded with the usual share in the contraband collected. British officers were authorized to enter and to search houses suspected of holding smuggled goods without the necessity of judicial due process.[35]

George III had ascended to the throne of Great Britain in 1760 and had an unbounded confidence in his own judgment, a confidence that was not supported either by his intelligence or experience. He approached his role in British government more aggressively than did his predecessors, and he sought to win support within Parliament for the greater powers he wished to assume. He fully supported the Townshend policy of exercising greater control over the colonies. With Lord North as prime minister he schemed to win support in Parliament by granting pensions, titles and bribes.[36]

The conclusion of the French and Indian War left Britain with a national debt of £140 million. The Prime Minister, Lord Grenville, proposed to levy a tax on the colonies to pay the cost of maintaining standing forces in America to provide protection against Indian attacks and to preserve order. Against the strong protest of the colonies and despite the counsel of Benjamin Franklin that British troops were not required in America and that the colonial militia was fully capable of protecting against Indian incursions in the absence of French incitement, the Parliament decided to permanently station a force of ten thousand British regulars there. The expense of maintaining this force was to be paid, at least partially, by the colonies through a proposed stamp tax. The colonial legislatures were sounded out on the proposed tax and were requested to recommend an alternative plan for raising the neces-

34 Ibid., 304
35 Ibid.
36 Ibid., 305

sary funds if they found the stamp tax repugnant. In due course most of the colonies argued strongly against the stamp tax but none offered an alternative. Parliament passed the Stamp Act in March 1765. A total of fifty-four kinds of documents were subject to the new fees.[37]

Charles Townshend, defending Parliament's right of taxation over the colonies, asked whether "these Americans, children planted by our care, nourished up by our indulgence until they are grown to a degree of strength and opulence, and protected by our arms, [would] ... grudge to contribute their mite to relieve us from the heavy weight of that burden which we lie under?" A biting response was given by Col. Isaac Barre, who had served with General Wolfe at Louisburg and Quebec: "They planted by your care? No! Your oppression planted them in America.... They nourished by your indulgence? They grew by your neglect of them... They protected by your arms? They have nobly taken up arms in your defence, have exerted a valour amidst their constant and laborious industry for the defence of a country whose frontier, while drenched in blood, its interior parts have yielded all its little savings to your emolument."[38]

The Stamp Act was repealed in 1767 when British merchants complained that the colonies had stopped buying their products, and British exports suffered. The repeal of the Stamp Act confirmed that Parliament was responsive to complaints from British merchants but not to complaints from American colonists. A succession of petitions from the colonies seeking redress from these oppressive taxes and other forms of abuse had gone unanswered. However, when merchants based in the home Isles complained of economic harm, prompt action was taken. To further underscore Parliament's contempt of the views of the colonies, the repeal of the Stamp act was accompanied by the Declaratory Act in which Parliament re-asserted its right of taxation over the colonies.

In his nine months at Elizabethtown, Hamilton had established a number of relationships that he would foster throughout his life. He made great strides towards attaining a classical education and grounded himself in American politics to the point where he thought of himself as an American. At the conclusion of his studies at the Elizabethtown Academy he had to

37 Ibid., 306
38 Brands, *The First American*, Anchor Books, New York, 2002, 362

choose a college for his professional training. The College of New Jersey, the seat of academic Presbyterian influence in America, seemed a natural choice. Hugh Knox and his other sponsors on St. Croix had implied their preference that he study at the College of New Jersey. The President of the College, Dr. John Witherspoon, interviewed Hamilton and agreed that he was fully qualified to enter the college. However, when Hamilton requested that he be granted the same right of independent study at Princeton that he had at the Elizabethtown Academy, Witherspoon hesitated. Later in life Mulligan was to recall,

> I went with him to Princeton to the House of Dr. Witherspoon, then the president of the College with whom I was well acquainted, and I introduced Mr. Hamilton to him and proposed to him to Examine the young gentleman which the Doctor did to his entire satisfaction. Mr. Hamilton then stated that he wished to enter either of the classes to which his attainments would entitle him but with the understanding that he should be permitted to advance from Class to Class with as much rapidity as his exertions would enable him to do. Dr. Witherspoon listened with great attention to so unusual a proposition from so young a person and replied that he had not the sole power to determine but that he would submit the request to the trustees who would decide, which was done & in about a fortnight after a letter was received from the President stating that the request could not be complied with because it was contrary to the usage of the College and expressing his regret because he was convinced that the young gentleman would do honor to any seminary at which he should be educated. [39]

One must speculate on John Witherspoon's motives in refusing Hamilton's request to advance through his collegiate studies as fast as warranted by his own attainments. Certainly such a request was not without precedent; only a few years earlier a similar request was granted to a young Virginia scholar named James Madison who completed the prescribed curriculum of four years in only two. Whatever Witherspoon's reasoning, history may have been the beneficiary of this decision. Had Hamilton attended the College of New Jersey in its peaceful rural setting he would have been isolated, to an extent, from the political clamor and contention that he experienced in New York where he attended King's College. The high pitch of political turmoil in New York stimulated his interest and involvement in nationalistic pursuits, allowed him to become a well-known figure, gave him an individual political stance and, through his political connections in New York, gave him a better

---

39 Schachner, *Narratives of Robert Troup and Hercules Mulligan*, William & Mary Quarterly, April 1947, 209

opportunity for entering the armed conflict than he would have had in New Jersey.

In his interview at King's College, Alexander Hamilton made the same request to be permitted to advance as his personal accomplishments justified. Dr. Myles Cooper, then president of the College, granted this request. Cooper was an ordained priest in the Anglican Church. He was born in England, graduated from Oxford University there and was ordained into the priesthood at twenty-two years of age. King's College under Cooper's presidency was a stronghold of Loyalist sentiment. Through his classmates at King's College Hamilton was exposed for the first time to Tory politics and the extreme intolerance they had for any dissenting viewpoints.

Despite their philosophical differences Hamilton seems to have gotten on well with President Cooper. They shared similar literary tastes and Hamilton's precocity interested Cooper as he watched young Hamilton rapidly progress through his studies. Hamilton's roommate, Robert Troup, noted, "He was studious, and made rapid progress in the languages, and every other branch of learning, to which he applied himself. He had originally destined himself to the Science of Physic [medicine]; and with this view, he was regular in attending the anatomical lectures, then delivered at the College by Dr. Clossey. The General [Hamilton] never graduated; the College having broken up, before his course of study was completed."[40]

Hamilton always made good use of any opportunity to use a good library. He hoarded the books that had originally belonged to his mother, and read voraciously from the libraries of Hugh Knox, William Livingston and Elias Boudinot. Similarly he devoured the books in the library at King's College, many of which had been acquired as gifts; "Joseph Murray, Esq. bequeathed his Estate and library; The Rev. Dr. Bristow of London bequeathed his library, ab. 1500 books. Sundry Gentlemen of Oxford gave Books whose names are in them."[41]

40 Ibid. 212
41 Mitchell, *Alexander Hamilton — Youth to Maturity*, 59

CHAPTER 2. GAINING MATURITY IN WAR

The French and Indian War resulted in a number of actions being taken by Great Britain that hastened and assured the revolution of the American colonies. As noted above, the war was concluded in 1763, leaving Britain with the staggering debt of £140 million. England viewed the American colonies as a great source of taxable revenue to help to defray this debt. Their first attempt to tap this revenue source was through the series of taxes imposed by the Stamp Act, enacted in 1765 and repealed in 1767 when the colonial embargo on British goods caused British merchants to raise a loud protest against these painful taxes. Parliament later imposed a tea tax on the colonies that went essentially unnoticed and the colonies imported tea from Britain when they were unable to smuggle tea from Holland.[1] Britain then gave to the East India Company a monopoly on the colonial tea trade through the Tea Act of 1773. It was Britain's intent to benefit by two means in granting this monopoly. First, the payment of the tea tax was assured, as the colonies had no other lawful source for tea but through the East India Company. Secondly, the profits gained by the East India Company could also be taxed to help to pay the debt incurred by the defense of India as a British possession during the French and Indian War.

---

1 Brands, H., *The First American*, 464

In New York and Philadelphia the reaction was quick and certain. The colonial outrage reverted to the previously successful policy used to combat the Stamp Act whereby no American merchant would buy English merchandise. In Boston other distractions slowed the reaction to this new offensive form of taxation. Yet when Boston did become aware that not only were they being taxed on tea without their assent but also that the East India Company had a monopoly on the tea imported to the colonies, their reaction was violent. In late November of 1773 the British merchant ship *Dartmouth* arrived in Boston harbor bearing the first shipment of East India Company tea. A confrontation between the Sons of Liberty and the consignees of the shipment resulted when the colonials became aware of the cargo *Dartmouth* was carrying. Samuel Adams called for a series of demonstrations where thousands of colonials turned out for mass meetings to protest the presence in Boston harbor of East India tea. The protestors were openly hostile toward Parliament and Colonial Governor Hutchinson for attempting to force their tea on the Bostonians. On the evening of December 16 the largest meeting to date was held at Boston's Old North Church, where in excess of eight thousand patriots demonstrated. While the meeting was being held, fifty colonials disguised as Indians boarded the *Dartmouth* and two sister ships which had arrived after the *Dartmouth*, the *Eleanor* and the *Beaver*. The men broke into the lockers containing the tea, opened the chests and dumped all of their contents into the bay. By morning they had destroyed £10,000 of tea. No other cargo on the ships had been touched.[2]

This event, dubbed the Boston Tea Party, was viewed as an inexcusable outrage by Parliament and to make clear to the colonists that this was unacceptable conduct, they passed four punitive laws that closed the port of Boston until such time as the colonies paid for the damages incurred by the East India Company. Called "the Intolerable Acts," the new laws gave the governor the power to appoint officials, provided that colonists accused of capital crimes could be removed to England for trial, and renewed the Quartering Act whereby colonists were required to house and feed the British troops assigned to their colony.

The protests over the closing of the Port of Boston reverberated across the colonies. In April, New York held its own Tea Party. The merchant ship *London* sailed into New York harbor, ignoring warnings against unloading its

2 Ibid., 465

cargo of tea. Captain Chambers attempted to bluff Alexander McDougall, denying he had tea aboard. When this lie was discovered he claimed that he was not in support of the Tea Act and that the cargo of tea belonged to him, not to the East India Company. But during the process of unloading the tea, as tally clerks checked his crates against his manifest, colonists disguised as Indians dumped the tea into the bay.[3]

Following the enforced closure of the port of Boston, the Massachusetts colony appealed to the other colonies to join in resistance against Great Britain and to re-institute the non-importation policy that had been successful earlier in defeating the Stamp Act. In New York the existing Committee of Correspondence, consisting mainly of conservatives and Tory sympathizers, was dissolved and a new Committee of 51 was appointed, this time consisting of a majority of moderates. Isaac Low chaired the committee, and John Alsop was his vice-chair. The first action of the committee was to form a subcommittee to respond directly to Boston. In this response New York consoled Massachusetts for the Intolerable Acts but stated that they did not have sufficient support in New York and so declined to re-institute the non-importation policy. Rather, they agreed to be bound by the decision of a general congress (the First Continental Congress), that should be called in Philadelphia for this specific purpose. As New York's delegates to the Congress, the committee appointed Philip Livingston, John Alsop, Isaac Low, James Duane and John Jay.[4]

The First Continental Congress met in Philadelphia during the period of September to December 1774 for the purpose of deciding a united response to the series of abuses for which they held both Crown and Parliament responsible. They felt that only four options were open to them. The first of these, to bow before the authority of Parliament, was not a serious consideration. All delegates recognized that to purchase peace from Britain by accession to the Tea Act was to acknowledge Parliament's full authority over them and would surely invite a multitude of additional taxes, greater control of colonial legislatures by Parliament and other restrictions. The second option was to petition Parliament or the King for redress of their grievances. The response they had received from Great Britain to past petitions convinced Congress of the futility of this option. Past petitions either had been ignored

3Champagne, *Alexander McDougall and the American Revolution in New York*, 50
4 Stokes, *Iconography of New York*, 316 - 317

or spurned, a response that worsened, rather than improved, their relationship. A third option was for the colonies to unify and place an embargo on the importation of all British goods and manufactures. This action had been successfully employed in obtaining repeal of the Stamp Act nearly a decade earlier. The earlier unified action of the colonies to enforce a non-importation agreement did not, of itself, motivate Parliament to reconsider the wisdom of its action. Rather, it was the British merchants' complaint of economic hardship that led Parliament to repeal the Stamp Act. The last available option was to strike for independence.

Still, as late as December of 1774, few if any influential colonists viewed independence as a desirable goal. They saw themselves as Englishmen with an allegiance to the King, able to conduct their own affairs and being desirous of social and economic intercourse on the world stage as an integral part of the British Empire. The problem from their perspective was simply that Parliament did not recognize that the spatial separation of three thousand miles disqualified them from effective governance of people fully capable of governing themselves. In recent decades the colonies had matured as cultural, political and economic entities. They saw little value for themselves in a continued dependence on Great Britain; especially in the terms which Parliament defined this dependency. Recent actions by Parliament were seen as intended to enforce subjugation, to prohibit the development of effective self-defensive capability and to deter, through unwarranted and excessive taxation, the commercial development of the colonies.[5]

The Continental Congress chose the course of action that seemed to offer the most reasonable probability of success without causing evils worse than the primary cause of their actions. They chose a boycott of all imports from England, Ireland and the West Indies. They further decided to prohibit all exports to these regions so that Great Britain would be denied the advantages of having American products so long as the contentious disputes continued.

To ensure full compliance each colony established committees to inspect all ports of entry and mercantile warehouses. It was left to the individual colonies to determine the action appropriate to any discovered violations of these non-import, non-export prohibitions. The response to these congressional actions was overwhelmingly supportive. It was understood by the

---

5 Irving, Washington, *George Washington — A Biography*, Da Capo Press, New York, 1994, 149

Americans that all that was necessary to ensure the success of the recently demonstrated British strategy of oppression was for the colonies to do nothing. The non-importation, non-exportation action decided on by Congress was an act of resistance not requiring bloodshed.

There were, however, Loyalists who opposed any confrontational actions against Parliament. An Anglican cleric by the name of Samuel Seabury published a pamphlet on November 16, 1774, which he entitled *Free Thoughts on the Proceedings of the Congress at Philadelphia,* under the pseudonym, *A Westchester Farmer.* In this publication Seabury trivialized the complaints of the colonies in regard to the usurpation of their natural rights and liberties and summarized the dispute as having no more significance than the three pence per pound tax on tea imposed by the Tea Act. He expressed his disappointment in the congressional action by saying of the Congress, "The eyes of all men were turned to them. We ardently expected that some prudent scheme of accommodating our unhappy disputes with the mother country would have been adopted and pursued. But alas! They are broken up without ever attempting it: they have taken no step that tended to peace: they have gone from bad to worse, and have either ignorantly misunderstood, carelessly neglected, or basely betrayed the interests of all the colonies."[6]

Seabury tried to excite opposition through fear when he said, "Can we think to threaten, and bully and frighten the supreme government of the nation into compliance with our demands? Can we expect to force a submission to our peevish and petulant humours, by exciting clamors and riots in England? We ought to know the temper and spirit, the power and strength of the nation better. A single campaign, should she exert her force, would ruin us effectually."[7] He concluded with the memorable passage, "Will you be instrumental in bringing the most abject slavery on yourselves? Will you choose such Committees? Will you submit to them, should they be chosen by the weak, foolish turbulent part of the country people? Do as you please: but, by HIM that made me, I will not...No, if I must be enslaved, let it be by a KING at least, and not by a parcel of upstart lawless Committeemen. *If I must be devoured, let me be devoured by the jaws of a lion, and not gnawed to death by rats and vermin.*"[8] With this statement he substantially increased the hostility

---

6Vance, Clarence H. (ed.), *Letters of a Westchester Farmer*, White Plains, 1930, 43
7 Ibid., 46
8 Ibid. 61

between "Patriot" and "Loyalist" and rather than instill fear he determined many to no longer to be bullied and abused by Parliament..

Hamilton defended the actions of Congress in two publications of his own. The first, dated December 16, 1774, he entitled, *A Full Vindication of the Measures of the Congress, Etc.*[9] Hamilton cited clearly and concisely the argument posed by the colonies as the basis of their protests of Parliamentary abuses, and he made the argument that Parliament's actions were founded on base and self-interested motives.

> That Americans are intitled to freedom is incontestable upon every rational principle. All men have one common origin: they participate in one common nature, and consequently have one common right. No reason can be assigned why one man should exercise any power, or pre-eminence over his fellow creatures more than another; unless they have voluntarily vested him with it. Since then, Americans have not by any act of theirs impowered the British Parliament to make laws for them, it follows they can have no just authority to do it....[10]

> A vast majority of mankind is intirely biased by motives of self-interest. Most men are glad to remove any burthen off themselves and place them upon the necks of their neighbors. We cannot therefore doubt, but that the British Parliament, with a view to the ease and advantage of itself, and its constituents, would oppress and grind the Americans as much as possible.[11]

Seabury was quick to respond. On December 24, 1774 he published a third essay regarding the continuing disputes between the colonies and the mother country [a second pamphlet entitled *The Congress Canvassed, Etc.*, was published less than a fortnight after his first but this essay did not enter into the running debate between "A. W. Farmer" and Hamilton and will not be addressed here]. This pamphlet, entitled *A View of the Controversy Between Great Britain and Her Colonies in a Letter to the Author of a 'Full Vindication of the Measures of the Congress,'* contained both a biting criticism of the writing style and wisdom of Hamilton in his *Full Vindication* essay and a full defense of the righteous authority of the British government (King, Lords and Commons, in his words). Where Hamilton had been so careless as to use the phrase "independent colony" in his essay, Seabury chided him, pointing out that the words "independent" and "colony" convey mutually contradictory meanings.

---

9 Syrett, *Papers of Alexander Hamilton*, Vol. I, 45; Lodge, Henry C., *The Works of Alexander Hamilton*, 2nd Edition, G. P. Putnam's Sons, New York, 1904, Vol. I, 3

10 Syrett, *Papers of Alexander Hamilton*, Vol. I, 47; Lodge, Henry C., *The Works of Alexander Hamilton*, Vol. I, 6

11 Ibid., 53 — 54; Lodge, Henry C., *The Works of Alexander Hamilton, Vol. I, 16*

It was apparently Farmer's intention to confound the reading public by misrepresenting Hamilton's arguments. In his *Full Vindication* essay Hamilton had argued that laws to which he has not consented either personally or through his representative do not bind a man. Farmer twisted this by pointing out that, since only land-owning males voted in the British Empire, fully ninety per cent of English subjects were, in fact, bound by laws which they had no part in drafting nor approving. He ignored the fact that even the landed males in the colonies were without direct means of influencing British laws governing the colonies. Through similar wiles he attempted to discredit each of Hamilton's arguments, although he failed in each instance to address fully the underlying arguments made.[12]

The most revealing statement written by A. W. Farmer is made in the first third of his essay where he states, "Great Britain still retains the power of binding the colonies by such laws as she shall think necessary to secure and preserve the dependence of the colonies on the mother country; ... to promote their particular welfare or the welfare of the whole empire collectively."[13]

Hamilton's response to this pamphlet was entitled, *The Farmer Refuted.* Hamilton examined the fundamental purpose for human laws and cited Blackstone, who reasoned, "The principal aim of society is to protect individuals, in the enjoyment of those absolute rights, which were vested in them by the immutable laws of nature; but which could not be preserved, in peace, without that mutual assistance, and intercourse, which is gained by the institution of friendly and social communities. Hence it follows, that the first and primary end of human laws, is to maintain and regulate these absolute rights of individuals."[14] Hamilton thus asserted that life, liberty and property are natural rights given man by his Creator and that man instituted laws to provide security for these rights in a collective sense. To the extent that parliament had abused these rights, then, they were morally wrong and alienated the fundamental purpose of government. He summarized, "[Parliament] are subversive of our natural liberty, because an authority is assumed over us, which we by no means assent to. And they divest us of that moral

12 Vance, *Letters of a Westchester Farmer*, 111
13 Ibid., 116
14 Syrett, *The Papers of Alexander Hamilton*, Vol. I, 88; Hamilton, John C. (ed.), *The Works of Alexander Hamilton*, Vol. II, 44

security, for our lives and properties, which we are intitled to, and which it is the primary end of society to bestow." [15]

Hamilton then proceeded to show that Parliament was constitutionally wrong when it assumed to legislate for the colonies.

> The right of Parliament to legislate for us cannot be accounted for upon any reasonable grounds. The very aim and intention of the democratical part, or the House of Commons, is to secure the rights of the people... It is the unalienable birthright of every Englishman, who can be considered as a free agent to participate in framing the laws which are to bind him, either as to his life or property. [16]

Through his studies Hamilton had come to the conviction that to the degree that checks and balances are effective in controlling abuses in government, to that same degree are the rights and liberties of the governed secure. It follows directly that where these checks and balances are prejudiced, the rights of man, lacking a strong champion, become insecure.[17]

While polemics were being offered on both sides of the dispute between the colonies and Great Britain, most colonists, patriots as well as loyalists, were focused on solving the present crisis within the framework of the existing relationship. It often happens in a crisis situation that if rational thinking and constructive action are not able to resolve the issue, events in due course will intervene to determine the outcome. In Massachusetts the British military governor, General Thomas Gage, received word that the colonial militia in the village of Concord was storing a large deposit of weapons and ammunition. With as much secrecy as possible he directed Light Infantry and Grenadier units under the command of Lieutenant Colonel Francis Smith and Marine Major John Pitcairn to discover this cache and to destroy it or to return it to the Boston garrison. When on April 19, 1775 the British troops crossed the Charles River and began their nighttime march to Concord, Paul Revere began his storied ride to sound the alarm to the militia at Lexington and at Concord. At dawn the British troops entered Lexington and encountered the Lexington militia, armed and ready to stop them. Here was fired the "Shot heard round the world." The militia began to disperse before the British surrounded them. In the scuffle someone fired a shot. The British,

15 Syrett, H., *Papers of Alexander Hamilton*, Vol. I, 88; Hamilton, J. *Works of Alexander Hamilton, Vol. II, 48*
16 Syrett, *The Papers of Alexander Hamilton*, Vol. I, 92; Hamilton, John C. (ed.), *The Works of Alexander Hamilton*, Vol. II, 48
17 Syrett, *The Papers of Alexander Hamilton*, Vol. I, 95

thinking the militia had fired, returned a volley killing eight and wounding ten colonials. The British then force-marched on to Concord, where they encountered the militia of that village. The British were routed and attempted an orderly retreat to Boston but were impeded by resistance from other militia in small groups who outflanked, out shot, and once again, routed them. In Lexington they met a reserve unit of British regulars that saved this royal unit by providing sufficient firepower to permit a reformation and orderly retreat.[18] The time for meaningful discussion and pandering petitions was over; the American Revolution had begun.

In New York the controversy between patriot factions and loyalists became heated. Late in April 1775 a flyer was distributed, addressed to "Myles Cooper and several other obnoxious gentlemen." They were held responsible for the bloodshed that had occurred in Massachusetts. They were warned to flee America or risk their lives to mob action. On the night of May 10 an angry crowd, including many of New York's Sons of Liberty, marched on King's College to make good their threats against Rev. Cooper. When their intentions became clear Hamilton and his friend Robert Troup stood on the steps to the college and harangued the crowd, arguing that this type of action would disgrace the noble cause of liberty for which they were striving. They commanded the attention of the crowd long enough for Cooper to escape. He fled to England and never returned to America.[19]

Although it was Hamilton's intent to secure the civil rights of Cooper over the irrational anger of the mob, this and similar actions later caused him to be accused of being a monarchist at heart. Hamilton was plagued by this unjustified accusation for much of his public life and for the better part of a century following his death.

Unsuccessful in their attempt to bring their idea of justice to Cooper, the mob descended on the home and business of James Rivington, the printer of Cooper's loyalist writings. Friends of Rivington diverted them from their mission; James Rivington escaped that night and likewise sailed to England. In late November Isaac Sears, a former leader of New York's Sons of Liberty movement and one of the extremists of that group, led an armed contingency from New Haven for the purpose of arresting Samuel Seabury (A. W. Farmer) and other Tories at Westchester. After the intended captures

---

18 Irving, G. W., *George Washington — A Biography*, 158 - 163
19 Flexner, *The Young Hamilton*, 78

in Westchester they traveled onto New York City, broke into and wrecked the printing business of James Rivington and destroyed all of the type they could discover.[20]

During the period of uncertainty and unrest Alexander Hamilton and his friends prepared themselves for the eventuality of war with military drill exercises. As their training officer they had the benefit of the experience of retired British Major Edward Fleming, who had held the position of Regimental Adjutant in the British Army. He lived in New York and was known as an excellent disciplinarian. Hamilton threw himself into this training experience with the intensive commitment that was characteristic of all his endeavors. Robert Troup later recalled, "The General [Hamilton] was constant in his attendance, and very ambitious of improvement. He became exceedingly expert in the manual exercise. The Company continued to exist until public events compelled Major Fleming, General Hamilton, Mr. Troup and other Members to join the American Army." [21]

The Second Continental Congress convened in Philadelphia on May 10, 1775 and directed New York to form a militia that was to be trained and armed. This militia was to be deployed in the city for protection against an invasion by the British. It was not until January 6, 1776 that the Provincial Congress authorized the formation of an artillery company. Hamilton immediately applied for a commission in this company. He obtained a certificate of proficiency from Stephen Bedlam, who was an expert artillery officer. The Provincial Congress gave him the commission of Captain of the Provincial Company of Artillery.[22]

Parliament had issued a general order to the governors of the colonies dictating that the military stores of the militia be gathered under British control. The military engagement in Massachusetts and the fear of armed reprisals in the rest of the colonies made the issue of a united American response of paramount importance to Congressional delegates. A resolution was proposed to submit a humble and docile petition to the king but was soundly defeated by loud voices of strong opposition. John Adams called this resolution, "an imbecile measure of submission" and said that "its passage would embarrass the proceedings of Congress." Instead Adams proposed a

20 Ibid., 84
21 Schachner, "*Narratives of Robert Troup and Hercules Mulligan,*" William & Mary Quarterly, April 1947, 218 - 219
22 Randall, *Alexander Hamilton — A Life*, 99

course of action which was both forceful and immediate. Adams's resolution allowing Congress to assume and exercise the powers of a federalized authority was carried. A Confederation of the various states was formed for their common defense in which each colony was free to conduct its affairs in accordance with its own constitution; Congress was given the power of peace and war, making treaties and governing general commerce.[23]

Congress soon passed provisions for the formation of a federal army; enlisting troops, procurement of provisions and the construction of forts in various locations throughout the colonies. George Washington was made commander-in-chief of the Continental Army. To defray the expenses of these actions the emission of notes in the amount of two million dollars was authorized, based solely on the faith of the confederacy to assure their redemption.[24]

The issuance by the Confederation of these notes, unsecured by any hard specie, soon resulted in their serious devaluation. The lack of specie throughout the country that necessitated the use of this unsecured money assured that America would be unable to meet the financial burden of the war and placed the future of the Confederation in the hands of foreign allies who, it was hoped, would fund the war through international loans. This dismal fiscal system existed for fourteen years until Alexander Hamilton, as Washington's Secretary for the Treasury, created the financial system and polices which finally secured stability for the United States government.

Washington's first job as commander-in-chief was to put substance into the Army of New England that was attempting to corral the British army within the confines of the City of Boston. If the Army was neglected, it would surely dissolve and the British would be free to ravage New England for their defeat at Concord. More importantly, if New England fell, it was doubtful the lower nine colonies could resist the might of the British Army.

Bolstering the numbers of his small army, training them, and obtaining provisions, occupied Washington for the following nine months. Surrounding the garrison at Boston, Washington's army isolated the British Army, deprived them of all sources of fresh food supplies, and attempted to incite them into battle or starve them into departing Boston. The lack of artillery hampered Washington's siege of Boston through the second half of 1775 and

---

23 Irving, *George Washington — A Biography*, 165
24 Bobrick, Benson, *Angel in the Whirlwind*, Simon & Schuster, New York, 1997, 123

into early 1776. Washington directed Henry Knox to procure what artillery pieces there were in New York along with shells and powder and then to travel to the forts along Lake Champlain to requisition their artillery supplies. The successful accomplishment of this expedition was to be one of the heroic epics of the Revolution. General Knox returned to Boston with eighty sleds loaded with artillery pieces and shells in February. On the night of March 2–3, Washington had the guns fire all night onto the British in Boston.[25]

While Washington and his generals were engaged in resolving these critical shortages, word was received that Parliament had communicated to the British commanders in Boston a plan for taking possession of New York and Albany. The plan relied upon the assistance of Governor Tryon of New York and the support of the mainly Tory-dominated population in New York. The Hudson and East Rivers were to be taken by small men-of-war and cutters who were to sever all communication between New York, New Jersey and Philadelphia, effectively isolating New York and New England from the rest of the colonies. This intelligence fit well with observed British action, which showed their preparations to abandon Boston. A fleet of cargo ships was being loaded in Boston harbor and troop transports were being readied to embark the British Army from the siege at Boston.[26]

Late in June the British fleet arrived in New York harbor to begin the battle for New York. To one American soldier, the harbor contained so many British ships that it resembled a wood of pine trees. He stated that he thought all of London was afloat. On July 12, the British commander-in-chief of the British forces, Admiral Richard Howe, arrived in New York.[27] While the British forces were assembling in New York harbor, in Philadelphia on July 2 Congress voted in favor of the Declaration of Independence; on July 4 the Declaration was signed.

New York's Provincial Congress gave its approval to the Declaration on July 9. On the evening of that day the Declaration was read to Washington's troops assembled on the Commons. As part of the ensuing celebration, a statue of George III which had been erected in 1770 was pulled down, the head placed on a spike for all to see and the rest of the statue, consisting of

25 Ibid., 165
26 Irving, W., *George Washington — A Biography*, 217 - 218
27 Bobrick, Benson, *Angel in the Whirlwind*, 206

four thousand pounds of lead, was hauled off to Connecticut to be melted into musket balls.[28]

During the Battle for New York the militia fought under General Washington, in coordination with the Continental Army. On the night of August 23 the New York revolutionary militia undertook to seize the two dozen cannon that had defended the Battery beneath Fort George. The British gunship *Asia* had been alerted that the rebels intended to confiscate these cannon. A patrol boat of riflemen was dispatched to repulse any such attempt. This patrol boat spotted Captain Alexander Hamilton and his men pulling the cannon into the city with stout ropes. The Redcoats opened fire with musket; the Americans fired back, killing one Englishman. On observing this skirmish the *Asia* drew near and opened an assault with a single gun. Hercules Mulligan, the friend and mentor of Hamilton, was a member of Hamilton's company. He later reported that when the shelling commenced, Hamilton took Mulligan's rope, asked him to hold his musket and proceeded to drag the cannon away. Mulligan left Hamilton's musket in the Battery and quickly retired from the incoming cannon shots. He was intercepted by Hamilton, who inquired where his musket was. When Mulligan told him, Hamilton raced back to retrieve his musket under the continuing bombardment from the British gunship. Mulligan was to recall later in life that the New Yorkers got twenty-one of the twenty-four large guns left by the British.[29]

Dealings between the opposing forces were made difficult by the contemptuous British attitude toward the American revolutionary forces. The British would emphasize their derogation of colonial officers by not giving formal recognition of their rank or offices. General Washington had earlier insisted that he be addressed with due recognition of his office; anything less was an insult to the American Confederacy. When, under a flag of truce, a letter intended for Washington was presented to Colonel Reed, the American delegate to the truce meeting, he immediately noticed the letter was addressed to Mr. Washington. He denied there was any such person in the American Army, which stalemated the discussion and ended the truce meeting. A week later a British Colonel Patterson was sent, again under a flag of truce, to attempt to establish correspondence between the opposing commanders. Patterson was brought before General Washington, who formally

28 Irving, *George Washington — A Biography*, 245 - 247
29 Schachner, Nathan, *Alexander Hamilton Viewed by His Friends: The Narratives of Robert Troup and Hercules Mulligan*, William & Mary Quarterly, April 1947, 210

greeted him in full dress uniform. Patterson addressed General Washington as "your excellency" and asked permission to present the same letter, this time addressed to Mr. Washington, Esquire, etc., etc., hoping that the et cetera's could imply everything; but Washington observed that they could also imply "anything," and therefore the letter could not be properly delivered.[30]

Colonel Patterson, in parting, stated that Lord Howe and his brother had been nominated as commissioners for the promotion of peace and that they would be most pleased were they able to effect some accommodation. He hoped that his visit would serve as a preliminary step toward the achievement of that end. Washington replied that to his understanding the brothers Howe were given powers only to grant pardons. Since those who had done no wrong had no need of pardons, he could see no benefit to Americans, who were merely defending their indisputable rights, in reaching an accommodation with Admiral and General Howe.[31]

The battle for New York began in late August of 1776. The British who had earlier landed on Staten Island were divided into two divisions. Approximately twenty thousand men were ferried across the harbor entrance to Long Island where they landed unopposed. There General Cornwallis led his reserve detachment to Flatbush. The rest of the British forces distributed themselves from the Narrows to the village of Flatland. Cornwallis, with two battalions of light infantry with limited artillery attempted to advance through the central pass through the hills that form a spine down the middle of Long Island. The pass, however, was well defended by Colonel Hand and his Pennsylvanian rifleman. Rather than engage prematurely Cornwallis was content to bivouac for the night in Flatbush. Generals Putnam and Sullivan shared the defensive responsibility for Long Island. Putnam was stationed to defend Brooklyn Heights while Sullivan, with twenty-eight hundred men defended the Heights of Guan. Only four roads crossed this rocky ridge so Sullivan's meager force should have been able to defend the ridge, even against vastly superior numbers of the British forces.[32]

By some error in planning only very light Colonial forces were assigned to guard the northern-most pass at Jamaica, an error which did not escape the notice of a civilian, likely a Tory. General Clinton was notified of this defensive flaw and he encouraged General Howe to attack in large numbers.

30 Irving, *George Washington, - A Biography*, 248 — 251
31 Ibid.
32 Ibid., 257 - 263

In an overnight march ten thousand British regulars, along with two companies of colonial loyalists, marched down the Jamaican Pass and behind the
forces of General Sullivan. In front of the Americans five thousand Hessian
attacked the next morning on signal. With the Hessians to their front and
the British to their rear, the result was a devastating slaughter. Those who
were not bayoneted or shot were captured, including General Sullivan. At
Gowans some nine thousand British regulars attacked two thousand militiamen commanded by General Alexander. Though fighting valiantly the
Americans were in an untenable position because of the collapse of Sullivan's troops earlier in the day. Great loss of life within General Alexander's
forces did purchase the escape of hundreds of American soldiers to safety in
Brooklyn Heights. General Howe hesitated in pressing the attack. In the following days rain impeded further British offensives and presented General
Washington with the opportunity to ferry what troops remained on Long
Island across the East River to join the main army on Manhattan. While
this escape in small personal craft is heralded as emblematic of the bravery
and commitment to independence of the colonists, General Israel Putnam
was later to write, "General Howe is either our friend or no general. He had
our whole army in his power and yet suffered us to escape without the least
interruption."[33]

The lessons of the campaign of Long Island were clear. It was not only
the superior numbers but also the training and discipline of the British Army
that bought the overwhelming victory for England. The Americans, officers
as well as soldiers, still had much to learn. Until they were fully seasoned by
experience and their confidence bolstered by significant victories, the American forces would remain vulnerable to the British in any frontal encounter. The success enjoyed by the British army was not untarnished by serious
concerns, however. This war was extraordinarily costly for them to conduct
from a distance of three thousand miles. All supplies, military stores, men,
clothing and equipment had to be transported across the Atlantic. With a
good ship's crossing requiring six weeks, it took England a minimum of three
months to respond to a material need. Washington saw that his best chance
of victory was by way of attrition, where he would harass the enemy at every
opportunity that did not require an open confrontation. Eventually the cost

to feed, clothe, equip and replace soldiers would exceed even Britain's ability to bear the financial burden of continuing the war.

In a series of fateful battles on Manhattan, the well disciplined, well-trained and well-provisioned British Army overwhelmed Washington's forces and the Battle for New York was lost by mid-November. General Washington led his defeated and disheartened army south through New Jersey to Trenton, where they crossed the Delaware River to find sanctuary in Philadelphia. As part of the New York militia supporting General Washington's Continental Army, Captain Hamilton continued to command his artillery company. Early in the retreat across northern New Jersey, Hamilton's artillery provided essential bombardment of the advancing British troops, permitting Washington's army to avoid an open conflict which would surely have finished the Revolution.[34]

When Washington led his army across the Delaware River all of New Jersey except for the contingent wintering at Morristown was yielded to the British. With Howe settled into winter quarters in New York, minimal British forces were distributed across New Jersey from the Delaware River to Brunswick. The Hessians were stationed along the Delaware in the vicinity of Trenton and British regulars and Tory militia were distributed from Trenton to Brunswick to serve as advance guards against any offensive move by the American forces.[35]

Washington's army was in disarray, poorly provisioned and at a very low morale. Many of the enlistments were to expire at the end of December and the men were not responding to enticements to prolong their tour of duty. The mood of the country was not supportive of the war, reflecting the long series of defeats in New York and the general inglorious retreat across New Jersey. Washington knew that news of some success was needed or, by spring, the revolution would be finished. Washington decided to risk all on a Christmas night raid on the Hessians at Trenton. He reasoned that, given the total disdain that the enemy held for his forces, the Hessians would celebrate Christmas in unbridled drinking and in the following early morning hours would be vulnerable to attack.[36]

At sunset on Christmas Day he launched twenty-four hundred troops in three prongs across the Delaware River. The main force under Washington

34 Flexner, J., *The Young Hamilton,* 122 - 123
35 Irving, W., *George Washington — A Biography,* 326
36 Leckie, *George Washington's War,* Harper Perenial, New York, 1992, 317 - 319

himself was to land at McKonky's Ferry (now Taylorsville), about nine miles above Trenton. They were to march to Trenton where the Hessian force of some fifteen hundred men was billeted. A second column under General Ewing was to land about a mile below Trenton, secure a bridge over the Assunpink Creek, and prevent any retreat of the Hessians by that route. General Putnam, along with troops under General Cadwalader, was to land near Burlington and attack the lower posts under Count Donop. Unfortunately, these last two columns were prevented from crossing the river by the ice floes, critically weakening Washington's planned offensive.[37]

Washington planned for the simultaneous attack at five o'clock in the morning. However, battle plans seldom are accomplished as planned. An insurrection in Philadelphia kept General Putnam and some of his forces in the city to maintain security there. He detached about six hundred of his Pennsylvania militia under Colonel Griffin to accompany Washington's raiding party. The transport of twenty-four hundred men, their artillery and stores took much longer than was planned due to the large amount of loose ice floating in the river. It was four in the morning before Washington was prepared to march from McKonky's Ferry. It was not until eight o'clock, daylight already, that the Americans were in Trenton.[38]

Washington had guessed correctly that the Hessians would celebrate the holiday heavily and be ill prepared to answer an offensive threat. During the night the Hessians had received and ignored numerous intelligence reports of the approach of the American forces. The ensuing attack caught the Hessian commander completely off guard. The response was uncoordinated and erratic. As Washington Irving described it,

> The outposts were driven in. They retreated, firing from behind houses. The Hessian drums beat to arms. The trumpets of the light horse sounded the alarm. The whole place was in an uproar. Some of the enemy made a wild and undirected fire from the windows of their quarters. Others rushed forward in disorder and attempted to form in the main street, while dragoons hastily mounted, and, galloping about, added to the confusion.

In the end approximately one thousand Hessians were captured. This number would have been considerably larger but many were able to escape by retreating over the routes that Generals Ewing and Putnam were to have secured.[39]

---

37 Irving, *George Washington — A Biography*, 329-331; Leckie, *George Washington's War*, 319
38 Irving, 334
39 Ibid., 336 - 337

Barely two days following their return to Pennsylvania Washington was anxious to return to the Jerseys and to press the Hessian remnant that had been able to escape capture during the Christmas contest. The commander of the remaining Hessians force, Count Donop, had divided his small force, sending part to Princeton and leading the remainder to Brunswick. It took fully two days for Washington's army to cross the Delaware with artillery and baggage. By that time it was year's end and many of his troop had enlistments that ran out on December 31. It would be folly for Washington to pursue his planned offensive without these men, so he persuaded many of them, with the added enticement of ten dollars bonus, to extend their enlistment for six additional weeks.[40]

When General Howe, in winter retreat in New York, received word of the Christmas rout of his forces at Trenton, he recalled Cornwallis who was at the point of embarkation on a planned trip to England and sent him back to correct the reverse experienced by the Hessians. Soon Lord Cornwallis, with his main force, which greatly outnumbered Washington's, was closing in on Trenton. They appeared prepared to trap the Americans between their forces and the frozen Delaware River. As it was late in the day and his troops weary from the long march he chose to bivouac his army for the night, stating confidently that he would "bag the fox in the morning."[41]

Studying his position Washington determined that they could not stay and fight the British with their greatly superior numbers. However, if he left under the cloak of night the British could cross the Delaware and take Philadelphia unopposed. At the same time, even if he were on the Pennsylvania side of the river, he could not prevent the large British force from capturing Philadelphia if they chose that course of action. On the other hand, many of the forces of Cornwallis' had recently left Princeton, where they must have left large quantities of baggage and stores. Washington could leave Trenton covertly and attack the meager force at Princeton early in the morning, capture the supplies there and march on to Morristown and more secure winter quarters. Washington presented this plan to a council of war with his commanders, who adopted it with enthusiasm.

The Americans circled around Trenton and Cornwallis in the night and marched toward Princeton. The main body of soldiers under General Wash-

---

40 Ibid., 341 - 342
41 Ibid., 343 - 345

ington took the principal road while a secondary detachment under General Mercer took a parallel road called Quaker Road. Mercer's regiments were observed and attacked by some British detachments that had been ordered to Trenton from Princeton, where they had spent the night. At the height of the battle General Washington came on the scene and in one of his storied examples of leadership rallied and cajoled the Americans, who then inflicted heavy losses on the British. Finally able to disengage from the Americans, the British made a full retreat to Trenton. The battle of Princeton cost the life of General Mercer, who was repeatedly bayoneted and left for dead. At daybreak Cornwallis learned that the Americans had escaped his trap and fled. Concerned that they might march to Brunswick and capture huge caches of British military stores, he began a forced march to intercept them. When Washington was advised of Mercer's fatal wounds, he petitioned Cornwallis that Mercer's aide-de-camp and nephew, Colonel George Lewis, be permitted to attend to Mercer until the latter's death, which occurred after several days of suffering.[42]

Washington meanwhile had reconsidered going to Princeton and Brunswick to scavenge enemy supplies. Recognizing that his men were fatigued from a sleepless night and the early morning battle he decided to go instead to winter quarters at Morristown. General Putnam arrived from Philadelphia and took Princeton, giving the Americans a presence in New Jersey from Princeton to Morristown while the British were confined to northern Jersey, near to the Hudson. In late 1776 and early 1777 the Americans had completely turned the war around. The equipment and experience of the British forces had early dominated and demoralized the Americans and had essentially driven them from New York and the Jerseys. Now, by the surprise victories at Trenton and Princeton Washington served notice that the Revolution was not to be a short conflict easily concluded. Britain's continued domination of America would come at a staggering cost.

Later during the winter of '76–'77, Washington needed to add to his staff a new aide-de-camp. Five generals nominated Alexander Hamilton. On earlier occasions Lord Sterling and Nathanael Greene had offered Hamilton the post of aide-de-camp in their respective headquarters. Captain Hamilton had declined their offers, feeling that he could contribute more substantially to the Revolution as a line officer and commander. When the offer came from

---

42 Ibid., 346 — 350

the commander-in-chief, however, Hamilton accepted. As of March 1, 1777, Alexander Hamilton assumed his new role in George Washington's "family" at the rank of Lieutenant Colonel.[43]

Soon after assuming the post of aide-de-camp, Hamilton committed to a weekly letter exchange with the New York Committee of Correspondence, an informal group of prominent citizens formed as a pseudo-governmental body intended to create a constitution for the state of New York and to direct that state's participation in the revolution. Hamilton continued this correspondence throughout the war to keep that body abreast of the conduct of the war as seen from General Washington's headquarters. In his correspondence with the New York Committee he was drawn into a discussion of the form of government that had been drafted for that state. He gave early evidence of his support of a representative democracy form of government, stating, "When the deliberative or judicial powers are vested wholly or partly in the collective body of the people you must experience error, confusion and instability. But a representative democracy, where the right of election is well secured and regulated and the exercises of the legislative, executive and judiciary authorities, is vested in select persons, chosen *really* and not *nominally* by the people, will in my opinion be most likely to be happy, regular and durable."[44] This was Hamilton's first expression of his philosophical support of a representative democratic government. Although his actions, writings and public statements bore proof of his advocacy of a democratic form of government, he would be charged by his political opponents with being a monarchist at heart.

Throughout the war both the Congress and General Washington were deluged with applications for high-ranking positions from European soldiers of fortune. Many of these applications resulted from letters of recommendation sent by Dr. Franklin or Silas Deane, both American representatives in France. Some of the foreign applicants actually profited America considerably by their military skills and fortitude; examples include such notables as LaFayette, Kosciusko and Von Steuben. Other officers, given the rank of general by Congress, created dissension among American-born officers who were superseded in rank. During the early months of 1777 Silas Deane

---

43 Mitchell, *Alexander Hamilton — Youth to Maturity*, 104 - 105
44 Syrett, *The Papers of Alexander Hamilton*, Vol. I, 254 - 256

recommended an Irish-born officer, Colonel Conway, to General Washington. Col. Conway represented himself as a veteran of thirty years service to France and claimed to be a recipient of the honor of being named Chevalier of the Order of St. Louis. Following an interview with Conway, General Washington wrote to Congress that, while he had no first-hand knowledge of Conway's experience and accomplishments, on the surface his application seemed to qualify him for the rank of brigadier general, the rank he had applied for. His performance, however, did not match his claimed experience. By personality he was boastful and presumptuous. By character he was prone to intrigues designed for self-aggrandizement. He will be encountered later in this story acting in the role of intriguer, plotting for the downfall of the commander-in-chief.[45]

Late in the month of May 1777, General Washington broke camp from winter quarters at Morristown and realigned his troops at Middlebrook, near Brunswick. General Howe, with some fresh German troops as well as some re-enforcement redcoats, spent the month of June attempting to draw Washington and the American army out of their stronghold at Middlebrook into an open confrontation in which both commanders knew the British would be decisively victorious. When, after a month of such attempts, he proved unable to entice Washington to weaken his position and render himself vulnerable to a frontal attack, Howe returned to New York, embarked his army on transport ships and sailed to the open sea from the New York harbor. It was supposed in the American camp that the final destination of the British army was Philadelphia, although whether they would attempt their assault via the Delaware Bay or further south through the Chesapeake was uncertain.[46]

While Washington was focused on defeating the anticipated British attack on Philadelphia, the enemy opened a second, most threatening offensive. This offensive, conceived by the Colonial Secretary Lord George Germain, consisted of a three-pronged effort. The flamboyant Major General John Burgoyne was to lead one column that would attack New York from Canada, down through Lake Champlain. Howe, with another column, would move up the Hudson River from New York City, joining with Burgoyne at Albany.

45 Irving, *George Washington — A Biography*, 358 - 361
46 Ibid., 360 - 361

The third column, under Lt. Col. St. Leger, was to travel up the St. Lawrence River to Oswego, capture Fort Stanwix and move down the Mohawk Valley, joining with Howe and Burgoyne at Albany. Burgoyne's army consisted of 3700 British, 3016 Germans, 250 Canadians and 400 Indians. In addition he had some 470 artillerymen; the total of the British army involved in this invasion was nearly 8000 men.[47] Were this offensive to be successful, the British would cut New York and New England off from the southern states, crippling America's combined capability to conduct the revolution.

Major General Philip Schuyler, assisted by General Horatio Gates, headed the Americans opposing Burgoyne. In anticipation of the enemy's offensive these commanders had seen to the reinforcement of Fort Ticonderoga and felt that capturing this fort would be extremely costly to the British. Unfortunately, the Americans erred in thinking that Sugar Loaf Hill, overlooking the fort, was inaccessible by foot and doubly so to any artillery. The British managed, in just one night, not only to mount the hill but also to drag cannon and shot up with them; in the morning their view from the top dominated Fort Ticonderoga. The Americans had been warned by Polish born military engineer, Tadeusz Kosciuszko, that if the enemy were able to locate cannon on that hill the fort would be at the mercy of their guns.

When the Americans realized their position was within range of the British guns on Sugar Loaf, they were forced to abandon Fort Ticonderoga and were chased and harassed through miles of woodland, eventually finding security at Fort Edward, approximately fifty miles north of Albany. The British entrenched themselves approximately twenty miles north of Fort Edward to prepare for their final assault. Burgoyne envisioned garrisoning the captured Fort Ticonderoga with Canadians under General Carleton where all his supplies could be transported and stored to be transported by wagon from there as needed. It turned out, however, that Carleton was unable to garrison the fort, requiring that Burgoyne parcel out one thousand of his troops for this purpose.[48]

The seeds for Burgoyne's disastrous defeat were contained in his battle plan. Dividing the attack force into three columns reduced the effort required of the Americans to defeat him by a factor of three. It was impossible to synchronize the efforts of the three advancing columns, so the Americans

---

47 Ibid., 365 - 371
48 Leckie, George Washington's War, 382 - 388

were able to deal with them one at a time. In addition, the fact that he chose to begin his journey in Canada complicated his problem of continuous supplies, requiring them to be transported hundreds of miles through hostile territory over mean and treacherous roads. Still, with his inflated confidence in his own generalship and the combat skills of the British Army, combined with his dim view of the American fighting force, he envisioned nothing but victory.[49]

General Burgoyne led his Army of British regulars and Hessian mercenaries down the length of Vermont on Lake Champlain, taking control of Fort Ticonderoga, and across the New York wilderness toward Albany. With each mile, however, his supply lines grew longer and soon were so extended and perilous that they constituted a major threat to his success. More and more of his troops needed to be employed in moving his supplies and in guarding the supply train. Barely fifty miles from his objective at Saratoga, Burgoyne was drawn into an attack where his forces, being so extended, were unable to withstand the assault of Generals Gates and Arnold with the American forces. On October 17, General Burgoyne was forced to surrender to General Gates. It has been a continuing debate whether Gates or Arnold was responsible for the American victory, although General Gates was quick to claim full credit.[50]

The resounding American victory at Saratoga gave renewed hope to the country that the Revolution would eventually succeed. It also gave credibility to the American cause in capitals around the world. Specifically the French and the Dutch were motivated, for their own purposes, to give critically needed support. The Dutch offered loans and the French committed both money and essential military assistance, helping the Americans while at the same time serving the French national objective of weakening the British.

For several months General Washington was concerned with countering General Howe's attempt to capture the capital, Philadelphia. Late in August, Howe landed his fleet in the Elk River at the top of the Chesapeake Bay. The British faced difficult terrain to Philadelphia, seventy miles to travel, fording deep streams and crossing rugged, wooded land to achieve their objective. There would appear to have been numerous opportunities for Washington's

---

49 Bobrick, *Angel in the Whirlwind*, 245 - 246
50 Irving, *George Washington — A Biography*, 419 - 426

forces to trap the British at some geographical obstacle. But the skill and discipline of the British army and the superior leadership of General Howe prevailed at the battles of Brandywine Creek and Paoli's Tavern and the British eventually marched into Philadelphia unopposed, on September 26.

Desperate for a victory and anxious to evict the British from the capital city, Washington decided to wage one more battle prior to going into winter quarters. Cornwallis occupied the capital with two battalions each of British regulars and Hessians. A significant portion of his force had been dispatched to New Jersey to capture the fort at Billingsport. Howe was outside of Philadelphia in Germantown, along the Schuylkill River with nine thousand men, having dispatched three thousand to expedite and escort a shipment of provisions from Elkton, Maryland.[51] Washington took this opportunity to go on the offensive and to attack Howe at Germantown. On the night of October 3, Washington launched a well conceived but complex offensive in which four separate columns were to march approximately sixteen miles in the dark and converge on the hamlet of Germantown simultaneously at daybreak. [52]

This battle plan would have been a challenge for experienced officers and soldiers to synchronize and was doubly daunting for the mostly inexperienced men in Washington's army. The Americans approached the British nearly in unison but later than planned; the sun was fully up before the first shot was fired. The British resisted until Anthony Wayne's division charged Colonel Musgrave's light infantry with bayonets. Spirited and seeking revenge for the massacre they had suffered several days previously, the Americans charged, chanting, "Have at the bloodhounds." The British force retreated before this onslaught and twice attempted to counter charge. Wayne's forces pressed the attack. When the British broke, retreated and called for quarter, none was given. Although the American officers tried to restrain them the soldiers continued their attack, killing all they encountered.[53]

During the British retreat Musgrave and some 120 men sought refuge in the stone country house of Benjamin Chew, Chief Justice of Pennsylvania prior to the Revolution. From this stronghold vantage point Musgrave's soldiers fired on one of the American columns. In a very animated debate held at General Washington's headquarters some officers, including Alexander Hamilton and Col. Timothy Pickering, argued that it was best to give the

---

51 Leckie, *George Washington's War*, 359
52 Ibid.
53 Ibid., 359 - 362

house a wide berth and continue the attack; however, General Knox in-sisted that that tactic violated the cardinal rule of warfare, which dictated that an occupied castle should never be left to one's rear. By this time in the war Washington was increasingly turning to Hamilton for his viewpoint in military decisions; in this case, however, Washington deferred to Knox's reasoning and ordered that the Chew house be taken. One American unit after another was diverted to barrage and silence the Chew house, but to no avail. These diversions did, however, disrupt the simultaneity of the multi-columned attack. When the coordination was broken, mayhem resulted. In the mist and smoke of battle, two American forces, headed by Generals Ste-phen and Greene, stumbled onto one another and a "friendly fire" fight broke out. Eventually both units retreated. General Sullivan's troops were running out of ammunition and likewise retreated. Wayne's division mistook a large contingent of Americans as the enemy and also retreated.

At this point the British reformed and pressed their gratuitous advantage and, reinforced by Cornwallis with a cavalry of light horse from Philadelphia, completed the generalized American retreat. This retreat continued for more than twenty miles until the Americans reached a safe haven at Perkiomen Creek.[54]

Washington's report of the disastrous reversal said, "It is with much cha-grin and mortification, I add, that every account confirms the opinion I at first entertained that our troops retreated at the instant when victory was declaring herself in our favor. The tumult, disorder and even despair which, it seems, had taken place in the British Army, were scarcely to be paralleled, and it is said, so strongly did the ideas of a retreat prevail that Chester was fixed on for their rendezvous."[55]

On October 28 Colonel James Wilkinson stopped at Reading, Pennsylva-nia en route to Philadelphia, carrying Gates' report to Congress concerning his victory at Saratoga. During his stop Wilkinson dined with Lord Ster-ling and told him of a letter written by General Conway to General Gates. In this letter he cited Conway as saying, "Heaven has been determined to save your country, or a weak general and bad councilors would have ruined it." This derogatory opinion of Washington must have given encouragement to Gates, who already entertained aspirations of replacing Washington as

54 Bobrick, *Angel in the Whirlwind*, 267 - 269
55 Irving, *George Washington — A Biography*, 435

commander-in-chief based on his victory at Saratoga. Upon receiving word of this quotation from Conway's letter, Washington immediately drafted a note to Conway, questioning the incident.[56] Although Conway denied being the author of this quotation, he had already committed himself to the ouster of Washington. Earlier in October 1777 Washington had warned Richard Henry Lee in Congress that a proposed move to raise Conway to the rank of major general would be a most serious blow to the army because there were a number of more brave and more capable brigadiers who would not serve under him. This rejection of his aspirations drove Conway into a faction with General Mifflin for the displacement of the commander-in-chief. This alliance became known as the Conway Cabal and the intrigues generated thereby spread throughout the army and infiltrated Congress itself.[57]

---

56 Leckie, *George Washington's War*, 448 - 449
57 Ibid., 450 - 451

Chapter 3. Valley Forge to Yorktown

The American Army spent the winter of 1777–1778 at Valley Forge, outside of British occupied Philadelphia. In the memory of America, Valley Forge represents the epitome of suffering of the soldiers struggling to gain independence. Whether or not the Congress or the Quartermaster General had done all that was within their power to provide for the needs of the Continental soldier at Valley Forge, the truth remains that the American Army, throughout the Revolution, suffered chronic needs for the bare necessities of clothing and food as well as for arms and wages.

These winter quarters, twenty miles from Philadelphia, were remote enough that the Americans would not be frequently pestered by British patrols yet were sufficiently near to be able to respond to any further British aggression. The most immediate need faced by the Americans was to acquire shelter, food and adequate winter clothing. Those soldiers who were physically fit and had at least some warm clothing and shoes were given the task of constructing log huts. Washington's regulations stated that the log huts would have a base measuring fourteen by sixteen feet. The six and half-feet high walls would be chinked with clay, split logs forming the roofing. A hut would house twelve non-commissioned officers and men. A general officer would occupy a hut by himself. Washington shared the hardships of his troops, living on the grounds in a tent until all of the men were located in their meager huts. Thereafter Washington and his wife took up residence in a stone house on the premises.[1]

During the winter at Valley Forge, General Washington looked forward to his spring offensive to displace the British army from the capital in Philadelphia. The most pressing need he had to support this offensive was an influx of fresh, well-equipped soldiers. Following the army's autumn victory at Saratoga, there existed in Washington's mind a prime source for the replacements so desperately needed by Washington's army. General Washington delegated Lieutenant Colonel Hamilton to ride to a meeting with General Gates in Albany to explain the need for reinforcements and to requisition men and arms from General Gates' army. As a demonstration of Washington's confidence in his young aide-de-camp, Washington drafted a letter to Alexander Hamilton in which he gave only a broad description of the objective and scope of Hamilton's direction. Hamilton was given wide latitude in dealing with Gates; he was to decide if any plans for action that General Gates presently was considering offered benefits to the army greater than those offered by Washington's plans to retake Philadelphia. Providing that Hamilton was convinced of the merits of Gates' plans, he was to adjust the quantity of men ordered to Philadelphia.[2]

When he arrived in Albany, Hamilton found Major Robert Troup, an old friend from King's College. Troup was an aide to General Gates and had recently been released from a prisoner-of-war camp. Troup confirmed that Gates had planned to send Washington no reinforcements and added that General Putnam at Peekskill was sending no reinforcements, either. Exercising the authority given to him by Washington, Hamilton ordered Putnam to send the New York militia under his command to Washington. He based this order on information that General Clinton had sent most of his troops to Philadelphia to bolster General Howe's numbers.[3]

When Hamilton met with General Gates on the matter of reinforcing Washington's army, Gates was adamant that he could not offer Washington any support. Gates took personal offense in the fact that Washington had sent so young and inferior an officer to dictate troop movement strategy to an officer of his rank and prestige. Gates cited three arguments against conforming to Hamilton's directions: (1) General Clinton might decide to

1 Bobrick, *Angel in the Whirlwind*, 287
2 Randall, *Alexander Hamilton — A Life*, 140 - 141
3 Ibid. 141

come up the Hudson River and attack Albany; (2) without all of his troops he would be unable to retake Fort Ticonderoga; and finally, (3) even if he were to offer assistance to Washington it would have to wait until the roads were frozen to transport artillery.[4]

Hamilton was greatly embarrassed at not being able to obtain the critically needed assistance from Washington's inferior officer. He sensed that Gates had acquired a broad base of support on the account of his Saratoga victory and that his support extended even to Congress. To collect his thoughts and plan for round two of his encounter with Gates, Hamilton took leave and visited his mentor and friend, Phillip Schuyler, at the latter's house outside of Albany. Schuyler welcomed Hamilton and took the opportunity to fill him in on the military and political intrigues involved in Gates' strategy. During this visit Hamilton became reacquainted with Schuyler's daughter, Eliza, who would, in little more than two years, become his bride.[5]

Upon revisiting General Gates, Lieutenant Colonel Hamilton rescinded his earlier acquiescence to Gates' position and required that maximum support be given to Washington's urgent need. No argument of Gates' filled the condition to which Washington referred in his letter regarding plans that might provide greater benefit to the country than the objective of retaking Philadelphia. This time Gates conceded and within days twenty two hundred Continentals were marching to Valley Forge. Hamilton left Albany when he saw the troops afoot. At Peekskill, Hamilton was astonished to see that General Putnam had not proceeded to send his troops south as ordered. Hamilton told Putnam, "How (your) noncompliance can be answered to General Washington you can best determine." He then gave Putnam written orders to send the entire Continental troops under his command immediately. The Connecticut troops under Putnam refused to move until they were paid at least part of their back wages. Hamilton took matters into his own hands and arranged with Governor George Clinton for a loan to meet this demand and got the troops on the march.[6]

In addition to the added troops provided by Hamilton's negotiation with General Gates, the one positive occurrence that winter was the arrival at Valley Forge of the German officer, Baron von Steuben. He claimed the Prussian rank of Lieutenant General where, in fact, he had never held a rank higher

4 Ibid., 142 - 143
5 Ibid.,
6 Ibid., 142 - 146

than Captain. He arrived at Washington's headquarters attired in uniform and riding in a horse-drawn sleigh with a greyhound sitting proudly beside him. At the side of the sleigh were five grooms, three servants, a cook and three French aides and interpreters. Among the aides was Pierre L'Enfant who one day would design the City of Washington. He challenged General Washington to permit him to serve the American army as a volunteer until Washington himself decided upon his appropriate rank based on his demonstrated capabilities. He insisted that he desired no command until he learned "the language, the genius and the manners of the people."[7]

Upon examination of the army Steuben was appalled at the conditions he saw. Officers and men alike were without uniforms of any kind; many did not have adequate clothing or shoes. No units were at full strength. He identified one company that consisted of but one solider, a corporal. One regiment found that consisted of only thirty men. All of the muskets were dirty and rusting, many had no bayonets. Those soldiers who did have bayonets often used them as cooking utensils. [8]

Steuben saw in addition that the Americans lacked discipline and to Steuben that spelled the need for drill. Up to that point each unit followed drill practices of their own invention with no uniformity across the army. Von Steuben undertook to select a cadre of veterans, seasoned by combat and hardened by privations, and treated them as raw recruits who knew nothing of discipline or drill. This cadre of soldiers he would train and instill with discipline. They in turn would train less experienced soldiers. It took Steuben a month to compose a drill manual for the army, hampered mainly by the language barrier. Steuben would write the drill instructions in French. Du Ponceau would translate these into English. Nathanael Greene and Alexander Hamilton would further translate them into "American" that was understandable to the soldiers. [9]

That being accomplished, Von Steuben in a very short time transformed the army into an integrated unit that could march with as much precision as any European army. Steuben himself was impressed that the Americans could maintain their unity and under combat conditions were able to maneuver and alter formation on command. Steuben was astute enough to recognize the basic difference between the American soldier and the Europeans

---

7 Leckie, *George Washington's War*, 438 - 440
8 Ibid., 440 - 442
9 Ibid.

he was used to. To the European soldier he could say, "Do this," and he would do it. To the American soldier he had to say, "This is why you should do this," and then they would do it.[10]

He taught the marching drill, and instituted training that combined classical military thinking and the battle tactics developed by the Americans (fighting in rapidly moving, loose formations rather than in close order, stand up formations). He identified and trained sharpshooters and organized them into light infantry. He taught the Americans how to fight and to defend themselves with the bayonet. He showed them how to fire their muskets to improve their accuracy. All of this he accomplished with a ribald humor and the ability to curse in three languages — characteristics that quickly endeared him to the soldiers. Washington had expected and hoped for much from Steuben, and was overjoyed at the results produced by springtime. Washington recommended that Von Steuben fill the position of Inspector General at the rank of Major General.[11]

Washington increasingly relied on Lieutenant Colonel Hamilton for participation in strategic planning meetings; he was used on a number of occasions as personal emissary for Washington, and Hamilton was a principal negotiator for the American Army in prisoner exchange discussions. Still, with his fertile mind, Hamilton was not content to expend all of his energies on assigned tasks. He had recognized, along with numerous others, the weakness of the Confederation. He understood that for America to survive independence, once it was won, a more stable form of government would have to be established. A strong central government, to which the states would assume a subordinate position, was essential in his mind to provide the stability necessary for the grand experiment in republicanism to endure.

Hamilton held the position that the weakness of the central government made Congress impotent to acquire and provide the necessary funds to conduct the Revolution. Based on their recent experiences with the monarchy and Parliament, Americans held a resentment and fear of any form of centralized government as a potential source of tyranny. Each of the states was jealous of its sovereignty and was adamant that the central government not be given powers of taxation, guarding that prerogative for itself. According to the provisions of the Articles of Confederation, Congress had no fixed

---

10 Ibid.
11 Ibid., 441 - 442

source of income and was dependent upon voluntary contributions of the individual States.

During the Revolution one of the great weaknesses was the lack of a stable national system of finance to support and spur the economy. Hamilton set himself the task to examine and identify the parameters requisite for the creation and operation of an efficient system of finance. What would be the operating cost of the central government he envisioned? What part of the economy could most readily support taxation without hindering the free operation of commerce? What is required for the national monetary system to be stable and for the value of the specie underwriting the monetary system to be respected on the world market; and, what is needed for the notes of exchange to be free from the runaway speculative depreciation recently suffered by the Continental notes? To answer these and other critical questions Hamilton consulted the world's writers on economy and finance. He kept personal copies of David Hume's *Political Discourses* and Postlethwayts's *Universal Dictionary of Trade and Commerce*. At night, after completion of his tasks supporting Washington, he studied these tomes and began to formulate his own concepts and arguments that would eventually evolve into the Treasury system of the United States when he became its first Secretary.

In his role as aide-de-camp to General Washington, Alexander Hamilton was in a position to recognize the weakness and failings of the country as defined under the Articles of Confederation. In 1780, James Duane, a congressman from upper state New York and a friend of Hamilton's, wrote to ask his opinion on the defects of the Confederation government and for suggestions on ways to improve its effectiveness.

As was his style, Hamilton replied with a rather lengthy letter in which he enumerated the faults of the current government: (1) Congress was too weak to unify and direct the country; (2) Congress suffered the lack of a strong and efficient administration; (3) The Congress needed to have an adequate, independent power to raise revenue sufficient to accomplish the tasks it assumed; (4) The embarrassing and fluctuating constitution of the army continuously threatened the country's ability to continue the revolution. His recommendations were well conceived and to a large extent presaged the results of the Constitutional Convention that was yet seven years in the future. He recommended that Congress be given powers consistent with the needs for public security, felicity and stability. He strongly promoted that Congress be given sovereignty over the States in regards to war, peace, finance, and the management of foreign affairs. He saw Congress as a deliberative body, needing a separate branch of Administration to execute the dictates of the Congress. Hamilton's idea of a suitable Administration included a chief magistrate and a consultative body, the Cabinet, to administer the various departments of government. As a separate concept, Hamilton introduced the idea of a national bank as an institution to secure the public credit.[12]

In a move that was highly controversial in the British army at Philadelphia, General William Howe was replaced by General Henry Clinton as commander of the British army in America. General Howe left Philadelphia to return to England on May 25, 1778. Clinton's first responsibility, as he saw it, was to secure the British position in New York. He was aware that a French fleet, under Comte d'Estaing, was on its way to America and might well blockade the Delaware River, closing Clinton's only seaward escape route. To protect his army from possible defeat by the French naval forces, Clinton decided to move overland to New York. He shipped his cavalry, his artillery and 3,000 Tories by sea. The rest of his army, about 8,000 men, Clinton led on a march across New Jersey along with 1500 wagons of baggage that stretched out for twelve miles.[13]

This thinly spread line of the British army presented a tempting target for General Washington. Washington assigned Alexander Hamilton to reconnoiter the British movements to ascertain the route they were taking. Hamilton and his reconnaissance detachment were in the saddle for four nights and four days, reporting back to Washington regularly. On June 25 he reported to LaFayette that the front of the British column had turned onto the Monmouth Road. Hamilton's reports convinced Washington that the British were taking the shortest possible route to the sea and that they would shortly be out of reach if the American army did not attack soon.[14]

In a council of war Washington proposed to attack the British forces following the baggage train. General Charles Lee disagreed with this stratagem; however, when it was generally agreed upon, over his objections, he concurred and insisted on assuming the command position for the vanguard of the American attack. Afterwards he vacillated until Washington, in dis-

12 Syrett, H., *The Papers of Alexander Hamilton, Vol. II*, 400 - 411
13 Bobrick, *Angel in the Whirlwind*, 343; Leckie, *George Washington's War*, 463 - 465
14 Randall, *Alexander Hamilton — A Life*, 171 - 174

gust, gave Lafayette the command. Later, to appease Lee who by then was seething with resentment, Washington re-assigned him to the command, in a decision he would soon regret.[15]

On June 28, Lee and his advanced force of 5000 encountered the British rearguard at Monmouth Courthouse in Freehold, New Jersey. Washington was coming behind with the main army, ready to support Lee once combat was entered. Instead of fully engaging his troops, Lee shuffled their position back and forth, allowing only some of his units to engage the British. Lee's uncertainty caused confusion and loss of focus in the ranks. At one point Washington sent word asking for an explanation and Lee replied, "Tell the General I am doing well enough." Finally, Washington rode forward to assess Lee's operation, only to find all of Lee's forces marching away from the enemy. When Washington encountered Lee he demanded to know, "What is the meaning of this, sir? I desire to know the meaning of this disorder and confusion." "The American troops would not stand the British bayonets," Lee replied. Washington exploded, "You damned poltroon, you never tried them!" It was said that, although unaccustomed to using vile language, Washington cursed that day "till the leaves shook on the trees."[16]

Washington then took charge, reversed Lee's orders and led the fighting through the hot afternoon. In the evening both sides withdrew, having suffered the loss of 350 men apiece. Although Lee's villainy that day cost the Americans a significant victory, the discipline instilled in the soldiers by von Steuben allowed them to recover from Lee's retreat and to gain a draw in the day's battle. Alexander Hamilton participated in the reversal of the battle until his horse was shot out from under him. Hamilton was pinned beneath the fallen horse until some Rhode Island militiamen pulled him free. Clinton and his forces marched through the night and avoided further conflict, as the Americans were unable to overtake them before the British crossed over to New York.[17]

In the aftermath of the Battle of Monmouth, Lee tried to extricate himself from his disgrace by offering justifications of his actions in a letter to Washington. Upon receiving Washington's rebuke, Lee demanded an opportunity to exonerate his conduct in a court martial. Washington obliged him in this requests and charged Lee with

---

15 Bobrick, *Angel in the Whirlwind*, 344
16 Leckie, *George Washington's War*, 475 - 483
17 Leckie, *George Washington's War*, 483 - 484, Randall, *Alexander Hamilton — A Life*, 175

- Disobedience of orders in not attacking the enemy.
- Misbehavior before the enemy by making an unnecessary, disorderly and shameful retreat.
- Disrespect to the commander-in-chief in two letters, dated June 28 and July 1.

Lee was found guilty of all charges, although the word "shameful" was stricken from the record. He was suspended from his command for the period of one year. Congress approved the sentence and subsequently dismissed him permanently from the service on account of an insulting letter Lee wrote to the President of Congress.[18]

With Clinton safety quartered on Manhattan, Washington allowed his army time to catch its breath and then marched at an easy pace to the North River, where they crossed over to White Plains, meeting General Gates who had moved his northern army to White Plains some time earlier.

In a touch of irony, the two armies were now essentially in the same setting they had occupied some two years earlier. It was not, however, the same American Army facing General Clinton that had faced General Howe earlier. The new American Army had battle experience. They had tasted significant victories as well as disheartening defeats. There was no longer a sense of awe at the well attired, highly disciplined British army. They had seen the redcoats break into headlong retreat, and had soundly beaten them in battle. The American army had become confident of attaining victory and Britain's domination appeared to be in its twilight.

Perhaps the most memorable and surely the most dramatic contribution of the American Navy during the war came from a displaced Scotsman, John Paul Jones. He was born John Paul in Galloway Scotland in 1747, the son of a gardener. He was drawn to the sea as a young boy, often playing on and around moored ships in nearby Carsethorn. At age twelve he was apprenticed to a ship owner in Whitehaven. By the time he was nineteen he had worked his way up to first mate on a slaver. He was captain of a ship at age twenty-one. When he was twenty-seven he killed a sailor in his crew who was agitating for mutiny. Fearing that he would be tried in England for murder he fled to America, added "Jones" to his name and, when the Revolution began, he was commissioned a first lieutenant in the American Navy. He

---

18 Bobrick, *Angel in the Whirlwind*, 350 - 351

convinced Congress that to compete with the privateering fleet for crewmen the Congress would have to offer larger shares of captured cargo to the naval crews.[19]

Jones' early conquests included interruption of British shipping in American waters from Bermuda to Nova Scotia, seized the island of St. Kitts from the British and captured British sloops of war in the Gulf of Mexico. In the American sloop *Ranger*, he sailed the Irish Sea, captured the 250-ton ship *Lord Chatham* and sank a Scottish coastal schooner loaded with grain and imprisoned her crew. In the only American action of the Revolution conducted on British soil, Jones made a daring raid on Whitehaven, spiked some guns of the shore batteries and attempted to burn ships in the harbor. Before leaving Whitehaven the crew made an audacious trip to the local pub where they drank freely of Scottish liquor. He so thoroughly instilled fear in coastal Britain that Lord North determined to dispatch a squadron of ships for his capture once the threat of the Franco-Spanish invasion was resolved.[20]

With the Franco-American alliance in effect, Jones began to use French ports as his base. Soon he had assembled a marauding task force of four ships. His flagship, the *Bonhomme Richard*, named for Benjamin Franklin's *Poor Richard's Almanac*, had been used in the tea trade with India. The French had converted her into a forty-two-gun warship of mediocre seaworthiness. The thirty-gun frigates *Pallas* and *Alliance* and the twelve-gun brigantine *Vengeance* rounded out his fleet. On the evening of September 23 the *Bonhomme Richard* and her escort of gun ships fell on the British warship *Serapis*, sporting fifty guns and under the command of Captain Richard Pearson. When the ships approached one another Jones let loose a barrage at point blank range into the *Serapis*. Unfortunately two of three heavy guns on that side ruptured when fired, killing their crews and doing structural damage to the deck above. In desperation Jones drew his ship to the Serapis and lashed the two ships together. As the battle raged the *Richard* took the worst damage and at one point a sailor on the *Richard* called for quarter. When Captain Pearson asked Jones for confirmation of the request, Jones made his memorable reply, "I have not yet begun to fight." As the battle continued the marines in the rigging of the *Richard* defeated their counterparts in the rigging of the *Serapis* and finally were able to lob grenades and to fire muskets onto the up-

---

19 Leckie, *George Washington's War*, 496 - 498
20 Ibid., 499

per deck of the *Serapis*. Eventually the explosion of a munitions locker on the *Serapis* set off a chain of explosions, causing massive damage and casualties. When the *Alliance* came alongside to assist *Richard* the battle was finished and Captain Pearson offered Jones his sword. This naval victory signaled to the British that their unchallenged mastery of the sea was at an end. The victory bolstered the morale of the American Congress and the Continental Army.

Unfortunately neither John Paul Jones nor the Continental Navy was able to capitalize on this victory. No additional significant naval engagements occurred through the remaining years of the revolution.[21]

Throughout his life Alexander Hamilton was acutely sensitive to personal attacks on his character or integrity. On a number of occasions he reacted with vitriolic anger to false accusations or insults where a more moderate approach of ignoring the affront or resolving it through mediation would have been successful. In July 1779, while Hamilton enjoyed a senior position in General Washington's "family," a congressional representative from Massachusetts, Francis Dana, accused Hamilton of publicly stating "that it was high time for the people to rise, join General Washington and turn Congress out of doors." Hamilton confronted Dana and demanded to know the source of this falsehood, threatening a challenge on the field of honor if necessary to resolve the issue. This incident was finally traced to a Dr. William Gordon, a Congregationalist minister. Unable to challenge a man of religion to a duel, Hamilton limited his reaction to a rancorous letter in which he accused Gordon of the falsehood and implied that Gordon was a man of little honor.[22]

In 1779 and 1780, the war in the South was going badly for the Americans. Successive defeats at Savannah, Charleston and Camden, South Carolina had drawn a pall over the prospects for independence. Washington continued to place his best hopes in a plan for the combined American and French forces to force a British evacuation of New York City. Washington, Knox and La-Fayette met with Rochambeau, commander of French forces in America, at Hartford, Connecticut on September 21, 1780 to discuss the general strategy of the war and to determine if they could agree on a combined offensive. Of this meeting Washington wrote, "We could only combine possible plans on the supposition of possible events." It was agreed that, provided the French

---

21 Ibid.
22 Syrett, *The Papers of Alexander Hamilton*, Vol. II, 99, 108, 141-143, 224

fleet arrived prior to fall, an offensive against New York could be considered. On September 23 Washington left Hartford, visited the French minister Luzerne at Peekskill, and planned to travel on September 25 to inspect General Arnold's fortifications at West Point.[23]

Unbeknownst to Washington, General Benedict Arnold had been persuaded by his new wife, Peggy (Shippen), to betray the American cause and to sell out for personal gain to the British. Arnold asked two things from the British: first, a command of equal status in the British Army and, second, compensation for the material losses he would suffer in abandoning his current position. He was seeking £10,000. General Clinton assigned to Major John Andre, his aide-de-camp, the task of communicating with Arnold and effecting this transfer. Although Arnold gave some sensitive information to the British as an act of good faith, they desired something substantial to come with Arnold in his perfidy. Together they agreed upon West Point as an important enough prize. Arnold had been assigned this command by a general order dated August 3, 1780.[24]

It was agreed that Major Andre was to visit Arnold at West Point, complete the conspiracy negotiations and return to the British lines with some form of evidentiary proof of Arnold's complicity. Andre, traveling under the *nom de plume* of Mr. Anderson, traveled aboard the *Vulture* to West Point and directed the ship's captain to await his return. Joshua Smith, the owner of a mansion across the Hudson from West Point, was directed by Arnold to row out to the *Vulture*, take Mr. Anderson aboard and to bring him to Arnold's quarters at West Point.[25]

During the night, Arnold provided plans of the fort showing each installation and its strength. During their discussions, Andre offered Arnold the command in the British army that Arnold had insisted upon. However, he was authorized only to offer him £6,000 instead of £10,000. Following a heated discussion, Andre agreed to ask General Clinton to provide the full amount, although both men knew that the die was cast. There was no turning back; Arnold no longer had any negotiating leverage in the matter.

During the night an American shore battery commanded by Colonel James Livingstone fired at the *Vulture*, driving it downriver. As a consequence Andre was forced to travel overland to return to the British lines. Andre and

---

23 Irving, *George Washing — A Biography*, 525 - 526
24 Leckie, *George Washington's War*, 560
25 Ibid., 563

Arnold thought it safer for Andre to travel to the British lines in civilian clothes rather than the British uniform he had come dressed in. When he was within sight of the British lines, in what appears to have been a chance encounter, a group of ragged highwaymen stopped Andre at the point of a gun and insisted that he give them his money. When Andre insisted that he had none, he was forced to disrobe; inside of one of his boots they found the plan that Arnold had given him of West Point's fortifications. Realizing this was an important document and hoping they could parlay it into some cash, they took Andre to the American garrison at North Castle and turned him over to a Lieutenant Colonel Jameson.[26]

Alexander Hamilton and James McHenry, who had been sent by Washington and Lafayette to advise Arnold of their imminent arrival, were breakfasting with Arnold when the rider dispatched by Jameson arrived and handed Arnold the fateful message. In a glance Arnold realized that Andre had not returned safely to the British lines and that, by then, General Washington must be aware of his treason. Arnold ran upstairs to tell his wife the distressing news and dashed off to board his personal barge. He ordered his boatmen to take him to the *Vulture*, supposedly on urgent army business.

Before Washington could arrive at Arnold's headquarters, Hamilton heard Arnold's wife upstairs in a state of hysteria. He went up to find out the cause of her distress and to attempt to console her. Her extreme agitation and her incoherent words, combined with Arnold's bizarre exit, convinced Hamilton of Arnold's treason. Hamilton attested to the persuasiveness of Peggy Arnold concerning her husband's treason in a letter that same day to his Eliza.

> In the midst of my letter, I was interrupted by a scene that shocked me more than any thing I have met with — the discovery of a treason of the deepest dye. The object was to sacrifice West Point. General Arnold had sold himself to Andre for this purpose.... I went in pursuit of him but was much too late..., and I could hardly regret the disappointment, when on my return, I saw an amiable woman frantic with distress for the loss of a husband she tenderly loved — a traitor to his country and to his fame, a disgrace to his connections.... She for a considerable time intirely lost her senses. The General went up to see her and she upbraided him with being in a plot to murder her child; one moment she raved; another she melted into tears, sometimes she pressed her infant to her bosom and lamented its fate occasioned by the imprudence of its father in a manner that would have pierced insensibility itself.[27]

26 Bobrick, *Angel in the Whirlwind*, 415 - 416
27 Syrett, *The Papers of Alexander Hamilton*, Vol. II, 441; Hamilton, John C., *The Works of Alexander Hamilton*, *Vol. I*, 186-187

Since Major Andre had been caught in civilian clothing rather than his military uniform, he was guilty of spying, which carried the mandatory punishment of death. He did, however, implore General Washington to permit him the more honorable death of the firing squad. Washington refused Andre's request and signed his warrant for death by hanging. On October 3 Andre was led to the gallows. When asked if had anything to say, he replied, "I have nothing more to say, gentlemen, but this: you all bear me witness that I meet my fate as a brave man."[28]

By the end of November 1780, with the army in winter quarters, Hamilton took his first leave from the army in four and a half years and, along with his friend James McHenry rode to Albany to take the hand of Elizabeth Schuyler in marriage. Schuyler mansion still stands today, a handsome three-story brick edifice overlooking Albany and a ten-mile stretch of the Hudson. They were wed on December 17, 1780 in the large second floor hallway. The clerk of the Dutch Reformed Church of Albany recorded the marriage of Colonel Hamilton and Elizabeth Schuyler.[29] During the six weeks following the marriage that Hamilton languished in Albany, he had ample opportunity to speak with his father-in-law and to refine his plans for his post-war life. It was decided that Alexander and Eliza would live at the Schuyler home while he studied law and until he was prepared to open his law practice in New York City. This future, Hamilton knew, would be enhanced if he could distinguish himself with a meritorious combat command, and he had pressed General Washington to give him such an opportunity.[30]

Washington's primary interest remained the campaign for New York. Meanwhile trouble was brewing within his headquarters. Since the beginning of the revolution Alexander Hamilton had desired to have a field command, and he had been petitioning General Washington for some months to give him a command position in a combat unit. On each occasion Washington had put him off with the argument that he could not give Hamilton the combat command opportunity over other, more senior officers. Although Hamilton understood this argument, he became increasingly frustrated with the passing of time. Whether this contention contributed to the following incident in any way can only be guessed at since there is no evidence that either party to the incident acted from any ulterior motive.

28 Leckie, *George Washington's War*, 579 - 581
29 Flexner, *The Young Hamilton*, 321 - 323
30 Randall, *Alexander Hamilton — A Life*, 220

On February 16, 1781 at Washington's headquarters in New Windsor, New York, Washington and Hamilton passed one another on the stairs and Washington indicated that he wished to speak with Colonel Hamilton. At the moment Hamilton was on his way to deliver to Colonel Tilghman a letter of a pressing nature to be sent to the Commissary. On his way back to see General Washington he was stopped by the Marquis LaFayette, an interruption on a matter of business which, according to Hamilton, took no more than half a minute. When he returned to the top of the stairs the General was waiting for him and Hamilton quoted Washington as saying, "Col. Hamilton, you have kept me waiting at the head of the stairs these ten minutes. I must tell you, Sir, you treat me with disrespect." Hamilton, in relating the story to his father-in-law, stated that he replied to the General firmly but without petulancy, "I am not conscious of it, Sir, but since you have thought it necessary to tell me so, we part." In retrospect Hamilton said he felt certain that his absence that caused the dispute did not last so long as two minutes.[31]

Less than an hour afterwards, the General sent Tench Tilghman to relay the General's high regard for Alexander Hamilton and his wish that they could put that ugliness behind them and continue their relationship in their common cause of securing independence. Hamilton replied that he could not so easily revoke such a decision and that, while he would agree to a conversation with the General, he would prefer to avoid the disagreeable scene such a meeting would surely produce. Hamilton wished to impose no difficulty on the commander-in-chief by his leaving and agreed to continue in his position until a suitable replacement could be found. Hamilton stressed to his father-in-law that he in no way intended to exit the service, but to find a command position in a combat unit.[32] Again, Hamilton displayed a prickly ego that was more concerned with correcting a personal affront than with seeking reconciliation.

By the spring of 1781 Virginia had become the center of the most vigorous activity. At the end of 1780 a small British fleet, under the command of Benedict Arnold, had entered the Chesapeake Bay and sailed up the James River, and plundered Westover and Richmond. General Cornwallis, who earlier had enjoyed military successes in the South had recently been bested

---

31 Flexner, *The Young Hamilton*, 330 - 331
32 Mitchell, *Alexander Hamilton — Youth to Maturity*, 228 - 229

in battle and doggedly pursued by General Nathanael Greene and had moved north into Virginia to avoid Greene's army and to participate in the conquest of Virginia. In late March a force of 2300 men under Major General Phillips landed at the mouth of the James River under orders to assist Cornwallis.

General Nathanael Greene kept the British forces in the South from moving northward to assist Cornwallis and Phillips. Washington had dispatched Marquis LaFayette to capture Arnold and to prevent Cornwallis' forces from ravaging Virginia. When Cornwallis crossed over into Virginia and joined forces with General Phillips, he commanded an enlarged force of 7200 men. Throughout the late spring and summer Lafayette and Cornwallis sparred with one another across the state of Virginia. The force that Cornwallis commanded was large but ponderous in its movements. Lafayette's force of 3000 men was far too small to fully engage Cornwallis but was mobile enough to skirmish and irritate him. The British inflicted terrible damage on the civilian population, burning and looting as they went. The Virginia governor, Thomas Jefferson, had his estate ransacked after he fled before the onslaught of the British.[33]

Late in June after vandalizing warehouses in Richmond and burning what they didn't need, Cornwallis turned his army eastward toward the coast. LaFayette followed, but at a respectful distance, occasionally engaging with Cornwallis' rearguard. At this time Washington and Rochambeau were holding a conference discussing the most advantageous joint offensive they could conduct. Washington continued to view taking New York as his most important objective. The whereabouts and itinerary of the second French fleet under Admiral de Grasse remained the pivotal open question. The participation of this fleet would be essential to any operation that Washington and Rochambeau planned. Word arrived on June 13 that de Grasse's fleet would arrive in American waters by summer's end. DeGrasse stated that he planned for only a short stay in American waters and he requested that plans for his participation be completed. Rochambeau replied by message that was couriered by frigate that New York was the prime objective but for him to stop in the Chesapeake on the way to "give the Americans a strategic opportunity there."[34]

33 Bobrick, *Angel in the Whirlwind*, 442 - 443
34 Ibid., 447

On July 31, after Hamilton had all but given up his hope for a combat command, his wait was rewarded by a General Order from Washington, establishing a new Light Infantry battalion to be commanded by Lieutenant Colonel Alexander Hamilton with Major Fish as his adjutant. This battalion consisted of two companies of New York Light Infantry and two companies of New York militia.[35]

In July and August both General Washington and General Clinton were distracted by the Virginia campaign. At the start of this period Clinton was concerned over the French forces that had been encamped in Newport and that recently had moved to White Plains, re-enforcing Washington. Generals Washington and Rochambeau were engaged in the development of plans to re-take New York, dependent upon the arrival of the long-awaited second French fleet under Admiral de Barras. Then, in communications from Lafayette, Washington learned that Cornwallis had chosen to sequester himself in a defensive posture in the Virginia village of Yorktown to await reinforcements from General Clinton. It was Lafayette's assessment that the British in this position were vulnerable to a naval siege.[36]

Washington must immediately have seen a greater opportunity in this situation; his writings at the time become curiously quiet in regard to any military plans. In his reply to Lafayette on August 17 Washington was very secretive and stated only that he was sending the letter with General du Portail who would explain in full Washington's plans.[37] He did provide Rochambeau with a travel itinerary, in an August 17 communication, for movement of the French Army into New Jersey, detailing the suggested travel schedule in their march as far south as Trenton.[38] Washington also communicated with Admiral de Grasse to coordinate French and American efforts.[39] It is clear that Washington was seeking to prevent any intelligence from falling into British hands in order to prevent their providing assistance to Cornwallis.

The diary of an American soldier records,

> Our situation reminds me of some theatrical exhibition where the interest and expectation of the spectators are continually increasing and

---

35 Flexner, *The Young Hamilton*, 348 - 349

36 Irving, *George Washington — A Biography*, 565

37 Leckie, *George Washington's War*, 637

38 Fitzpatrick, John C. (ed.), "The Writings of George Washington," United States Government Printing Office, Washington, D. C., 1932 — 1944, Vol. 23, 6 — 7

39 Ibid., 7 - 11

> where curiosity is wrought to the highest point. Our destination has been for some time [a] matter of perplexing doubt and uncertainty. Bets have run high on one side that we were to storm the ground marked out on the Jersey shore to aid in the siege of New York. And on the other that we are stealing a march on the enemy and are actually destined to Virginia in pursuit of the army under Cornwallis. [40]

On August 19 the lead detachments, one battalion of which was under Lt. Col. Hamilton, departed New York bound for Virginia. They were to march overland to the mouth of the Elk River in Maryland and embark on ships and be transported down the Chesapeake to Williamsburg.[41] On September 5 as Washington was riding out of Philadelphia en route to the Elk River, he received word by messenger that de Grasse had entered the Chesapeake with twenty-eight ships of the line. The arrival of de Grasse's fleet gave the allies a clear superiority in naval power in the Chesapeake, indeed in the western Atlantic. Admiral de Grasse also had 3,000 soldiers aboard which, when combined with Lafayette's army, constituted a force strong enough to ensure that Cornwallis would be unable to escape his Yorktown encampment. The allied net was beginning to close on Cornwallis.[42]

When de Grasse arrived in the Chesapeake, he anchored his main fleet in the Bay off the Virginia coast and dispatched 1500 of his seamen to ferry the 3,000 infantry up the James River to Williamsburg. While he awaited their return, British Admiral Graves appeared in the Chesapeake with twenty sail of British ships. De Grasse, intent on protecting the fleet of de Barras who was expected from Rhode Island, sailed for the open sea, hoping to draw Graves into a limited action, thereby covering de Barras' arrival in the Bay. Admiral Graves pursued de Grasse and a heated engagement took place in the afternoon of September 7. After sunset de Grasse disengaged and assessed the result of the battle. For four days the fleets remained in sight of one another and effected repairs to their vessels. When de Grasse learned that de Barras had arrived in the Bay, he withdrew and joined forces with him, effectively blockading Cornwallis from receiving any assistance or provisions by sea. Admiral Graves, realizing that the combined French fleet was too superior a force for him to engage, left Cornwallis and Virginia and sailed for New York.[43]

---

40 Irving, *George Washington — A Biography*, 567 - 568
41 Ibid., 566 - 567
42 Bobrick, *Angel in the Whirlwind*, 449 - 451
43 Leckie, *George Washington's War*, 644 - 648

Washington and his army arrived in Williamsburg on the Virginia peninsula late on September 14. On the morning of September 28, the American and French armies marched the twelve miles from Williamsburg to Yorktown and prepared their positions for the assault. By the first of October the allied armies were in place to commence the siege. These forces were positioned in a semicircle about Yorktown, both ends of which were on the banks of the York River. The French fleet barricaded the York River, cutting off access to Cornwallis' position. With Tarleton across the York at Glouster, Washington sent three thousand troops to entrap this British force with their backs against the river. The investment of Yorktown was complete, the blockade prevented any re-provisioning and shortly its effect was felt. One British soldier wrote, "We get terrible provisions, putrid meat and wormy biscuits that had spoiled on the ships. Many of the men have taken sick here with dysentery or the bloody flux and diarrhea....Foul fever and we have had little rest day or night." [44]

Cornwallis sent a number of blacks out of Yorktown whom he had intentionally infected with smallpox, hoping to create an epidemic in the Allied ranks. Cornwallis had earlier attempted this despicable tactic in other battles, an act that in modern warfare would raise cries of barbarism and constitute recognized war crimes. [45]

On the afternoon of October 9, the shelling of Yorktown began. In the first day of cannonading approximately forty-five large caliber guns were in use, dealing deadly destruction to the British fortifications. On successive days the number of guns increased and the shelling continued throughout the night. On October 11 Cornwallis wrote Clinton, "Against so powerful an attack we cannot hope to make a very long resistance." One British officer wrote, "I now want words to express the dreadful situation of the garrison.... Upwards of a thousand shells were thrown into the works this night." [46]

Two British redoubts, numbers 9 and 10, had to be taken to destroy the security of the British fortifications at Yorktown. [47] The task of storming these redoubts were given to Lt. Col. Hamilton and to the Chevalier de Lameth. At eight o'clock in the evening the signal to begin the assault, three rockets fired in quick succession, was given. Hamilton and his men began

---

44 Bobrick, *Angel in the Whirlwind*, 457
45 Ibid.
46 Ibid., 460
47 Ibid., 460 - 461

attacking redoubt number 10 from one side while on the opposite side the French Lt. Col. Gimat stormed the same redoubt. Not waiting for the men to clear the abatis and other obstructions, Hamilton and his men climbed the parapet and stormed the Hessian defenders at the point of the bayonet. Within ten minutes the Hessians were overwhelmed and the redoubt was taken with few casualties. The French brigade on redoubt number 9 was also successful but due to meeting heavier defenses, the cost in casualties was significantly higher.[48]

On October 17, the anniversary of Burgoyne's surrender at Saratoga, the British signaled that they desired a parley. A British officer waving a white handkerchief approached the American lines carrying Cornwallis' request for terms of capitulation. The next day Washington called for a joint meeting to be held behind the allied lines where a document of surrender consisting of fourteen articles was drawn up. These were submitted to Cornwallis on October 19 together with Washington's direction that they be signed by eleven o'clock.[49]

At noon, the American and French forces formed parallel lines leading to the allied commanders, between which the British could march to their surrender. Brigadier General O'Hara rode out of Yorktown; Cornwallis, pleading illness, sent his deputy. O'Hara first approached the French Admiral Rochambeau and offered him Cornwallis' sword. Rochambeau simply nodded toward General Washington. When O'Hara went to offer the sword to the Commander-in-Chief, Washington nodded to General Lincoln; he would not accept the sword from Cornwallis's deputy. The beleaguered O'Hara handed the sword to General Lincoln, who first accepted it and then ceremoniously returned it and called for the surrender to begin. Out came the British and the Hessian survivors of Yorktown, sullen-faced, with eyes downcast. They surrendered their arms, throwing their muskets down forcefully enough to damage them. The defeated army paraded to their surrender as the British band played the tune from the song, "The World Turned Upside-Down."[50]

Lieutenant Colonel Tench Tilghman, one of Washington's devoted and long-term aides, was given the honor of carrying the news of victory to the Congress. After the news was read before the assembled body, they marched to church for a special service of thanksgiving. It was so indicative of the

---

48 Leckie, *George Washington's War*, 657; Bobrick, B., *Angel in the Whirlwind*, 461
49 Irving, *George Washington — A Biography*, 588 - 589
50 Leckie, *George Washington's War*, 657 - 658

state of the Confederation at the time that, in order to compensate Tilghman for the expenses of his trip, it was necessary for each member of Congress to contribute a dollar, the treasury being empty.[51]

When news of Cornwallis' inglorious defeat at Yorktown was received in London, Lord North reacted as if he had received a "ball in the chest," according to Lord Germain who delivered the news to him. "Oh God, it is all over," cried North. King George received the bad news more stoically and expressed resolve to continue the effort, while admitting that some alterations may well be necessary.[52]

Following Yorktown, Parliament voted against the continuation of the war. This led directly to the failure of Lord North's reign as prime minister. His replacement, Lord Shelburne, was also opposed to granting independence but without funds allocated by Parliament he was forced to seek those gains he could achieve at the negotiation table. The British retained their garrisons in New York, Charleston and Savannah as well as the forts in the contested region of the northwest. The American forces were impotent to dislodge the British once the French had withdrawn their forces from American shores. The most that America could hope to accomplish was to be a sufficient military presence to discourage the British from renewing offensive operations.[53]

Arriving back in Albany, Hamilton, on extended leave from the military, was welcomed into the most normal family life he had ever experienced. For fully two months he was so ill as to require almost fulltime bed rest. During Hamilton's recuperation the New York Assembly passed an ordinance making it easier for war veterans to enter the legal profession.

As far back as his King's college days Hamilton had exhibited a propensity for the law. The new dispensation applied to young men who had been studying law at the time the war for independence broke out; it set aside the traditional requirement that aspirants spend three years as clerk to a practicing attorney. Near the deadline of April of 1782, Hamilton traveled to the temporary state capital of New York in Poughkeepsie and applied for qualification under that exemption. He based his arguments on the study he

---

51 Ibid., 659
52 Ibid.
53 Flexner, *The Young Hamilton*, 380

had done at King's College. He won a six-month extension to complete his studies and avoided the three-year clerk requirement.[54]

As soon as he had received his exemption from the state of New York, Hamilton began to study, using the extensive law library of his friend, James Duane. This library was well stocked with treatises on British law that were the basis for and closely resembled New York law. His friend Robert Troup was also residing in the Schuyler mansion and had been admitted to the New York bar at the same time that Hamilton had begun his law studies; no doubt he was of assistance to Hamilton in these studies. By July 1782 Hamilton passed the bar exam after only three months of study and was licensed to argue cases before the Supreme Court of the state of New York. By October he had obtained certification as a counselor, which meant that he could argue cases in court.[55]

54Ibid., 374 - 375
55 Randall, *Alexander Hamilton — A Life*, 253 - 256

Chapter 4. Creating the New Government

The paper currency issued by Congress early during the revolution, as its sole attempt at establishing an independent source of funds, had failed miserably. By the spring of 1781 the Continental currency had become so devalued that one thousand dollars bought only a single dollar in specie. The popular phrase "not worth a Continental" reflected the essentially worthless currency.[1]

Other income sources considered by Congress included the requisition process that had been used since the Confederation had been formed. In this system, when Congress needed funds to support the war effort, they issued requisitions to the states, apportioning the levies by land area or population. The various states responded unevenly to such requisitions issued by the Congress. Since there was no approved method for Congress to coerce compliance of the states, the needs and objectives of state governments often took precedence over the Congressional requisition. Congress considered seeking the authority to compel the states to respond to its requisitions for funds. However, since amendments to the Articles of Confederation required unanimous approval of the states, those states most often delinquent in responding to requisitions could be counted on to veto such proposals.

Congress could seek financial support in the form of loans from wealthy private citizens, a practice that did provide significant income to the Con-

---

1 Ketcham, R., *James Madison*, 116

federation while Robert Morris was Superintendent of Finance. This source of national funds was both limited and suspect, in that it carried the suggestion that wealthy private individuals could purchase influence over the government.

Foreign loans was yet another source of money for Congress. While France and the Netherlands were willing to advance America financial support during the war, following independence these pockets effectively dried up. These European allies had extended themselves to the limit that made sense for them to support fledgling America against their old rival, England. Also, the fact that no income was being realized from loans already made raised serious questions regarding America ever being able to repay the loans.

It became apparent that the national legislative body required the authority to impose and collect taxes. Only through such a reliable source of income could the government ever hope to repay their war debt and to conduct the legitimate business of the country.

Alexander Hamilton was selected by the New York legislature as one of its five delegates to the Confederation Congress scheduled to reconvene in November 1782. Hamilton, like others (notably James Madison), devoted his early months in Congress to the need to secure a permanent source of revenue to enable Congress to effectively conduct the business of government. The proponents for giving Congress taxation authority argued that foreign creditors were looking to America to see how the war debt to European supporters would be retired. The participation of America in world trade was dependent upon its public credit. The re-establishment of America's public credit required that Congress have an adequate and independent source of revenue to meet its obligations. This need had been one of the highest priorities throughout the war; only the loans from France and Holland had spared Congress a devastating financial collapse during the war. In late 1782 and early 1783 the problems of unfulfilled obligations were undermining the public's faith in the Congress and, for many, in the Confederation itself. The army had not been paid in many months; Congress was unable even to address the half-pay for life commitment it had made to the officers of the Continental Army, or the cash settlement option. Obligations for clothing, rations and materials were unpaid for long periods. Government officials were badly underpaid; Congressmen reported that their salaries met only two-thirds of the most meager living expenses.[2]

A growing tension existed between the Army and Congress over the continuous and abusive failure of Congress to meet the salary obligations of the Army. Congress was justifiably concerned that the army might use force to obtain their wage arrears. Should the peace negotiations with the British fail and active warfare resume, the army would again be called upon to prevent British incursions. If they remained unpaid and unsupplied, how could the army be depended upon to meet the country's needs? And, should a permanent peace be confirmed, how could the army be disbanded without granting the back pay owed to them?

George Washington was the only man in the country who had the necessary stature, confidence and respect to soothe the passions and temper and the resolve of the army. Hamilton wrote to Washington on February 13, 1783, confiding his assessment of the dilemma and encouraging Washington's strongest and wisest efforts to avoid the looming potential for disaster. Washington's response to this confidential letter, dated March 4, 1783, was in full accord with Hamilton's recommendations. The army is skeptical, Washington wrote, that it will ever realize the back pay it is owed. "The prevailing sentiment in the Army is, that the prospects of compensation for past service will terminate with the war."[3] When he considered the reasonableness of the claims of the army, the justice involved and the potential for mischief if they were denied, Washington was incredulous that the States would fail to supply the necessary means. "The states cannot, surely, be so devoid of common sense, common honesty and common policy as to refuse their aid on a full, clear and candid representation of facts from Congress."[4]

The discontent within the Newburgh garrison where General Washington and his army were encamped increased in early March to the point where Washington was concerned that the men might resort to mob action in an attempt to redress their grievances. In a letter to Hamilton dated March 12, Washington stated that the very real concern of the army was that "Peace may take place and prevent any adjustment of accounts which they say would inevitably be the case if the war was to cease tomorrow." He told

---

2 Ibid., 265 - 269
3 Syrett, *The Papers of Alexander Hamilton*, Vol. III, 278
4 Ibid., 279

Hamilton that he would meet with the officers and make one last attempt to settle their concerns.[5]

This meeting was held on March 15; Washington prepared to discourage the officers from making a show of force to intimidate Congress into settling their accounts. For the first time Washington confronted an audience of his own officers who were hostile to anything the Commander-in-Chief might say. Washington addressed them sternly, saying that any rebellion would only threaten the liberties they all had fought so long to secure. He had a letter from a congressman he wanted to read but was unable to bring the words into focus. He reached for his glasses and commented, "Gentlemen, you will permit me to put on my spectacles, for I have not only grown gray but almost blind in service to my country." The sight of their commander, admitting to his frailty, brought about by the struggle in which they had all suffered, rejuvenated the sense of unity and brotherhood that had sustained them for eight years. With a reconciliation of their differences, Washington agreed to personally lobby Congress on their behalf. A committee chaired by Alexander Hamilton agreed to a pension payment to the officers of five years full pay. This commitment was made and agreed to by Congress even though they still had no fixed revenue on which to base this promise.[6]

During his tenure in Congress Hamilton established an important personal relationship with James Madison in Congress, one that was to prove mutually supportive in promoting the strength of the central government. Unlike the brash, confident and eloquent Hamilton, Madison was shy, withdrawn and somber in appearance. Eight years Hamilton's senior, Madison was possessed of a keen intellect, having graduated from the College of New Jersey at age twenty. He had been a member of Congress since 1780 and was considered a seasoned legislator and exhibited a judgment that was widely hailed as fair and sound. When Hamilton wrote his famous letter to James Duane in 1780, Madison shared boarding facilities with Duane and surely read Hamilton's letter and discussed it with Duane.[7] Hamilton and Madison shared a common vision of America becoming a strong, prosperous and prominent country among the community of nations. To achieve that goal they believed the country required a central government having the vitality to unite the states, to mandate laws governing areas where conflicting

---

5 Ibid., 287
6 Ellis, *Founding Brothers*, 130; Mitchell, B., *Alexander Hamilton — Youth to Maturity*, 304
7 Ketcham, R., *James Madison*, 95, 113, 117-118

state laws could result in internal discord and to win popular support. To be strong, the central government had to possess sufficient independent and perpetual resources to reclaim the public credit by retiring its war debt, both foreign and domestic, and to conduct those aspects of business necessary to ensure the continued freedom and happiness of the people.

The depressed state of the economy, a foreign debt that had been delinquent too long in being serviced made clear the survival of the Confederation depended upon an effective solution to this challenge. States' rights advocates, fearful of the potential for tyranny in an independent central government, strongly opposed providing Congress with an independent and perpetual source of revenues. They jealously guarded the prerogatives of state sovereignty.

By August Hamilton was back in Albany with his family. His nine-month stint in Congress had instructed him on the strength of the sentiment for autonomy of the states. He understood now that, flawed as was the structure of the Confederacy, there was still much resistance to the changes he thought necessary to strengthen the union. In a letter to General Greene, Hamilton said,

> There is so little disposition either in or out of Congress to give solidity to our national system that there is no motive to a man to lose his time in the public service; who has no other view than to promote its welfare. Experience must convince us that our present establishments are Utopian before we shall be ready to part with them for better.[8]

The news from Europe became increasingly favorable to the prospect of peace between Britain, France, Spain and America when a separate peace initiative was unexpectedly offered to America by Great Britain. There was great and justifiable concern that signing this separate peace treaty would alienate both France and Spain. This provisional treaty, signed by the American negotiation trio of Benjamin Franklin, John Adams and John Jay on November 30, 1782, was not reported in Philadelphia until March 12, 1783. At first Congress took a wary view of the treaty being separately executed with England, but after lengthy and heated debate, the treaty was ratified and went into effect on September 3, 1783.[9]

The British evacuation of New York was finally completed on November 25, 1783, a day that was celebrated in that city for more than a century. In mid

---

8 Syrett, *The Papers of Alexander Hamilton*, Vol. III, 376
9 Leckie, *George Washington's War*, 660

November Hamilton received word of his brevet promotion to full colonel. With receipt of this recognition Hamilton determined to join General Washington and the army for their entry into New York following the departure of the British. On November 25 Hamilton joined General Washington, Governor George Clinton and a number of selected officers in leading a thousand men in a march across Manhattan. This military parade was met at some point by a crowd of refugees who had left the city when the British occupied Manhattan in 1776 and had spent seven years in exile from their homes.

Following ratification of the Peace Treaty and the subsequent British evacuation, Washington made a ceremonial visit to New York. While he was in New York, Washington publicly recognized the patriotic contributions that had been made by some who had been generally suspected of being Tories and of collaborating with the British.

Washington had held the army together through two years of inactivity while the peace negotiations were in progress. Now, at last, there remained no further cause for the nation to maintain the Revolutionary Army. On December 4 he met with his principal officers at Fraunce's Tavern. On entering the presence of these officers, these comrades in arms, these men with whom he had shared so much, his emotions overcame his usual self-confidence. With his glass raised he spoke movingly, "With a heart full of love and gratitude I now take my leave of you, most devoutly wishing that your latter days may be as prosperous and happy as your former ones have been glorious and honorable.[10] His officers escorted Washington to the Hudson River, where he caught a barge to take him to New Jersey and the start of his journey to a long anticipated retirement at Mt. Vernon. Alexander Hamilton and his family moved to New York. Their first residence and his law office were located at 57 Wall Street.[11]

Prior to the initiation of hostilities in the revolution, American colonists held a broad spectrum of views and interests on the relationship with Great Britain. There were those who strongly advocated independence. The great majority sought reconciliation with England, on terms that would allow America greater autonomy in its political and commercial life. Still others wanted a return to full colonial status with the protection of England's military might. This last group was known as Loyalists or Tories. Each of these

---

10 Irving, *George Washington — A Biography*, 618
11 Mitchell, *Alexander Hamilton — Youth to Maturity*, 332

views were based on various understandings of principle, plus both political and personal interests. The merchants who controlled the trade with Great Britain were influenced by the continued profit they would realize; they tended to be strong supporters of the king and parliamentary rule. Those who favored independence viewed the English dominance as suppressing the growth, development and prosperity of America. Most Americans were ambivalent toward continued British rule and did not view the cost, the danger and the turmoil of a revolution as being justified.

All of this changed at Lexington and Concord. No longer would Britain be viewed as a beneficent protector of American interests. Britain had showed its willingness to use deadly force to protect its own interest to the detriment of its colonies. The popular response in America was a decided sense of betrayal. The choice now seemed simpler: accept subservience enforced by the sword or fight for independence. Those who chose to fight for independence knew the struggle against the greatest military power in the world would be arduous and long. They looked scornfully on the Tories who, as they felt, in their cowardice and self-interest would willingly sacrifice those involved in the patriotic fight for independence.

Early in the revolution many Tories left America for England or its territories. After the war was over, Patriots and Tories looked to one another to resolve their differences or to re-kindle their animus.

Following the evacuation of the British, a wave of resentment fueled reprisals against the Tories who chose to remain in the city. Governor Clinton lent the prestige of his office to the vilification of the Loyalists, decrying the "cruelty and rapine" they had committed upon "the ruins of this once flourishing city." The Sons of Liberty, active once again, held a large demonstration where the more notorious Tories were tarred and feathered.[12] Editorials in the patriot press called for exile for any Loyalist who refused to leave America. A series of laws enacted by the New York Legislature were in direct conflict with the articles of the peace treaty. In 1779 the Confiscation Act, enacted in New York, permitted seizure of Tory estates. The 1782 Citation Act placed obstacles in the way of British creditors collecting debts from patriots.[13]

---

12 Randall, *Alexander Hamilton — A Life*, 295
13 Mitchell, *Alexander Hamilton — Youth to Maturity*, 338 - 339

By 1785 the floundering financial system in each of the states began to collapse. Public credit was non-existent, debts were not being paid and the interest owed on them was mounting, trade between the states was hampered by exorbitant tariffs and international trade also suffered from import fees — but most of all because the real wealth of the country had diminished so seriously that public credit was insufficient to support foreign trade. The state of affairs in the country was so tenuous that the expected influx of immigrants failed to materialize, seriously depreciating land values. Despite the growing financial crisis, the states were less able and less willing to provide the funds necessary for the functioning of a strong central government.

To the laws enacted to discriminate against the Loyalists, Hamilton had this response.

> Nothing is more common than for a free people, in times of heat and violence, to gratify momentary passions, by letting into the government, principles and precedents which afterwards prove fatal to themselves. Of this kind is the doctrine of disqualification, disfranchisement, and banishment, by Acts of Legislature. The dangerous consequences of this power are manifest. If the Legislature can disfranchise any number of citizens at pleasure, by general descriptions, it may soon confine all the votes to a small number of partisans, and establish an aristocracy or oligarchy. If it may banish at discretion, all those whom particular circumstances render obnoxious, without hearing or trial, no man can be safe, nor know when he may be the innocent victim of a prevailing faction. The name of liberty applied to such a government would be a mockery of common sense.[14]

With patriotic emotions running high and popular sentiment highly antagonistic toward any Loyalist in New York, Alexander Hamilton risked his political future and professional success in denouncing all measures taken in prejudice against Tories. His view was that the Peace Treaty forbade acts of reprisals against citizens who did not take up arms against America during the war. In a legal sense New York was taking actions in direct opposition to the treaty, which, having been ratified by Congress, was the law of the land. If the states can choose to ignore laws enacted by Congress to obligate the nation, America would be projecting a pitiful national image to the world.

He focused the country's attention on the real objectives of America's noble experiment in republican government when he wrote,

> The world has its eye on America. The noble struggle we have made in the cause of liberty, has occasioned a kind of revolution in human sentiment. The influence of our example has penetrated the gloomy regions of

---

14 Syrett, *The Papers of Alexander Hamilton*, Vol. III, 485; Lodge, Henry C., *The Works of Alexander Hamilton*, Vol. IV, 232-233

despotism, and has pointed the way to inquiries which may shake it to its deepest foundations.

> With the greatest advantages for promoting it that ever a people had, we shall have betrayed the cause of human nature. Let those in whose hands it is placed, pause for a moment, and contemplate, with an eye of reverence, the vast trust committed to them. Let them retire into their own bosoms and examine the motives which there prevail. Let them ask themselves this solemn question: Is the sacrifice of a few mistaken or criminal individuals an object worthy of the shifts to which we are reduced, to evade the Constitution and the national engagements?[15]

Hamilton took part in a number of cases resulting from business affairs that took place during the British occupancy of New York. He represented the Patriot position in some of these and the Tory in others. He consistently upheld the supremacy of national over state laws in suits that opposed the articles of the Peace Treaty. His efforts won a number of supporters to his view of the supremacy of national law. He argued that, since the Confederation was given the power to wage war, actions taken by Congress in fulfillment of this responsibility bore with equal weight on all states and took precedence over state laws. The articles of the Peace Treaty, being the conclusion of this responsibility, were included in the sovereignty of the Confederation.

Hamilton performed in actions what he professed in writing. In a 1783 suit tried under the Trespass Act, one Elizabeth Rutgers charged a debt owed by a Tory, Joshua Waddington, over the latter's use of a brewery originally owned by Mrs. Rutgers. Public sympathy was on the side of Mrs. Rutgers, who portrayed herself as a poor, defenseless widow. Hamilton took the defense of Waddington and reaped popular hostility for this stance. In 1778 Rutgers had rented to Waddington a brewery and malt house. Waddington found the property to be in very poor order and stripped of everything of any value except "an old Copper, two old pumps and a leaden Cistern full of holes." A sum of £700 was spent on the renovation before the brewery could be put into production. From 1780 to 1783 the Waddington family paid an annual rent of £150 to a Tory attorney named John Smyth, Esq. as administrator of a children's orphanage in New York that had been assigned as beneficiaries of the property by the British military commander of New York. When the Americans returned to take control of New York, General Birch

15 Syrett, *The Papers of Alexander Hamilton*, Vol. III, 557; Lodge, Henry C., *The Works of Alexander Hamilton*, Vol. IV, 289-290
557

ordered Waddington to pay rent from the first of May, the termination date of the rent paid to Smyth, to the son of Mrs. Rutgers. Rutgers refused this rent and demanded back rent from the period of British occupation. Rutgers would make no allowance for the improvements that had been made to the property by Waddington, nor give consideration for the rent paid out to Smyth under British orders. Finally Waddington refused to pay any rent and surrendered the property back to its owners. During this period the brewery burned to the ground, resulting in further loss to Waddington for equipment and stores amounting to £4000.[16]

Hamilton argued that the peace treaty, which had been ratified by Congress, making it common law, forbade the suit. He showed, by citing Vattel, that an occupying army had the right to use all property on conquered territory. According to this view of laws governing war, Rutgers had no claim to the brewery during the British occupation of New York. He persuaded that the State of New York was obligated to conform its laws to the law of the nation as defined by that treaty. Hamilton's arguments prevailed although his reputation suffered. It was typical of Hamilton that his actions were not dictated by popular opinion but by his own judgment of right. The case was tried in the mayor's court headed by James Duane, five aldermen and the city recorder, Richard Varrick. Duane gave a written opinion, agreeing with Hamilton's legal arguments. Mrs. Rutgers was awarded £800 damages, not the £8000 she had requested. The award was to cover rent for the first two years of Waddington's occupancy.[17]

The industry of slavery had been flourishing in America for well over a hundred years by the mid 1780s. In the South commerce was based mainly on the cotton and tobacco industries, and the principal markets for their products were the mills and drawing rooms of Europe. To offset the high cost of shipping products to European markets, the South depended on the cheap labor offered by the system of slavery. The odiousness of the institution of slavery was rationalized by its economic necessity. The inconsistency and indeed hypocrisy of a country having freed itself from a form of bondage, embracing popular liberty and proclaiming, "all men are created equal," and yet still harboring and defending the concept of slavery troubled many people.

---

16 Randall, *Alexander Hamilton — A Life*, 298 - 299
17 Ibid., 299

In 1775 a Quaker-based antislavery organization was founded in Philadelphia and spread to other regions of the country. George Washington, at the time of the Revolution, held one hundred slaves. By 1786 he owned twice that number and told Robert Morris, "There is not a man living who wishes more sincerely than I do to see a plan adopted for the abolition of slavery."[18]

Thomas Jefferson owned about two hundred slaves at Monticello and was particularly sensitive to the contrast between his high-minded words of liberty contained in the Declaration of Independence and the reality of slavery that was so heatedly defended throughout the South. Despite his efforts to devise a scheme whereby Negroes could be freed from bondage, in the end pressures from other sources forced him to shelve or abandon these plans.[19]

For Alexander Hamilton the question of slavery had been settled in his early childhood. He had seen, and likely participated in, the auctioning of slaves just disembarked from the ships that had brought them from Africa. He had witnessed the horrible condition of many of them following the dehumanizing experience of the slave ships. To him no economically based rationalization or pseudo-humanitarian concern for the welfare of "wretches incapable of caring for themselves" could make right the inherent evil of the trade.

The depressed economy of the country, brought about primarily by the oppressive public debt, continued to worsen, as there was no generally accepted plan to reverse the trend. Men of knowledge and influence continued to promote, as a solution to the financial ills of the country, the strengthening of the Confederation and to provide the Congress taxation authority to make that institution independent of the whims of the individual states. Political leaders in some states saw this proposed remedy as a threat to the authority of the states and to the revenue sources upon which those states depended. These parochial jealousies inevitably led to abuses that threatened to tear the Confederation asunder. States having large seaports collected revenues on all imports while neighboring states were among the consumers for these goods and paid the cost of these taxes in the prices paid without receiving any benefit from the imposts. Large taxes were imposed on goods traded across state lines, sometimes exceeding the imposts on foreign products. In

18 Chernow, *Alexander Hamilton*, 212
19 Ibid., 212 - 213

the midst of these pecuniary interstate rivalries the Congress struggled for its survival. The large national war debt was going unserviced; not even the interest on foreign loans was being paid. Some states seemed content to allow the Congress to languish rather than relinquish any of their own prerogatives and revenue to strengthen it.

One concept for stimulating commerce originated among a group of Virginians spurred mainly by James Madison and entailed the development of a series of canals to join the Ohio and the Potomac Rivers. Through this canal the products of the western territories could be shipped cheaply to eastern markets and, by way of the Chesapeake Bay, to foreign markets. Since Virginia had ceded to Maryland the control of the Potomac River in 1776, Madison involved Maryland in his great canal scheme and wanted to arrange joint jurisdiction of the Potomac River and the Chesapeake Bay between the two states so there would be no trade-suffocating taxation issues on the canal project. The delegates from the two states met in a convention held at Alexandria, Virginia in the spring of 1785 and later moved to Mount Vernon to establish the groundwork for this venture. At the Alexandria convention Maryland's delegates began the negotiation by taking a hard-line stand, demanding that Virginia agree not to impose any taxation of goods upon entering the Chesapeake Bay. Maryland proposed that tolls should be limited to the sites of waterfalls along rivers entering the Bay and along a toll road that might be constructed. Virginia's delegates came to the convention with instructions not to negotiate on issues of tolls; however, as it appeared that the convention was going to collapse before it accomplished anything unless this compromise was made, the Virginia delegates agreed to the toll recommendation put forth by Maryland. Thomas Stone of Maryland proposed a partial solution to the interstate tax rivalry by recommending that Maryland and Virginia cooperate to regulate the currencies issued by the two states, to regulate import duties and to hold annual meetings to review cooperation on joint commercial interests. A follow-up meeting was scheduled for May 1786 to be held in Annapolis, Maryland. The delegates agreed to invite Pennsylvania and Delaware to attend the meeting. It was understood that these states likely would invite their neighboring states.[20]

In 1786 Alexander Hamilton once again decided to run for election to the New York Assembly and was elected as one of the delegates for the city and

20 Randall, *Alexander Hamilton — A Life*, 310 - 311

county of New York. Hamilton was subsequently appointed as one of five New York delegates to attend the Annapolis Convention.[21]

The number of states that sent delegates to Annapolis was too few to justify the convention undertaking the commercial challenges before them. It seemed clear to the delegates that the commercial disputes between the states and Congress' inability to effectively address the public debt were but surface appearances of an overall flaw in the governmental system that needed to be understood and corrected.

Hamilton believed that for America to survive as a nation required that the states, be united by a strong central government. The ineffectual union of the Confederacy Hamilton attributed to mankind's innate love of power. The states held the power of the purse and had sovereignty over their regions, and guarded these powers jealously. The individual states, being representative of local communities, naturally gave their first allegiance to the interests of those communities. No consideration was recognized or given either to the concerns of neighboring states or to the interests that the states shared in common — except for that of defense. State governments passed laws, collected taxes, and exercised police powers according to the needs and dispositions of that state.

Even during the Revolution a number of states found it burdensome to raise funds to support their state militias and were unwilling to find additional funds to support Congress's efforts to finance the Continental Army. With no power of enforcement, Congress had no recourse to the recalcitrant states and was forced to rely on foreign loans to support the Revolution. After the Revolution, the states' interest in national defense still did not rise above their parochial needs and interests; they rejected all proposals for raising funds to pay the interest due on those foreign loans that had supported the national fight for independence.

The delegates to the Annapolis convention, by unanimous consent, decided that yet another convention was needed to address in detail these flaws in the Articles of Confederation. They resolved, "To meet in Philadelphia on the second Monday in May next, to take into consideration the situation of the United States, to devise such for the provisions as shall appear necessary to render the Constitution of the Federal Government *adequate to the exigencies*

---

21 Ibid., 313, 317

of the Union and to report such an act for that purpose to the United states in Congress assembled."[22]

The Revolutionary War left in its wake, an economy overwhelmed by debt, both foreign and domestic, and a monetary system crippled by lack of circulating secured currency and by a flood of paper money, issued with little or no backing, that had deteriorated seriously in actual value. The effect of these economic troubles was felt nowhere more strongly than in Massachusetts. The state government attempted to establish a system of taxation that would permit them to at least meet the accrued interest on their debt. The mostly agrarian western part of the state experienced great difficulty in this financial crisis. The constantly depreciating value of the state-issued paper money meant that equal produce grown on the farms of Massachusetts brought less buying power from year to year. Realizing less real income from their farms meant that farmers were increasingly unable to meet their tax assessments. Increasingly farmers found themselves involved in lawsuits brought by their creditors. More and more ended up in debtor's prison or at the risk thereof. A number of men took up arms in an attempt to force the state government to take measures to relieve the financial plight of the farmers. Shay's Rebellion, as it became known, alerted the country to the potential for anarchy and violence stemming from the general weakness of the Confederation. The timing of this insurgency instilled a sense of urgency in the work of the upcoming General Convention that would be convened in Philadelphia.

The Philadelphia Convention was scheduled to start on May 14. Congress had given support to the convention in February of 1787. On that day only the Pennsylvania and Virginia delegations had a majority of their members present; it was nearly two weeks later, on May 25, when the states of New York, New Jersey, Delaware, North Carolina and South Carolina were represented by a quorum of their delegates. The delegates were aware that their charter was limited to amending the Articles of Confederation. Many of them were also aware of the fatal flaws in the existing structure of government, which could not be corrected by amendments. Without the structure to operate as a government and without independent funds to conduct the

---

22 Syrett, *The Papers of Alexander Hamilton*, Vol. III, 688; Hamilton, John C., *The Works of Alexander Hamilton*, Vol. II, 339

rightful business of government, the Confederation languished and the states alone retained sovereignty and independence. This was the situation in the spring of 1787 and the charter of the Philadelphia Convention was to create the governmental structure that would give to the Union strength, vigor and credibility and one that would be acceptable to the people.

The delegates coming to Philadelphia had their individual views of what was wrong with the Confederation and what was likely to provide the required remedy. There were those like George Washington, James Madison and Alexander Hamilton who thought that a strong, independent, central government was necessary to secure the strength and stability of the union. Others such as Luther Martin and Edmund Randolph continued to support state sovereignty, while admitting that some structural revisions were necessary. There were those delegates such as Robert Yates and John Lansing of New York who came to Philadelphia under strict orders from Governor George Clinton not to vote for any measures that lessened the importance, or sovereignty, of New York. Other delegates, mainly Southerners, such as John Rutledge, were adamant in the defense of slavery. They took the stand that, for the Union to survive the Philadelphia Convention, there must be a formal recognition and acceptance of slavery in the generated articles. Two men of distinction, John Adams and Thomas Jefferson, did not attend as both were in Europe engaged in business for the Confederation. The Convention delegates understood that the structure of the existing government was destructive of the Union and also threatened the survival of the individual states. Only twelve states would be represented in Philadelphia; Rhode Island chose not to participate and would be the last state to ratify the new Constitution.

On Friday, May 25, a total of twenty-nine delegates were present, representing seven states. On this Friday the credentials of the new delegates were read and a three-man committee was named "to prepare the standing rules and orders." The convention selected Major William Jackson of Philadelphia as secretary. Robert Morris nominated George Washington as president of the Convention; John Rutledge seconded and by unanimous vote Washington was so appointed.[23] James Madison appointed himself the task of keep-

---

23 Madison, James, *Notes of Debates in the Federal Convention of 1787:* May 25; Ashbrook Center for Public Affairs, Ashland University, accessed April 21, 2005; available from http://www. teachingamericanhistory.org/convention/debates

ing as accurate and complete a record of the proceedings of the Convention as was possible at that time.

On May 28, Chancellor Wythe gave the report of the Rules Committee. The proposed operating rules followed closely the rules used in Congress with which many delegates were familiar. Four of the rules were particularly important in defining the style and operation of the Convention.

> 1. Voting was to be done by states with each state having one vote. [The committee recognized that, while the Convention would have to recognize, in the proceedings, the priority that large states have over smaller states through voting rights based on population, it would be injudicious to impose this rule on the smaller states before detailed deliberations could confirm this reality.]

> 2. The Convention was to be conducted with a decorum befitting a gathering of gentlemen. A prohibition on side conversation, exchanging of notes and extraneous reading was imposed. "When the house shall adjourn, every member shall stand in place, until the president pass him."

> 3. There was a provision that allowed for reconsideration of any decision already determined by a majority. [It turned out this was a most useful provision. Members could discuss and vote upon a resolution one day and, with improved insight from further deliberations, could later resurrect the original decision for further consideration.]

> 4. The rules imposed a strict secrecy on the deliberations of the Convention. Nothing that was discussed or decided upon was to be revealed in any manner outside of the Convention. [There was understandably great interest among the public in the proceedings of the Convention but also an understanding and acceptance of the wisdom of this veil of silence. The temptation was removed from the delegates to play to popular opinion. The rule of silence also removed inhibitions that may have existed if delegates had reason for concern over seeing their speeches or statements replayed in the press].[24]

---

24 Madison, *Debates*, May 28

Convention Delegates
(Name, (Age), Date of 1st Attendance)

New Hampshire John Langdon, (46), July 23 Nicholas Gilman, (32), July 23	*Delaware* George Reed, (53), May 25 G. Bedford, Jr., (40), May 28 John Dickinson, (55), May 29 Richard Bassett, (42), May 25 Jacob Broom, (35), May 25
Massachusetts Elbridge Gerry, (43), May 29 Nathaniel Gorham, (49), May 28 Rufus King, (32), May 25 Caleb Strong, (42), May 28	*Maryland* James McHenry, (33), May 28 Daniel Jenifer, (64), June 2 Daniel Carroll, (57), July 9 John F. Mercer, (36), Aug 6 Luther Martin, (39), June 9
Rhode Island No delegates appointed	
Connecticut William S. Johnson, (60), June 2 Roger Sherman, (66), May 30 Oliver Ellsworth, (42), May 28	*Virginia* George Washington, (55), May 25 Edmund Randolph, (34), May 25 John Blair, (55), May 25 George Mason, (62), May 25 George Wythe, (61), May 25 James McClurg, (41), May 25
New York Robert Yates, (49), May 25 John Lansing, (33), June 2 Alexander Hamilton, (30), May 25	
New Jersey David Brearley, (41), May 25 William Houston, (41), May 25 William Paterson, (41), May 25 William Livingston, (64), June 5 J. Dayton, (26), June 21	*North Carolina* Alexander Martin, (47), May 25 William R. Davie, (31), May 25 William Blount, (38), June 20 Hugh Williamson, (38), May 25
Pennsylvania Thomas Mifflin, (43), May 28 Robert Morris, (53), May 25 George Clymner, (48), May 28 Jared Ingersoll, (38), May 28 Thomas Fitzsimmons, (46), May 25 James Wilson, (44), May 25 Gouverneur Morris, (35), May 25 Benjamin Franklin, (81), May 28	*South Carolina* John Rutledge, (48), May 25 Charles Pinckney, (29), May 25 Charles C. Pinckney, (41), May 25 Pierce Butler, (43), May 25 *Georgia* William Few, (39), May 25 Abraham Baldwin, (33), June 11 William Pierce, (47), May 31 William Houstoun, (32) June 1

After the housekeeping business of accepting the procedural rules had been resolved, Governor Edmund Randolph of Virginia. Randolph gave a lengthy address in which he outlined the purpose for which the convention had been assembled. He described the generally accepted failings of the Articles of Confederation, the economic woes of the country that existed because of the oppressive war debt, the instability of the currency systems operating throughout the country and the perils to which the country was exposed as evidenced by the recent rebellion in Massachusetts.

The remedy he recommended was called the Virginia Plan. The essence of the Virginia Plan was that the Articles of Confederation were irremediable and must be replaced with a national government in many ways supreme to the states. This Virginia Plan was used throughout the convention as the model about which the deliberations of the convention were based.[25] The essential points of this plan were:

1. The Articles of Confederation needed to be corrected and enlarged to ensure the common defense, security of liberty and general welfare.
2. Voting rights in the national legislature to be based on funds contributed to the legislature or on the number of free inhabitants.
3. The National Legislature was to consist of two branches.
4. Members of the first branch to be elected by the people. The term of service, whether they could stand for re-election, the minimum age required of a delegate and the stipend for that office were left for the Convention to determine.
5. The members of the second branch were to be elected by the members of the first.
6. Both branches were authorized to originate legislation. The legislature was to deliberate on all cases where the states were incompetent or where the harmony of the United States required it. They were to be empowered to negative (veto) all laws passed by the states and to authorize the use of force against a recalcitrant state. [This last statement was the only provision in the Virginia Plan that established the National Legislature as being the Supreme deliberative body in the nation.]
7. That a national executive be instituted to serve a single term of duration to be determined by the convention.
8. That a national judiciary be established to consist of a supreme tribunal and of inferior tribunals as determined by the National Legislature. Members of the national judiciary to serve during good behavior.
9. That the executive and judicial act as a council to have negative power over the acts of the National Legislature.
10. That provision be made to admit new states into the Union.
11. That a Republican government and the sanctity of its territory be guaranteed each state by the United States.
12. That provision be made for the continuation of Congress until the new government is formed.
13. That provision be made to amend the articles of the Union.
14. That an allegiance oath to the articles of the Union be required of all state government offices.
15. That these new amendments to the Articles of Confederation be offered to state ratifying conventions. The state conventions were to be chosen by the people.[26]

Immediately following Randolph's presentation, objections arose. Elbridge Gerry of Massachusetts stated that to pass on Randolph's resolution would have the effect of dissolving the Confederation, which was clearly be-

---

25 Ibid., *May 29*
26 Mitchell, Broadus, *Biography of the Constitution of the United States*, Oxford University Press, New York, 1964, 53

yond the charter of the convention. In response to Gerry's challenge, Gouverneur Morris quipped, "We had better take a supreme government now than a despot twenty years hence, for come he must."[27]

The members thus set about their summer-long deliberations, meeting for a full four or five hours, six days a week, in unusually sultry summer weather. Evenings, Sundays and early mornings were given to committee, lobbying, correspondence and other necessary paperwork. The members shared a sense of destiny in their work, knowing that their product would likely affect generations of Americans stretching through the years, hopefully for centuries. Indeed, there was a global dimension to their work for the experiment they were creating was to determine whether man was capable of self-governance in justice and of defending liberty.

The matter of how the National Legislature was to be elected and of how state voting rights within the Legislature were to be apportioned would occupy the convention for half of the summer. Among the members of the convention there was a general distrust of the collective wisdom of the people. Roger Sherman felt that the people "should have as little to do as may be about the government. They want [lack] information and are constantly liable to be misled."[28] George Mason of Virginia presented a strong voice of opposition. If we recoil from the prospect of too much democracy, he argued, do we not run the risk of becoming mired in the opposite extreme? "We ought to attend to the rights of every class of the people...provide no less carefully for the...happiness of the lowest than of the highest orders of citizens," the concerns and aspiration of every class, every occupation, every region of the country.[29]

Inherent in the structure of the two branches of the National Legislature was the concept that the first, or lower, house was to be the vessel for expression of the wants and needs of the people, whereas the second or upper house was to provide the steadying influence of the government. The members of the second branch needed to be possessed of a calm perspective and of a wisdom that transcended the temporary passions of the moment — characteristics most often attributed to the aristocracy.

The smaller states, principally Delaware and New Jersey, were determined to preserve their equal suffrage in both houses as they had in the Con-

27 Bowen, Catharine, D., *Miracle at Philadelphia*, Atlantic Monthly Press, Boston, 1966, 42
28 Madison, *Debates* — May 31.
29 Bowen, *Miracle at Philadelphia*, 47

federation Congress. John Dickinson of Delaware summarized the small state position. "Some of the members from the small states wish for two branches in the general legislature, and are friends to a good national government; but we would sooner submit to a foreign power than ... be deprived of an equal suffrage in both branches of the legislature, and thereby be thrown under the domination of the large states."[30]

Later, on June 15, William Paterson of New Jersey presented an alternative to the Virginia Plan. The New Jersey Plan, as it was to become known, contained nine resolutions. It was structured as a series of amendments to the Articles of Confederation and provided for new powers allowing Congress to raise its own funds through imposts and a stamp tax. The Congress was to be given regulatory powers controlling commerce; and, power to compel states to respond to requisitions. An Executive as well as a Judicial Branch was to be created and the Executive was granted the power to summon the power of the confederated states to enforce the laws and treaties of the United States in recalcitrant states. These amendments also recognized acts and treaties of the Congress as carrying the authority of "supreme law of the respective states." [31]

On the day preceding the deciding vote on the Virginia vs. the New Jersey Plan, Alexander Hamilton took the opportunity to present to the convention his considered views on the structure of government. Hamilton had spoken little in the convention up to that time due, as he stated, to respect for the opinions of the other, more experienced men, and partly due to his delicate position on the New York delegation. Hamilton declared that he was unfriendly to both the Virginia and the New Jersey Plans. As he was convinced that no plan that left the states in possession of their sovereignty could possibly serve the public needs, he was particularly opposed to the New Jersey Plan.[32] The Virginia Plan carried the majority in a vote of 7-to-3 over the New Jersey Plan.[33]

In the formulation of an effective solution to the need for good government Hamilton explained some fundamental needs. The expense of operating a national government would be substantial. Raising the necessary Federal revenues, in addition to the cumulative tax revenues used to fund state

---

30 Madison, *Debates* — *June 15* (postscript note 4)
31 Ibid.
32 Ibid., June 18
33 Farrand, Max, *The Framing of the Constitution*, Yale University Press, New Haven, 1913, 87 - 89

governments, would be oppressive to the country. Therefore, the machinery of state governments would have to be drastically reduced, but this reduction would be consistent with the absorption of a great portion of their functions by the national government. Hamilton encouraged the convention to study the structure and efficacy of the British government in the creation of a national government for America. His opinion was that the British government was the best in the world and he doubted whether anything short of it would suffice in America.[34]

Hamilton outlined his idea for the structure of government, specifically with respect to the relationship between the legislative branch and the executive. He stated clearly his preference for, and support of, a republic form of government. He thought that the duration of terms of office was an important consideration, first to attract the right kind of person to seek those offices and secondly to provide the greatest assurance against abuse of power.

> That we ought to go as far in order to attain stability and permanency, as republican principles will admit. Let one branch of the Legislature hold their places for life or at least during good behaviour. Let the Executive also be for life. He appealed to the feelings of the members present whether a term of seven years, would induce the sacrifices of private affairs which an acceptance of public trust would require, so as to ensure the services of the best Citizens. On this plan we should have in the Senate a permanent will, a weighty interest, which would answer essential purposes. But is this a Republican Govt., it will be asked? Yes if all the Magistrates are appointed, and vacancies are filled, by the people, or a process of election originating with the people. He was sensible that an Executive constituted as he proposed would have in fact but little of the power and independence that might be necessary.... An Executive for life has not this motive for forgetting his fidelity, and will therefore be a safer depository of power. It will be objected probably, that such an Executive will be an elective Monarch, and will give birth to the tumults which characterize that form of Govt. He wd reply that Monarch is an indefinite term. It marks not either the degree or duration of power. If this Executive Magistrate wd. be a monarch for life — the other prop'd. by the Report from the Com'tte of the whole, wd. be a monarch for seven years. The circumstance of being elective was also applicable to both. It had been observed by judicious writers that elective monarchies wd. be the best if they could be guarded ag'st. the tumults excited by the ambition and intrigues of competitors.[35]

Whether due to misunderstanding or from malice, his political opponents, throughout his life, distorted this speech and accused Hamilton of preferring a monarchical form of rule for the country.

---

34 Madison, *Debates* — *June 15*.
35 Ibid., June 18

The task before the convention was formidable and all the delegates were aware of that fact. On every issue there were heated debates. On the key issue of equal, as opposed to proportional, voting in the legislature, the feelings were so strong that the issue could not even be raised. Every delegate knew that this issue must be resolved if they were to accomplish the goal of the convention.

Dr. Johnson of Connecticut argued to maintain the rights of the States on a par, declaring that "The fact is that the States do exist as political Societies, and a Government is to be formed for them in their political capacity, as well as for the individuals composing them." James Madison presented an opposing view, one that under the new government the States, as political entities, were to take on a greatly reduced significance. As such it was to place too much importance on states to grant suffrage rights to these entities, robbing, to some extent, the voting rights of individuals.[36]

Alexander Hamilton sided with Madison when he reasoned, "But as States are a collection of individual men which ought we to represent most, the rights of the people composing them or the artificial beings resulting from the composition?" On a different facet of this suffrage problem, Hamilton offered, "It has been said that if the smaller States renounce their equality, they renounce at the same time their liberty. The truth is it is a contest for power, not liberty. Will the men composing a small state be less free than those composing the larger? The state of Delaware having 40,000 souls will lose power if she has 1/10 only of the votes allowed to Pennsylvania having 400,000. But will the people of Delaware be less free, if each citizen had an equal vote with each citizen of Pennsylvania?"[37]

The great question of suffrage rights in the two branches of the Legislature continued to be heated by partisan concerns. When the issue to determine the suffrage policy for the first house came under deliberation, for two days heated polemics were exchanged with no prospects for reaching an accommodation. Dr. Franklin arose and, in an attempt to set the Convention back on a proper course, said,

> In this situation of this Assembly, groping as it were in the dark to find political truth, and scarce able to distinguish it when presented to us, how has it happened, Sir, that we have not hitherto once thought of humbly applying to the Father of lights to illuminate our understandings? In

36 Ibid., June 29
37 Syrett, *The Papers of Alexander Hamilton*, Vol. IV, 220 — 221; Lodge, Henry, C., *The Works of Alexander Hamilton*, Vol. I, 415

the beginning of the Contest with Great Britain, when we were sensible of danger we had daily prayer in this room for the divine protection. — Our prayers, Sir, were heard and they were graciously answered. All of us who were engaged in the struggle must have observed frequent instances of a superintending providence in our favor. To that kind providence we owe this happy opportunity of consulting in peace on the means of establishing our future national felicity. And have we now forgotten that powerful friend? Or do we imagine that we no longer need his assistance? I have lived, Sir, a long time, and the longer I live, the more convincing proofs I see of this truth — that God Governs in the affairs of men. And if a sparrow cannot fall to the ground without his notice, is it probable that an empire can rise without his aid? We have been assured, Sir, in the sacred writings, that "except the Lord build the House they labour in vain that build it." I firmly believe this; and I also believe that without his concurring aid we shall succeed in this political building no better, than the Builders of Babel: We shall be divided by our little partial local interests; our projects will be confounded, and we ourselves shall become a reproach and bye-word down to future ages. And what is worse, mankind may hereafter from this unfortunate instance, despair of establishing Governments by Human wisdom and leave it to chance, war and conquest.

I therefore beg leave to move — that henceforth prayers imploring the assistance of Heaven, and its blessings on our deliberations, be held in this Assembly every morning before we proceed to business, and that one or more clergy of this City be requested to officiate in that Service.[38]

Unfortunately no action was taken on this motion due to the fact that the Convention had been assigned no budget from which a clergyman could be paid for the proposed services.

On June 29, a vote on the motion to agree to the clause, "that the vote of suffrage in the first branch ought not to be according to that established by the Articles of Confederation" (one state, one vote) passed by a vote of 6-4-1. On the suffrage for the Senate, Oliver Ellsworth of Connecticut "moved that the rule of suffrage in the second branch be the same with that established by the articles of confederation." He was not sorry on the whole, he said, that the vote just passed had determined against this rule in the first branch. He hoped it would become a ground of compromise with regard to the second branch. The proportional representation in the first branch was, he said, "conformable to the national principle & would secure the large States against the small. An equality of voices was conformable to the federal principle and was necessary to secure the Small States against the large." He trusted that on this middle ground a compromise would take place. He did not see that it could on any other. He felt that it was well that a three-branch

---

38 Madison, *Debates* — *June 28.*

government (Legislative, Executive and Judicial) be formed but cautioned that they should not attempt too much. He was not normally a halfway man but in this instance would rather accomplish the partial good that was feasible than fail to accomplish anything at all. Perhaps, he said, experience will make us wiser and then the rest might be accomplished.[39]

Early in July, in a response to a motion by General Pinckney, a committee was formed consisting of one member from each state to generate a workable compromise position for voting rights in both houses of the legislature. At this point it was generally recognized that the success of the Convention rode upon the formation of a compromise acceptable to large and small states alike. Should the Convention fail, so would the American experiment in Republican government. The committee was given from Monday, July 2 until Thursday, July 5 to deliberate and prepare a report.[40]

The report made by that committee on July 5 contained two provisions and was made contingent on the acceptance (or rejection) of both provisions. It was recommended that the first branch of the national legislature be composed of members whose numbers were proportional to the population of their respective States. Each state was to have one delegate for each 40,000 population. This house was to originate all money bills and set the salaries for government officials. The second branch was not to have the ability to amend or modify any money bill. The second provision was that in the second branch each state was to have an equal vote.[41]

The debate over this proposed compromise continued for days. At its heart was the question of assigning the rules of suffrage within the two branches of the National Legislature. In reality the debates aired all of the local and regional prejudices that threatened the solidarity of the union.

The issue of slavery, so vital to the commercial success of the South, became a primary issue. In the apportionment of delegates in the first house, should slaves be included in the total population? It was argued by Northern delegates that the legislature was to represent the citizens. If the citizens themselves were to be assembled to vote on an issue, surely the slaves would not be present; therefore, they should not be included in the population count. The South countered that wealth is as valid a basis for delegate apportionment as population and surely slave labor produces as much wealth

---

39 Ibid., *June 29*
40 Ibid., *July 2*
41 Ibid., *July 5*

as free white labor, and therefore should be included. The great majority had agreed to count the slaves as 3/5 of a white man for the apportionment of taxation; it was argued that taxation and representation should be consistent, so blacks should be counted on the same 60% basis for delegate apportionment. Gouverneur Morris thought that Pennsylvanians would resent being equated with blacks to the extent that they would fail to ratify any Constitution having that provision.[42] After extensive arguments over the issue of slavery in representation and also over the initial distribution of representatives among the states, it was voted on July 10 that suffrage in the first house would be proportional to population.

The question of equal suffrage in the second branch carried its share of contentious debates as well. The sole argument of the small states in favor of the equal vote was the defense of their liberty. In a proportional voting system they envisioned their special interests trampled; the freedom and significance of their state governments minimized and their very identity diminished. Oratory from large state delegates questioned the reasonableness of these fears. Yet the small states persisted — they would participate in no national government that did not contain equal voting rights by the states.[43] The vote on the question of equal votes in the second branch was postponed until the morning of July 16, when it was passed in the affirmative by the narrow margin of 5–4.

Once this landmark decision was agreed, the business of the Convention took on a quicker pace. In the deliberation of the extent of the legislative powers to be given to the National Government, a clause was debated that stated, "And moreover to legislate in all cases to which the separate States are incompetent; or in which the harmony of the United States may be interrupted by the exercise of individual legislation."[44] Pierce Butler requested a more definitive explanation of the terms used, particularly "incompetent." He stated that the vagueness of the wording hampered his ability to decide on the merits of the clause.[45] Nathaniel Gorham said that it was the vagueness that gave merit to the clause. He explained that the Convention was establishing general principles; and suggested that the legislature would,

42 Ibid., *July 11*
43 Ibid., *July 16*
44 Ibid.
45 Ibid.

in the course of time and under specific tests, define precisely the extent of their legislative powers.[46]

Another clause, also relating to the extent of powers of the Legislature read, "To negative [veto] all laws passed by the several States contraverting, in the opinion of the National Legislature, the articles of Union, or any treaties subsisting under the authority of the Union."[47] Much discussion ensued concerning the impracticality of the clause and of the intrusion of the National Government into the process of state governments. Luther Martin offered a resolution that carried unanimously, "That the Legislative acts of the United States made by virtue and in pursuance of the articles of Union, and all Treaties made and ratified under the authority of the United States shall be the supreme law of the respective States, as far as those acts and treaties shall relate to the said States, or their citizens and inhabitants and that the Judiciaries of the several States shall be bound thereby in their decisions, any thing in the respective laws of the individual States to the contrary notwithstanding."[48]

The next resolution to be deliberated concerned the selection of the National executive, "To be chosen by the National Legislature." Gouverneur Morris took a stand in opposition. He preferred that the people elect the Executive. He argued, "If the people should elect, they will never fail to prefer some man of distinguished character, or services; some man, if he might so speak, of continental reputation. If the Legislature elect, it will be the work of intrigue, of cabal, and of faction."[49] Others argued that the Legislature would be in a much better position to know the men of merit. Some were fearful that the people would vote most preferentially for someone from their state and therefore, the Executive was certain to come from a large state. When it came to a vote on the question of election by the people, the resolution was defeated 1–9. The vote on the election by the Legislature passed unanimously. This decision was to be re-visited late in the convention.

On July 20 the topic of impeachment of the Executive was debated. The clause under analysis stated, "to be removeable on impeachment and conviction for malpractice or neglect of duty." What was meant by impeachment? Would the Executive be suspended from his duties upon impeachment and

---

46 Ibid.
47 Ibid., *July 17*
48 Ibid.
49 Ibid.

until vindicated by his trial? Specifically, what crimes should be punishable by impeachment? Should the chief magistrate be immune from impeachment altogether? These questions were debated for most of the day. In the end impeachment was found necessary by a vote of 8–2.

It becomes clear in reading through the daily deliberations that no delegate arose who had a preconceived, clear and detailed view of the manner in which the new republican government should operate. There was no one man who had so firm a grasp upon the first principles of political science, knowledge of the human behavior and the scope of the needs of the emerging nation whose wisdom could direct the thoughts and opinions of the Convention. Every speaker, wise and experienced in his own right, was feeling his way through the haze generated by the complex of conflicting influences.

Resolution 10 pertained to the power of the Executive to negative any measure enacted by the Legislature, subject to an override of two-thirds of the second branch. James Wilson introduced an amendment that would include the Supreme National Judiciary in this revisionary power. He felt that "Laws may be unjust, may be unwise, may be dangerous, may be destructive; and yet not be so unconstitutional as to justify the Judges in refusing to give the effect."[50] It was argued in favor of the amendment that the Judges would add "wisdom and firmness to the Executive" and they would have an extensive knowledge of the Laws that the Executive might not have. In opposition it was said that to extend the right of the negative over unwanted legislation was tantamount "to making Statesmen of the Judges; and setting them up as the guardians of the Rights of the People. It was making them the Expositors of the Laws, the Legislators, which ought never to be done."[51] The question of including the Judiciary in the revision process lost by 4–3. A unanimous vote in favor of Resolution 10, giving the Executive a qualified veto with no amendments, was cast.[52]

The Committee of Detail was given the task on July 26 to draft appropriate wording to express the resolutions that had been worked through to that point of time. The convention adjourned until Monday, August 6, to provide the committee time to fulfill this task. During this recess most delegates from distant states stayed in Philadelphia, catching up on their notes and "refreshing their spirits." Others from nearby districts went home to families

---

50 Ibid., *July 21*
51 Ibid.
52 Ibid.

to catch up on neglected businesses. George Washington, along with Robert and Gouverneur Morris, rode up to Valley Forge where they spent some time trout fishing and touring the grounds made famous by that winter of severe suffering by General Washington and his army.[53]

Upon reassembly the Committee of Detail laid their draft of the Constitution before the Convention. In addition to formalizing the resolutions enacted by the Convention, this draft established the following terms. The country was to be known as the United States of America; the two branches of the Legislature became known as the House of Representatives and the Senate, respectively; the Chief Magistrate was to be the President and the National Judiciary, the Supreme Court.[54]

With the resolutions in the emerging Constitution being presented more formally and concisely, the delegates were able to focus on the detail, the meaning and the innuendoes and potential ramifications, and were able to offer their suggestions more constructively and rapidly. The contentious elements of the deliberations were behind them, and they were able to mold and sculpt the document into the body of "general principles" they intended the Constitution to be. A few exceptions to the contention-free flow of deliberation were remarkable. The question arose once more regarding the apportionment of Representatives by population, with each slave being counted at 60% of a freeman. Again, the insight and eloquence of Gouverneur Morris was displayed:

> The admission of slaves into the Representation when fairly explained comes to this: that the inhabitant of Georgia and South Carolina who goes to the Coast of Africa, and in defiance of the most sacred laws of humanity tears away his fellow creature from their dearest connections and damns them to the most cruel bondages, shall have more votes in a Government instituted for protection of the rights of mankind, than the Citizen of Pennsylvania or New Jersey who view with a laudable horror so nefarious a practice.[55]

The Southern States, whose livelihood depended upon the institution of slavery, stood firm. If the Constitution were to place obstacles to its continuation, then at least Georgia and South Carolina would exempt themselves from the Union. John Rutledge said, "Religion and humanity had nothing to do with the question. Interest alone is the governing principle with nations.

---

53 Bowen, *Miracle at Philadelphia*, 192 - 195
54 Madison, *Debates*, August 6
55 Ibid., *August 8*

The true question at present is whether the Southern States shall or shall not be parties to the Union."[56] The matter regarding the importation of slaves was assigned to a committee which reported on August 24. In their report a compromise position was offered which prohibited a tax or duty on the importation of slaves prior to the year 1800. In the convention deliberations this limit was extended to 1808.[57]

Late in the proceedings of the Convention, on August 27, during discussions of the extent of the powers to be given to the Supreme Court, Samuel Johnson of Connecticut proposed that the Justices be given the power to interpret the Constitution.[58] James Madison opposed, saying he "doubted whether it was not going too far to extend the jurisdiction of the court generally to cases arising under the Constitution and whether it might not be limited to cases of a judiciary nature." Hence the Supreme Court would decide on matters relating to the Constitution but only when adjudicating a case testing the merits of a law according to the Constitution.[59]

Early in September the Committee of Eleven, whose task had been to make recommendations on Constitutional sections on which action had been postponed, gave a report. A principal feature of this report dealt with the manner of choosing the President. Their report recommended that electors chosen by a means to be determined by the individual States should elect the President. The number of electors would be equal to the sum of the number of Representatives and the Senators. The office of Vice President was defined, to be elected along with the President and to serve a four-year term with no definition of re-eligibility. In addition to serving as the replacement for the President should he leave office for any reason, permanent or temporarily, the Vice President was to serve as the President of the Senate, casting a vote only to break a tie. Should the election of the President not produce one winner having the majority of the electoral votes, the Committee recommended that the Senate elect one from a list of the five candidates having received the highest number of electoral votes.[60] The security issue was settled by requiring that a candidate for President be a natural-born citizen or be a citizen when the Constitution was adopted.[61]

---

56 Ibid., *August 21*
57 Ibid., *August 25*
58 Ibid., *August 27*
59 Ibid.
60 Ibid., *September 4*
61 Ibid.

On September 8 a committee was appointed by ballot to revise the style and arrange the articles that had been agreed to by the convention. By an abundance of evidence, Gouverneur Morris was the writer of the final form of the Constitution. In the words of James Madison, "a better choice than Morris could not have been made."[62]

During the discussion of the ratification process the general view was that the States would be asked to approve or disapprove the Constitution without amendments. There was a danger that the whole attempt to create a Union could fail if they had to convene a second convention to consider any such amendments. Edmund Randolph strenuously disagreed, on the grounds that offering the States no option but acceptance or refusal would assure its failure. He felt so strongly on this point, he said, that he would be unable to affix his name to the Constitution without a correcting amendment.[63]

As late as five days prior to the final signing of the Constitution George Mason raised the need for a Bill of Rights. He thought that such explicit protection for the rights of individuals would be warmly received by the people. It certainly would enhance the general reception of the Constitution. Roger Sherman pointed out that the State Declaration of Rights existed and had not been repealed by the Constitution, so that a Bill of Rights was not necessary. A motion to include such provisions in the Constitution was defeated.[64]

The delegates continued to deliberate each phrase and word until the close of business on September 15, when all States voted "aye" to the Constitution as amended. It was then decided that the Constitution be embossed. On Monday morning, September 17, the Constitution was read; Dr. Franklin rose to have a statement of his read by Mr. Wilson.

> I confess that there are several parts of this constitution which I do not at present approve, but I am not sure I shall never approve them: For having lived long, I have experienced many instances of being obliged by better information, or fuller consideration, to change opinions even on important subjects, which I once thought right, but found to be otherwise. It is therefore that the older I grow, the more apt I am to doubt my own judgment, and to pay more respect to the judgment of others.
>
> In these sentiments, Sir, I agree to this Constitution with all its faults, if they are such; because I think a general Government necessary for us, and there is no form of Government but what may be a blessing to the people if

---

62 Ketcham, Ralph, *James Madison — A Biography*, University Press of Virginia, Charlottesville, 1990, 225 - 226
63 Madison, *Debates — September 15*.
64 Ibid., *September 12*

well administered, and believe further that this is likely to be well administered for a course of years, and can only end in Despotism, as other forms have done before it, when the people shall become so corrupted as to need despotic Government, being incapable of any other. I doubt too whether any other Convention we can obtain, may be able to make a better Constitution. For when you assemble a number of men to have the advantage of their joint wisdom, you inevitably assemble with those men, all their prejudices, their passions, their errors of opinion, their local interests, and their selfish views. From such an assembly can a perfect production be expected? It therefore astonishes me, Sir, to find this system approaching so near to perfection as it does; and I think it will astonish our enemies, who are waiting with confidence to hear that our councils are confounded like those of the Builders of Babel; and that our States are on the point of separation, only to meet hereafter for the purpose of cutting one another's throats. Thus I consent, Sir, to this Constitution because I expect no better, and because I am not sure, that it is not the best. The opinions I have had of its errors, I sacrifice to the public good. I have never whispered a syllable of them abroad. Within these walls they were born, and here they shall die. Much of the strength & efficiency of any Government in procuring and securing happiness to the people depends, on the general opinion of the goodness of the Government, as well as of the wisdom and integrity of its Governors. I hope therefore that for our own sakes as a part of the people, and for the sake of posterity, we shall act heartily and unanimously in recommending this Constitution (if approved by Congress & confirmed by the Conventions) wherever our influence may extend, and turn our future thoughts & endeavors to the means of having it well administered.[65]

A last minute amendment was offered to increase the number of Representatives by changing the clause, "the number of Representatives shall not exceed one for every 40,000" to insert 30,000 for 40,000. At this point the president arose and added his support for that change, "although his situation had hitherto restrained him from offering his sentiments on questions depending the House," in order to reduce anticipated objections from the people. "The smallness of the proportion of Representatives had been considered by many members of the Convention as insufficient security for the rights and interests of the people." [66] The proposed amendment was passed unanimously.

Alexander Hamilton, wishing to encourage unanimity in the signing of the document, stated, "No man's ideas were more remote from the plan than his were known to be; but is it possible to deliberate between anarchy and Convulsion on one side, and the chance of good to be expected from the plan on the other."[67]

---

65 Ibid., *September 17*
66 Ibid.
67 Ibid.

The President asked what should be done with the records of the convention, whether copies were to be given to the members upon request. It was resolved that he retain the Journal and other papers, subject to the order of the Congress, if ever formed under the Constitution.

The members then proceeded to sign the instrument. Washington made a note in his diary that said, "The business being closed the members adjourned to the City Tavern, dined together and took a cordial leave of each other."

Major Jackson, the secretary of the Convention. was given the charge to travel the next day to take the Constitution to Congress at New York. The delegates each received a printed copy.[68]

When the Convention in Philadelphia sent the drafted Constitution on to Congress in New York, they did so with the hope that it would be studied and its advantages understood and appreciated. It still had to be ratified by each state, and it was hoped that Congress would transmit the Constitution with its approbation and a recommendation in favor of its ratification. And indeed, the Congress that received the Constitution inclined neither to controversy nor to exert its influence over the states under any circumstance. On September 28, Congress sent the Constitution to the States "in order to be submitted to a convention of delegates chosen in each state by the people thereof."[69]

The Signers of the Constitution knew that there would be spirited struggles in most states in order to gain ratification of their work. Most people throughout the thirteen states favored the concentration of power in the states, as it was under the Articles of Confederation. They had endured a long and arduous conflict to secure their independence from a centralized governmental power and were hesitant to revert to another central government, even one of their own making.

The Signers of the Constitution knew most of the arguments — they had debated them thoroughly in the Philadelphia Convention. They were also aware, where most Americans were not, that the Articles of Confederation contained fatal flaws that limited the effectiveness of Congress and would likely lead to a collapse of the Confederation in the near future. The Signers felt that the Constitution they offered to the country solved the weaknesses

---

68 Bowen, C., *Miracle in Philadelphia*, 262 - 264
69 Ibid., 269

inherent in the Confederation and provided for a government that would better provide for liberty, security and stability for the long term.

In the ratification conventions that were held in each of the states, those who favored the new Constitution, conferring more authority to the Federal government, were referred to as Federalists; those who wanted the ultimate sovereignty to reside with the state legislatures were called anti-Federalists. In most conventions anti-Federalists outnumbered the Federalist delegates, sometimes by considerable margins. The anti-Federalists agreed that the Articles of Confederation had weaknesses and flaws but thought that they could be solved with amendments to the existing articles. An entirely new constitution was not necessary, they argued, particularly one that gave ultimate authority to a central republican government.

The new Constitution provided protection from the abuse of power of the ruling few by the check-and-balance system that pervaded the governmental structure. The government defined by the Constitution would be republican in form, seeking to balance the rights of minorities as well as the majority, and to uphold the liberties of individual citizens. Many anti-Federalists disagreed that a republican government would be able to function over so large and diverse a landmass as the United States. The anti-Federalists considered that republics were most likely to succeed as small political entities where the government could consist of delegates selected from the people, were well known by the people and were intimately knowledgeable of the wants and needs of the people.

Governor George Clinton of New York found it difficult to see how a republican government could effectively rule over a land that had the climatic extremes presented by the heat of Georgia and Massachusetts's winters. The people were too diverse, ranging from agrarians in the south to manufacturers and foreign traders in the north. He could not imagine that the rulers of the republic could understand the problems and needs of so diverse a population.[70] James Madison, while he was still a Federalist, argued that the diversities pointed out by Clinton were more of a strength than a weakness for the new government. The special interests of the people, he stated, being generally of only local interest, would tend to cancel one another out so that

---

70 Spaulding, E. Wilder, *His Excellency George Clinton — Critic of the Constitution*, Ira Friedman, Inc., Port Washington, L. I., New York, 174

only those problems that are truly of national interest and importance would rise to the attention of the national legislature.

The anti-Federalists were opposed to granting so many powers to the central government via a constitution, especially the power to tax and to raise armies. The federal power of taxation encroached on what the anti-Federalists considered to be a state prerogative — and one which the states guarded jealously. They viewed the federal power to raise armies as oppressive of the liberties of the people. They further held the position that armies should only be raised in times of war. The war of 1812 showed the weakness of that approach.

The Federalists, through reasoned and thoughtful argument, persuaded the majority and won ratification in every convention. The anti-Federalists, for the most part, presented only vague arguments predicting dire consequences from the new Constitution, offered no well-thought-out alternative and were, in the end, won over by the reasoned and comprehensive arguments of the proponents of the Constitution.

The one argument put forth by anti-Federalists that was accepted and did improve the Constitution was the need for a Bill of Rights. This issue had been raised late in the Philadelphia Convention but was not acted upon. It was argued there that state constitutions had Bills of Rights and nothing in the federal Constitution nullified them or gave power to the federal government to nullify them in the future. But the anti-Federalists, led by Patrick Henry in Virginia, argued that the liberty of the individual is better provided for in explicit language in the Constitution than by reliance on the diminished power of state constitutions to assure them.[71]

The anti-Federalists were not able to offer a consensus alternative plan to the Constitution because they themselves were divided by numerous and often conflicting special interests. The states had been functioning since 1776 as separate and independent political entities. They passed their own laws, levied their own taxes, operated police powers, some engaged in foreign commerce, and had their own currency — all legitimate functions of sovereign states. Their political leaders had become accustomed to the responsibilities and perquisites attendant to the running of the state government. There were legislative agenda to work through, taxes to be levied and collected, ju-

---

71 Beeman, Richard P., *Patrick Henry — A Biography*, McGraw-Hill Book Co., New York, 1974, 162

dicial systems to operate and state militias to support and manage. In each of these functions there were political appointments to be made, transactions to be completed with firms contracting with the state and special interest groups to be served.

In the fulfillment of their various offices, the political leaders found ways for personal embellishment, most legal, some questionable. They could see in the new constitution that the functions they filled would be seriously diminished and their positions lessened in influence and importance. Certainly the new central government would be much stronger than any of the state governments they had known; more power, influence and money would be wielded by the national government and its leaders would be more powerful and influential than any political leaders in the state governments. It would, however, be difficult to win a prominent position in the new government as opposed to the relative security of the positions they currently held in the state government. These considerations were more than sufficient to generate resentment and opposition from the leaders in the state governments to the strong central government defined by the new Constitution.

There was yet another special interest that generated strong opposition from the anti-Federalists to the new Constitution — that of slavery. In 1790 the South was economically dependent upon the low cost of labor provided by slavery. In the North slavery was not so essential to the economy, and Northerners were increasingly repelled by the idea of slavery. Massachusetts had already abolished it.

During the Constitutional Convention the issue of slavery arose and the North-South polarization towards the institution came to the fore. Charles Cotesworth Pinckney of South Carolina had been a proponent of a strong central government before the Constitutional Convention, realizing the weaknesses of the Confederation. Being a slaveholder, he had experienced the extreme economic hardship in his state during the revolution when England had caused extensive damage to the crops and the plantations and then made off with many of their slaves. The reconstruction from this combined loss took several years for South Carolina's planters.[72] The memory of this loss made many Southern planters particularly sensitive to their economic dependence on slavery. In the Constitutional Convention, Pinckney was re-

---

72 Zahniser, Marvin R., *Charles Cotesworth Pinckney*, University of North Carolina Press, Chapel Hill, 1967, 74-75

solved that, while the new government they were defining needed to have considerable regulatory power, they must not allow any interference with the institution of slavery in the South. The postponement for ten years of any regulatory power of the federal government over slavery was a temporizing approach that did nothing to truly address an issue that eventually would have to be resolved.

Three men, James Madison, Alexander Hamilton and John Jay, combined to write a series of eighty-five articles that explained the Constitution, its need, and the functioning of the government under its guidance. These papers, written under the pseudonym Publius, were published three times a week in newspapers throughout the country. Even before the publication of the last article, they were being assembled into book form under the title, *The Federalist Papers*. As these articles were published they were read by a great many people; they influenced the more contentious conventions such as Massachusetts, Virginia and New York. In the intervening years *The Federalist Papers* has been cited by the Supreme Court in many decisions, and has been used as the basis for deciding the intended meaning of the Constitution. Today *The Federalist Papers* is accepted as a premier text on political science.

George Washington, always mindful of the mindset of his addressee, wrote tactfully to Patrick Henry, "I wish the Constitution had been made more perfect. But I sincerely believe it is the best that could be obtained at this time. It appears to me that the political concerns of this country are in a manner suspended by a thread and, if nothing had been agreed on by the Convention, anarchy would soon have ensued."[73]

The State of Delaware was the first to ratify the Constitution on December 7. Pennsylvania ratified it on December 12, followed by New Jersey on December 18. Georgia ratified on January 2, 1788.

The Massachusetts convention first met on January 8, 1788. There were 355 delegates in attendance. The delegates from the western districts were avid anti-Federalists; indeed, among their number were twenty-nine men who had fought with Shays. In the more populous eastern regions as well, any authority delegated to a central government was distrusted and hated. Countering their arguments were Rufus King, Nathaniel Gorham and Caleb Strong, each of whom had been delegates to the Constitutional Convention. Other Federalist delegates included fifteen state senators, twenty well-

---

73 Ibid.

known and respected clergy, a dozen prominent attorneys and sheriffs.[74] After extended debates, the Convention finally agreed to ratify the Constitution by the narrow margin of nineteen votes.

Maryland ratified on April 28 by a vote of 63–11. On May 23, South Carolina ratified. New Hampshire became the ninth state to ratify the Constitution on June 21,[75] beating out Virginia for this singular recognition.

The Federalists in Virginia had hoped to become the ninth and deciding state to ratify the Constitution when they met in full convention on June 2. In the Convention there were highly respected, eloquent speakers on both sides of the issue. Anti-Federalists made the same states' rights and special interest arguments that were made in other states. As in other southern states, the institution of slavery had strong support among the economic and political leaders of Virginia. Patrick Henry led a fight to add amendments to the constitution as a condition to their ratification of the Constitution. The Federalists made the argument that, considering the degenerated condition of the Confederation, the new government under this Constitution was the only avenue to continued liberty that could possibly avoid anarchy and civil war. On June 24, Chancellor Wythe called for attaching a Bill of Rights. On June 25 by a margin of a mere ten votes Virginia became the tenth state to ratify.[76]

The New York Legislature voted on February 1, 1788 to call a convention. Alexander Hamilton was elected in April as one of the state's delegates. As the sole Framer from New York favorable to the ratification, Hamilton felt great responsibility for securing an affirmative vote from his state. Hamilton gave his analysis of the question of New York's action on ratification in a letter to James Madison in early June. He projected the opposition to have, at that time, a 2/3 majority in the convention with a similar support in the community. Hamilton expected a lengthy adjournment of the convention rather than an outright refusal to ratify. This recess would give "an opportunity to see how the government works and to act according to circumstances."[77]

The anti-Federalists, with their majority, opposed the new constitution because of its intrusion into the rights and influence of the state legislature and out of fear of centralized power. The vocal spokesmen for the

74 Ibid., 282 - 284

75 www.factmonster.com/ipke'Ad6101025.html

76 Bowen, C., *Miracle at Philadelphia*, 300 — 304c

77 Syrett, H., *The Papers of Alexander Hamilton, Vol. V*, 3

"antis," Melancton Smith and Abraham Yates, argued that the constitution would have to be extensively amended to be acceptable. They wanted checks against the growth of federal power — limited tenure or rotation in office; they promoted limiting the jurisdiction of the Supreme Court and a formal Bill of Rights.[78]

The geographical boundaries between Federalists and anti-Federalists in New York were clear. The Federalists dominated New York City and some other sizable cities. The remainder of the state was strongly anti-Federalist. The farming population had a bias for self-sufficiency, requiring no outsider's guidance or dictates. Taxation was a minor issue for them, since most of New York's revenue had been derived from the taxation of imports at New York harbor.

The state politicians were anxious to defend the influence and importance of their positions, which the centralized government was certain to diminish. The general anti-Federalist philosophy was to "let well enough alone." They viewed the constitution as the antithesis of all they had fought for in the Revolution. They saw no reason for it, and wished not to be governed from a distant capitol, dominated by men from other states and oppressed by a standing army over which they could exercise no control.

These viewpoints either ignored or failed to appreciate the problems inherent in the Confederation and the long-term benefits offered by an emphasis on national interests that the Constitution provided.

On June 20, Hamilton first stood to address the convention. Hamilton gave an informed and reasoned address pointing out the fatal flaws in the Confederation as it existed. As a participant in the Philadelphia Convention he gave a strong defense of the measures contained in the Constitution. As in Massachusetts and Virginia, the anti-Federalist sentiment in New York was based mainly on conjecture, assumptions and fear fueled by the recent experiences with Great Britain and on sensationalized interpretations of the Articles in the Constitution. Hamilton persuaded with facts, reasoned thinking and historical examples.

The New York convention decided that a Bill of Rights would be essential. It became clear from the Federalists' unswerving stand that New York's ratification had to be unconditional. In response to Hamilton's arguments,

---

78 William & Mary Quarterly, July 1967, *Alexander Hamilton and Melancton Smith and the Ratification of the Constitution in New York*, Robin Brooks, 345

Melancton Smith finally proposed a change in the wording of his recommendation that urged Congress to consider the amendments most critical to New York. They finally agreed, on July 23, to attach these and other amendments as recommendations to their ratification. On July 26, by a vote of thirty to twenty-seven New York agreed to the ratification of the constitution.[79]

Following this decision there was rioting in Albany by anti-Federalists who publicly burned copies of the Constitution. In New York City there was celebration. A parade was held there in which the ship *Hamilton* — a frigate with thirty-two guns, fully rigged and manned by thirty seamen, was pulled down the street by ten horses. Eleven States had ratified, and Rhode Island and North Carolina would eventually come over to complete the Union. In the midst of a celebration in Philadelphia, Dr. Benjamin Rush, a signer of the Declaration pronounced, "Tis done, we have become a nation."[80]

---

79 *Ibid.,* , *348, 350, 354-356*
80Bowen, *Miracle at Philadelphia,* 306 - 310

Chapter 5. Fulfilling the Potential

There was a tacit understanding in the Constitutional Convention that the first Executive could be none other than George Washington. The noble bearing that Washington possessed, his integrity and his confident leadership, as well as the reputation he had gained by his generalship of the Revolutionary Army, had earned him the affections and trust of the nation. If the American experiment in Republican government was to succeed, it was essential that it take its first steps under the leadership that George Washington could provide. Where concern was expressed over too much power accruing to the Executive, it was directed at Washington's eventual successors.

At the conclusion of the War for Independence, Washington had eagerly retreated to his life as a gentleman farmer, while retaining a keen interest in the political life of the country. Only the summons to return to duty had brought him reluctantly out of this pleasant retirement to attend, and preside over, the Philadelphia Convention. Upon its completion, Washington once more sought the bucolic life of Mt. Vernon. When the national acceptance of the new Constitution became certain, a number of friends and supporters began writing to Washington, encouraging him to accept the inevitable call to serve as the new country's first President. Among these correspondents, Alexander Hamilton persuasively wrote, "The absolute retreat which you meditated at the close of the late war was natural and proper. Had the government produced by the revolution gone on in a tolerable train, it would have been most advisable to persist in that retreat. But I am clearly of the opinion that the crisis which brought you again into public view left you no alternative but to comply and I am equally clear in the opinion that you are by that act pledged to take a part in the execution of the government...It cannot be considered as a [mere] compliment to say that on your acceptance of the office of President the success of the new government in its commencement may materially depend."[1]

In his response to Hamilton, Washington revealed the management style he had so consistently used throughout the war and would continue to employ throughout his eight year Presidency; he sought the advice of respected councilors before making a final decision in any weighty matter. "I am earnestly desirous of searching out the truth, and of knowing whether there does not exist a probability that the government would be just as happily and effectually carried into execution, without my aid as with it. I am truly solicitous to obtain all the previous information which the circumstances will attend."[2]

From his law office in New York City, Hamilton maintained an active correspondence supporting Washington's nomination and further encouraged him to accept the eventual and certain call. Hamilton also spent time assessing the field of Vice Presidential candidates. As it became clear that the name of John Adams dominated the field, Hamilton considered his view of the Adams candidacy. He recalled that Adams, in the Continental Congress, was sympathetic to the Conway Cabal and had been less than supportive of Washington's performance as Commander-in-Chief. Would Adams's former opposition to Washington's leadership prevail in the new government and would this opposition limit Washington's ability to govern? In one letter Hamilton confides, "Mr. A(dams) to a sound understanding has always appeared to me to add an ardent love for the public good; and as his further knowledge of the world seems to have corrected those jealousies which he is represented to have once been influenced by, I trust nothing of the kind suggested in my former letter will disturb the harmony of the administration."[3]

---

1 Syrett, *The Papers of Alexander Hamilton*, Vol. V, 220 - 221
2 Ibid., 223
3 Ibid., 231

There remained in Hamilton's mind a nagging concern over the statistical possibility that an unbridled support for Adams could have the unhappy consequence that he could accrue more votes than Washington and himself become President. The Constitution specified that each elector would cast two votes; one vote must be for a man living outside of the elector's state. There was no provision to differentiate between votes for the President and Vice President; the one who received the highest number of votes, provided that number constituted a majority of the electors, became President and the runner up became Vice-President. Hamilton was concerned that some anti-Federalist electors might omit Washington's name from either of their votes, and create the possibility for Adams to receive the highest number of votes cast. Through his correspondence with knowledgeable political leaders across the country and as the names of the selected electors became known, his concerns subsided.[4]

The new Congress first met in Federal Hall in April 1789. New York had renovated the old City Hall for this use in an attempt to entice the federal government to make their permanent home in New York City. Among the early duties of the new Congress was a canvas of the electoral votes for the chief and assistant executive. Washington received a unanimous selection by the electors, and Adams received the second highest number of votes cast. Washington received word of his election by courier.

On April 16 he left Mount Vernon by carriage for the eight-day journey to New York. At Elizabethtown, New Jersey he took a barge to carry him across to New York. On April 24 Washington arrived in New York and moved into to his residence on Federal Square. That night the anti-Federalist Governor Clinton hosted a dinner in Washington's honor who, by his attendance, wished to signify that he was to be the President of all Americans, both those who opposed as well as those who supported his policies.[5]

On April 30 Washington took his oath of office, administered by Chancellor Robert Livingston. Washington, wearing a dress sword, was clothed in a suit of brown broadcloth with silver shoe buckles. Hamilton observed the inauguration from the crowd and must have felt a deep sense of accomplishment; for although he stated at the Constitutional Convention that no man's idea of government was more remote than his from the one being inau-

---

4 Syrett, *The Papers of Alexander Hamilton*, Vol. V, 248
5 Chernow, *Alexander Hamilton*, 276; Elkins, McKitrick, *The Age of Federalism*, 45

gurated that day, neither did any man labor with more dedication to assure that the country realize the advantages offered by this government over the Confederation. After taking the oath of office, Washington gave his inaugural address to a joint session of Congress in the Senate chamber. The short address, probably written by James Madison, was delivered in a tentative and barely audible voice. It was said that Washington was more agitated and embarrassed in giving this address than ever he was by the leveled cannon or pointed musket.[6]

President Washington was mindful that his early conduct in office would establish a precedent to decide the propriety of conducting formal relations with the President. He requested that Alexander Hamilton draft a list of considerations for him covering matters of protocol. In his response letter Hamilton stated foremost that,

> The public good requires, as a primary object, that the dignity of the office should be supported. Whatever is essential to this ought to be pursued though at the risk of partial or momentary dissatisfaction. Men's minds are prepared for a pretty high tone in the demeanor of the Executive; but I doubt whether so high a tone as in the abstract may be desirable. The notions of equality are yet in my opinion too general and too strong to admit of such a distance being placed between the President and other branches of government.[7]

Hamilton added considerations for determining who should have access to the President on business. He listed, as examples, department heads in the Cabinet, and Foreign Ministers. He drew examples from the governments of European countries as models for consideration. He asserted that Senators should have access on an individual basis, but not Representatives. He took note that this differentiation might cause some sense of discrimination but, in Hamilton's mind, was supported by the Constitution. He pointed out that the Senate was coupled with the President in the executive functions of treaties and appointments, making them, to an extent, his Constitutional counselors. By this reasoning they would have a peculiar claim to the president's attention.[8] Washington responded by letter, thanking Hamilton for his thoughts, and requested that Hamilton permit him to regularly seek his council "as occasions may arise."[9]

---

6 Ketcham, R., *James Madison*, 283
7 Syrett, *The Papers of Alexander Hamilton*, Vol. V, 335; Hamilton, John C., *The Works of Alexander Hamilton*, Vol. IV, 1
8 Syrett, *The Papers of Alexander Hamilton*, Vol. V, 337
9 Ibid., 337 - 338

In any period of separation from his wife, Hamilton maintained a lively and loving correspondence with her. During the early months of Washington's administration when Elizabeth Hamilton was visiting her family at the Schuyler mansion in Albany, Hamilton wrote,

> I am miserable My beloved angel that I cannot yet come to you; but this abominable business still detains us and will do it for some days. I would willing endure the fatigue of a journey to visit you, if it were but for a minute; but such is my situation and the expectation of those for whom I act, that I cannot get away for an hour. It cannot however much longer keep me from my beloved; and the moment I can I will fly to your bosom.[10]

The Constitution did not specify the cabinet positions to assist the Executive in his office so Washington requested Congress to establish the positions of Secretary of State, of Treasury, of War and Attorney General.

As soon as he was duly authorized to do so, President Washington asked Alexander Hamilton to serve as his first Secretary of Treasury. Washington had earlier asked Robert Morris to fill this role but Morris declined. He did, however, recommend to Washington that Alexander Hamilton was the man best qualified for this position. With Hamilton's assent, his name was placed in nomination for that post on September 11, 1789 and was approved by the Senate that same day.

In the Constitutional Convention Hamilton had pointed out the weakness of the Confederacy, and attributed this weakness to a natural tendency in human nature to restrict their interest and obligations to the smallest possible collective unit, in this instance the state. The parochial interests and jealousies that the state governments held for their powers and prerogatives derived from this human tendency. He cited the example of the ancient Greek city-states that were unable to develop an effective confederacy and eventually perished by foreign invasion. The German Diet was another example of the weakness of a confederated government which only succeeded by the ascension to great power of a monarch. Still another example he gave was the Swiss Cantons that refused any form of union and were frequently at war with one another.

Hamilton had long advocated the establishment of a strong central government. He proposed that, "we ought to go as far in order to attain stability

---

10 Ibid., 342 - 343

and permanency, as republican principles will admit."[11] With a sufficiently strong central government, having taxing authority consistent with its legitimate needs, the need for state legislatures will be greatly reduced because many of their functions under the Confederacy will be performed by the central government. Examples of the limited function of state governments favored by Hamilton included internal police, which relates to the rights of property and life among individuals, and to raising money by internal taxes. The central government would be responsible for the greater needs including all that relates to war, peace, trade, finance and the management of foreign affairs.[12]

When he was offered the position of Secretary of the Treasury, Hamilton was pleased to accept. He fully understood the dismal financial outlook of the country, he appreciated the urgent need for a solution, and he had a definitive plan to re-structure the country's finances. Within months of taking office, Hamilton proposed to Congress a plan for the consolidation of all of the government's debts, including the assumption of legitimate war debts owed by the states. He recommended re-financing the total debt and he suggested that a potential source of revenue could be tapped by granting the federal government the sole right of taxation over commercial imports. Later he proposed taxing alcoholic spirits, both imported and domestically distilled, to pay for the states' war debt. He submitted an extensive report to Congress on the establishment of a national mint, setting the dollar as the unit of monetary exchange. He gave a lengthy argument for the correct mixture of gold and silver in the minted coins so that American money would have a stable value both domestically and in foreign trading. As a capstone to his financial plan, Hamilton proposed that the Congress charter a national bank. A national bank would help to stabilize the nation's monetary system through the amount of gold and silver specie it would hold, expand the amount of money in circulation in the country, and serve as a transactional institution for the government.

Highest among Hamilton's priorities was the redemption of the public credit and stabilization of the monetary system. With its nearly boundless natural resources, a labor force that held all the talents, skills and energy necessary to transform the country into a highly influential economic power in

---

11 Madison's notes, June 18
12 Syrett, H., *The Papers of Alexander Hamilton*, Vol. II, 407-*408

the world. Hamilton's proposed plan for financial reform could transform the country's fiscal system and would move the economy toward prosperity.

The American Revolution was given an essential assist by loans from France and Holland. Under the poor fiscal arrangements of the Confederation these loans had gone unserviced and the interest in arrears was becoming a considerable debt in itself.

Early in his administration of the Treasury Department, Hamilton wrote a letter to the American chargé d'affaires in Paris, William Short, which evidenced that this issue was a serious concern to the American government. In this letter he admitted that payment of the principal owed to France was, at the moment, beyond the means of the United States and he suggested an approach that called for making interest-only payments for a period of five to six years, after which time the United States would resume principal payments. "It would be a valuable accommodation to the government of this country, if the Court of France should think fit to suspend the payments of the installments of the principal due, and to become due, for five or six years from this period on condition of effectual arrangements for the punctual discharge of the interest which has accrued." Hamilton preferred not to make this a formal request of France out of concern that such a request would do further damage to the present state of public credit. It was preferable that the Court of France suggest this arrangement as a voluntary and magnanimous offer.[13]

The House of Representatives issued a directive to Hamilton just prior to their adjourning for the fall, on September 21, requiring him to make a report to the House at its next meeting (in January 1790) with his recommendations for improving the public credit. The importance of the public credit, to the development of the country under its new government was well understood and accepted by the new Congress.

As early as 1781, in a letter to Robert Morris, Hamilton had observed that it would be through public credit, more than on the field of contest, they would win their goal of independence.[14] In response to the directive from Congress, Hamilton issued a report in which he described the importance of the public credit of the nation. "In dealings with foreign powers the public credit of a nation is of paramount importance. In trade, it is essential to prof-

13 Syrett, *The Papers of Alexander Hamilton*, Vol. V, 429 - 430; Lodge, Henry C., The Works of *Alexander Hamilton*, Vol. IV, 294-296
14 Syrett, *The Papers of Alexander Hamilton*, Vol. V, 429-430

itable commerce to be able to acquire credit at good rates. In times of war, the extraordinary expenditure rates will exceed the capacity of any country and all countries need to resort to loans to finance their campaigns; good public credit is essential in securing these loans and at rates that will not bankrupt the country in their repayment."[15]

In his *Report on Public Credit*, Hamilton reflected that, "If the maintenance of public credit, then, be truly so important, the next enquiry which suggests itself is, by what means is it to be effected? The ready answer to which question is, by good faith, by a punctual performance of contracts. States, like individuals who observe their engagements, are respected and trusted: while the reverse is the fate of those, who pursue an opposite conduct."[16]

In his report Hamilton itemized the benefits of correcting the unserviced status of foreign loans and improving the public credit, "To promote the encreasing respectability of the American name; to answer the calls of justice; to restore public landed property to its due value; to furnish new resources both to agriculture and to commerce; to cement more closely the union of the States; to add to their security against foreign attack; to establish public order on the basis of an upright and liberal policy."[17]

He went on to instruct that there is an additional benefit to properly servicing the national debt in which every citizen should be interested. "In countries in which the national debt is properly funded, and an object of established confidence, it answers most of the purposes of money. Transfers of stock or public debt are there equivalent to payments in specie."[18] If the United States demonstrated to the world that they had installed a revenue system adequate to meet the interest payments on their debts, as they came due, the national credit rating would soar and the public debt notes would become as respected as specie.

Fledgling America had always suffered from an extreme shortage of money. Throughout the colonial period and during the period of the Confederation the only legal tender accepted abroad was foreign coinage. What coinage did exist in America was continually being depleted through for-

---

15 Syrett, *The Papers of Alexander Hamilton*, Vol. VI, 67; Hamilton, John C., *The Works of Alexander Hamilton*, Vol. III, 2

16 Syrett, *The Papers of Alexander Hamilton*, Vol. VI, 66 — 68; Hamilton, John C., *The Works of Alexander Hamilton*, Vol. III, 1-3

17 Syrett, *The Papers of Alexander Hamilton*, Vol. VI, 70; Hamilton, John C., *The Works of Alexander Hamilton*, Vol. III, 5

18 Ibid.

eign trade. As with all agrarian societies, the balance of trade was negative, so more coins were outgoing then incoming. The use and stability of paper money in the first half of the eighteenth century in America had been remarkably successful. Its success likely proceeded from its good management and from the public need for a convenient circulating medium of exchange. The Revolution altered the stability of the American financial system to a great extent. The extended range of business transactions caused the paper emissions from one state to be offered in other states, perhaps even non-contiguous ones, wherein the confidence required for stability was either non-existent or unwarranted. When the Confederation Congress created its notes to compensate veterans of the Revolution, the little faith that the people had in that government transferred to these bills, which therefore quickly depreciated.[19]

Without an adequate money supply, commerce could never develop; but the economy, by itself, could never create a stable monetary system. It required the backing of a strong, stable government with adequate and reliable revenue sources to generate the faith in a monetary system necessary to give it stability. In Hamilton's view this would happen in the American system given adequate time. In the meantime he showed that the proper funding of the national debt could serve many of the same functions as a stable monetary system. He proposed that the national debt be re-financed through the sale of federal notes, backed by the security of the government and reliant upon the federal revenue system for reclamation. These notes were to be sold to foreign investors and governments as well as to private investors in America. It was in the trading of these notes that America would find its first stable monetary system.

Two major types of public debts attracted Hamilton's attention, in addition to the foreign debt. They were the domestic debt on the notes issued to the veterans of the Revolution in lieu of cash payment of their salaries, and the war debts that had been incurred by the individual States. Issues attendant to both of these classes of debt were heatedly debated in Congress; one such issue would destroy the friendship between Alexander Hamilton and James Madison and the other would fix the permanent seat for the nation's capital.

---

19 Ferguson, James, *Power of the Purse*, University of North Carolina Press, Chapel Hill, 1961, 14-19

At the conclusion of the war many of the soldiers and officers had not received any pay for years. Promises of severance or retirement settlements had been made to the officers that the government under the Confederation had been unable to meet. The government had issued promissory notes covering the commitments owed to these veterans. These notes were issued to the veterans without establishing any means of covering them when due. The states were no more likely to fund these requests than they had been to requisitions to service the foreign war debt. Consequently, the market value of these certificates plummeted and many veterans found themselves having to exchange them for specie at the best rate they could obtain, which was often no more than twenty cents on the dollar.

Hamilton had to confront the question that had been raised in various places of who should receive the profit arising from paying these notes at par. Many felt that the speculators should be paid only for their investment plus interest on that amount, but the soldiers should be compensated for the difference between par and the value they had received. Hamilton disagreed. He came down solidly on the side of the nature of contracts. When the government issued these notes they constituted a contract to the holder to pay the par value. They were made negotiable so that the holder, at any time, could choose to sell his share for the current market price. The buyer had the right to the par value when the note was redeemed, or likewise to sell it at his convenience. Aside from the impossible logistical problem of determining what each veteran had received for his notes, Hamilton said that the nature of contracts had to be respected and the holder reimbursed for the par value of the notes. Anything else would diminish the credit standing of the government, alienate creditors and violate the Constitution that specified, "all debts contracted and engagements entered into before the adoption of the Constitution shall be as valid against the United States under it, as under the Confederation."[20]

Hamilton understood the country's debt to the war veterans of the Revolution, but he was adamant that sentiment must not override the validity of contracts. The inviolability of contracts is at the heart of public morality, he argued. Hamilton's argument on the compensation issue, although it was beneficial to the long-term credit of the United States, was widely unpopu-

---

20 Syrett, *The Papers of Alexander Hamilton*, Vol. VI, 77; Elkins, S., McKitrick, E., *Age of Federalism*, Oxford University Press, New York, 1993, 117

lar, public opinion being on the side of the veterans whom they saw as suffering an injustice. Hamilton's reputation suffered greatly over this issue. At the time neither Hamilton (who was more an attorney than a diplomat) nor any apologist for him took the trouble to explain Hamilton's reasoning in terms that would have been understood and appreciated by ordinary citizens. To them Hamilton's dealings must have appeared high-handed and expressly designed to benefit the wealthy at the expense of the common man — although his approach may have been the only one practicable.

The real injustice done to war veterans stemmed from the issue of state autonomy. At the formation of the Confederation the states had agreed that common defense was the reason for and the responsibility of the Confederation Congress and that the states would respond, as a matter of commitment and honor, to legitimate requests for funding from the Congress to support the war effort. In actuality, many of the states fulfilled this commitment poorly, knowing that Congress lacked any coercive power.

It was the states' failure to fulfill their obligations that led directly to the depreciation of the veterans' certificates. It was the same failure of the states that necessitated the Congress to seek foreign loans to finance the Revolution. It was just such behavior that Hamilton spoke of in his *Report on the Public Credit* that countries that fail to meet their obligations will not be respected in the world's market place.

While it was not the determinant in who should receive the par value of the reclaimed notes, from a practical consideration, it was to the advantage of the country that the reclamation of the veterans' certificates be paid to investors rather than the individual veterans. Borrowing economic theory from David Hume, Hamilton held that the capital contained in the securities, if it was thinly distributed to the war veterans, would cease to function as working capital. Rather, the only effect it would have would be to prompt merchants to raise prices to profit from the additional money in circulation. It would be more beneficial to the country if the capital contained in the securities were concentrated in the hands of fewer men, specifically those who would invest it in uses that would produce a general economic growth and benefit.[21] By this time most of the Continental notes had indeed been bought as speculative investments by wealthy men involved in land development, commerce and large-scale agriculture. Many senators and congressmen were

---

21 Elkins, McKitrick, *Age of Federalism*, 117

also sizeable holders of these securities, so that the government approach to redeeming the speculators' claims seemed to be self-serving, although this consideration played no part in Hamilton's reasoning.

In addition to the foreign loans that the Confederation incurred during the war, the individual states had incurred substantial debt in support of the Revolution. The Confederation Congress had acquired some of its funding for the war effort through the process of requisition. When called upon for funding by the Army, Congress requisitioned those needed funds from the States in proportion to their population and land. Some States responded well, others moderately and some contributed nothing at all. Much of the support given by states to the Confederation Congress was derived from loans made by the states. In addition, state support for their militia drove them further into debt. Hamilton proposed that the national government assume these debts as, "a measure of sound policy and substantial justice." Hamilton suggested the policy of taking responsibility for states' war debts would "contribute in an eminent degree, to an orderly, stable and satisfactory arrangement of national finance."[22] This idea had been discussed in the Confederation Congress in 1783 but had been defeated. The states knew that if the Congress should assume their war debt they would also require independent taxing authority to assure their ability to pay those debts and the states were unwilling to relinquish that taxing prerogative.

On the issue of state debts, Hamilton was clear. It was both a matter of justice and an opportunity to cement the bonds of the individual states to the Union. There are, however, some rather difficult problems in determining the actual value of the war debts of each state. As an example, Virginia had already paid off much of its war debt and, unfortunately, could show few records of the expenses it claimed during the British invasion of 1780–1781.[23] Hamilton viewed the issue of a fair and uniform procedure for determining the value of state's debts as one of critical delicacy. He noted to the Congress that the matter "will require all the moderation and wisdom of the government." Whatever uniform criteria were applied to reconcile state war expenses and debts, there might well be cases where the state debts considerably exceeded their justifiable expenses, although in such cases the states would presumably argue that their expenses were all necessary and

22 Syrett, *The Papers of Alexander Hamilton*, Vol. VI, 78; Hamilton, John C., *The Works of Alexander Hamilton*, Vol. III, 13
23 Elkins, McKitrick, *Age of Federalism*, 119

justifiable war expenses. Hamilton recommended that the government side-step this incendiary subject and make a generous and equitable settlement with each individual states in the final accounting of war debts.[24]

Hamilton anticipated the arguments of the critics of assumption in his *Report on Public Credit*, noting that "it might be a satisfaction to the House to have before them some plan for the liquidation of accounts between the union and its members, which, including the assumption of the state debts, would consist with equity."[25] His plan would assure equity in the burden shared by the various states. The total debt calculated for each state would consist of "all monies paid and articles furnished to the United States, and for all other expenditures during the war, either towards general (aid to the Confederation) or particular (war expenses of the particular state, funding the militia, etc.), whether authorized or unauthorized by the United States."[26] Under this plan no state would be penalized for the amount of the debt paid off to date, and no state would realize an advantage for having not fully supported the Confederation during the war.

Once he had defined the various classes of debts that the government needed to deal with, he shifted his focus to the amount of the debts and his plan for dealing with them. The debts were summarized in his *Report* as follows: The foreign debt and interest in arrears amounted to $11.7 million; the domestic debt and its interest of $40.4 million; he estimated the state debts at $25 million. Hamilton also listed an unliquidated portion of the domestic debt, mostly continental bills of credit, which was not so well defined but might total $2 million, yielding a net total debt of $79.1 million. He calculated the annual cost of the interest payments alone, including state debts, at $4,587,444, based on the prevailing interest rate of 6%. Together with an annual cost of operating the national government of $600,000, the total annual revenue required by the government would exceed $5 million. This, in Hamilton's view, would strain the revenue-raising ability of the economy, leaving little or no room for contingencies.[27]

Hamilton's plan for meeting these obligations was ingenious, while not altogether novel. He projected that the 6% interest rate that was common

24 Syrett, *The Papers of Alexander Hamilton*, Vol. VI, 81 - 83; Hamilton, John C., *The Works of Alexander Hamilton*, Vol. III, 16
25 Syrett, *The Papers of Alexander Hamilton*, Vol. VI, 82
26 Ibid.
27 Ibid., 86-87

at the time would drop in the near future to 5% and within twenty years would drop further to 4% or below. This projection was based both on the current low rate of interest in Europe and on the projected increase in money capital in the United States, resulting from full funding of the public debt. Hamilton proposed that the entire debt of $79 million be refinanced in a new loan. Refinancing of the national debt would be accomplished through the sale of federal debt certificates. These certificates were to be offered to individuals and institutions, both domestic and foreign. He offered a variety of options for paying the interest on this loan, most of which embodied offering western lands as partial payment. Other options included creation of an annuity based on the reduced interest rates that he projected for the future and awarding a bonus to the note holder that would be paid off in land grants in compensation for these reduced rates.[28]

Hamilton's plan for repayment of the national debt offered seven options; differing in the interest rate applicable to each, together with an incentive for accepting an interest rate lower than commercially available. In most of the optional plans the incentive consisted of a partial repayment in grants to western lands. These plans bore resemblance in structure to plans which had been used by both France and England for paying off national debts with reduced interest rates. Hamilton was aware of these experiments and as early as 1780 he discussed the idea of a national bank, and proposed a plan of annuities be included in the bank's operation. In this proposal he referred to annuity plans as practiced in England.[29]

Hamilton's plan was that, once the total debt of the nation was transferred to federal debt certificates through a program of open sales, the revenue system that was principally based on import taxes would pay the accruing interest on those certificates. Although this plan did not immediately provide a means for retiring the debt, the existence of assured revenue to meet interest payments would provide stability to the nation's monetary system. The public confidence instilled by the stable value of the federal certificates made them an attractive instrument of investment. The fact that these certificates could be freely traded served much the same function as currency. This relieved, to a great extent, the critical shortage of currency in the country and provided a needed impetus to a sagging economy. Hamilton

---

28 Ibid., 90-96
29 Ibid., Vol. II, 400-411 (note)

suspended interest payments on that part of the federal debt that covered the war debts of the states. His justification for this was to provide an opportunity for the government to acquire creditors' approval for the federal assumption of these debts. More importantly, Hamilton intended to provide for interest payments on this portion of the debt with a planned excise tax on domestically distilled spirits. He would recommend to Congress that these excise taxes be introduced after one year to minimize the impact on the economy from the sudden introduction of multiple taxes.

Hamilton proposed that the main source of federal revenue be based on a system of taxation of imports. He reasoned that this taxation would have the least adverse effect on commerce. Under the Confederation states that had ports of international trade had traditionally taxed imports and that tax burden was indirectly passed on to the consumers of these imports. Hamilton argued that the federal government should be given the exclusive right to this source of taxation; otherwise, with both federal and state taxes imposed on imports the resultant increase in cost would induce the public to purchase less of the foreign materials, thereby suppressing the economy.[30] There had always been some unevenness among the states as to taxable assets. Some states, particularly the importing ones, were able to impose tariffs on imports as a means of financing their debts. Other states were bereft of a similarly lucrative source of revenue and were, accordingly, more heavily burdened to meet their war obligations. By endowing the federal government with the exclusive power of taxation over foreign commerce, this major inequity in revenue potential between the states was removed. With the responsibilities of individual states reduced by the strong national government, and the revenue capabilities more nearly the same, the competitive spirit between the states would be greatly reduced. With the federal government assuming all of the states' war debts, the loss to the states of import tax revenues could be considered a fair trade off. In addition, an excise tax was proposed for servicing the assumed states' debts, to be levied on those beverages which Hamilton considered luxury items, both imported and domestic, including tea, coffee, and wine and distilled spirits.[31]

Late in his *Report*, Hamilton expounded on an important consideration of fiscal philosophy. "Persuaded as the Secretary is that the proper funding of

---

30 Ibid., 79 - 97
31 Ibid., 79 - 80

the present debt will render it a national blessing: Yet he is so far from acceding to the position, in the latitude in which it is sometimes laid down, that 'public debts are public benefits,' a position inviting to prodigality, and liable to dangerous abuse — that he ardently wishes to see it incorporated, as a fundamental maxim, in the system of public credit of the United States, that the creation of debt should always be accompanied with the means of extinguishments. This he regards as the true secret for rendering public credit immortal."[32] Later in his career Hamilton was criticized for advocating a perpetual state of national indebtedness, but his policy statement regarding national debt effectively showed the inaccuracy of this charge against him.

Hamilton envisioned the post office as a potential source of revenue that could help pay the principal on the national debt. Hamilton cited the Postmaster-general as stating that under its current operating system the United States Post Office could produce a profit of at least $100,000 annually and, with proper management, had the potential to grow into a much larger revenue source for this purpose.[33]

Hamilton's *Report on Public Credit* generated controversy from the beginning. On January 19, 1790, shortly after Congress had re-convened, Hamilton gave notice that he was prepared to give his report. He preferred to present his report verbally; however, a conservative element in Congress, still struggling to define the relationship between the Legislative and Executive branches of government, felt that a verbal presentation would constitute an infringement by the Executive into the prerogative of the legislature. Hamilton acquiesced and sent his report in writing; Congress had it read aloud on January 14. The reading took some two hours. With the amount of detail contained in the report and the number of new and complex ideas introduced for handling the public debt, the reading created utter confusion. It was moved that the report be published so the Representatives could study it prior to debating its merits. Shortly after the report was published, it appeared in major newspapers across the country. Readers agreed that the report was ingenious, but there the agreement ended. Some felt it was too inclusive; others argued that it didn't go far enough.

Most of the thoughtful public had recognized for some time that the Confederation was not functioning well and that the numerous financial plans

---

32 Syrett, *The Papers of Alexander Hamilton*, Vol. VI, 106; Hamilton, John C., *The Works of Alexander Hamilton*, Vol. III, 41
33 Ibid., 106 - 107

in the various states were not generating fiscal stability but only a weak and ineffectual economy at best. The war debts that hung over the country and the individual states were a burden against which there had been no ready and promising solution. The plan that Alexander Hamilton offered to Congress in his *Report on the Public Credit* did offer a comprehensive solution to the financial woes of the country but at a price that many were unwilling to bear.

Hamilton's *Report* showed clearly the degree of national sovereignty the central government intended to exert over the states. The assumption by the federal government of the war-related debts of the states had a number of facets to it. Hamilton argued that the war debts of the states were unevenly distributed among the states, represented varying degrees of burdens to the various states and that the assumption of the debts by the federal government would be a unifying influence for the people. The assumption of states' war debts was a key element of Hamilton's financial reform plan to restore public credit. Improved public credit would improve foreign commerce by making credit readily available in foreign ports so that American shippers could buy those commodities so critically needed to America's continued expansion and as a spur to the economy. The country's growing economy helped all Americans by creating new jobs, placing more money in circulation and making a wider range of goods available at reasonable prices.

The assumption idea also gave the federal government an argument for assuming the right of taxation over the imports into the country. Those states that had major harbors and had engaged in foreign commerce had previously taxed the imports into their states as a major source of their revenue. Hamilton argued that, without the burden of their war debts, this source of taxation would not be needed by the states. It was essential that the federal government have an adequate and independent source of revenue to fulfill the cost of its legitimate governing responsibilities. Hamilton proposed that this taxation by the federal government be limited to imposts and various excises that he defined. The states, with significantly reduced responsibilities, would have sole rights to internal tax sources including land, stamps, and licenses.

To the South this degree of concentration of power of the central government was seen as a potential threat to the institution of slavery and, hence, to the financial stability of the South. Opposition to this centralization of power carried the urgency of survival. To those Southerners who were un-compromising proponents of slavery, the issues of states' rights and slavery became synonymous. Pierce Butler, who had been a delegate to the Phila-delphia Convention, stated, "The security the South'n States want is that their Negroes not be taken away from them, which some gentlemen within or without doors, have a good mind to do."[34]

When news of Hamilton's Plan reached Europe, the investment houses in Holland gave American securities, particularly the controversial veterans' notes, par value in the currency market. Their agents in America were buy-ing the Continental securities that American speculators would have liked to purchase, at 20 to 50 cents on the dollar, and shipping them to Holland where they sold at par. Coincidentally, crop failures in Europe drove the price of American commodities up dramatically. Temporarily the balance of trade improved for America; less European money was available for buy-ing American securities and their market value dropped. Still, the American speculators were cash poor and unable to capitalize on the opportunity.[35] Even before Congress enacted Hamilton's Plan for improving the public credit, the financial rating of America soared on the world market.

While the defects of the Confederation were clear to all, Hamilton's rec-ommended solution of a strong central government and vigorous economic policies were not uniformly accepted. America had grown from its earliest settlements as an agrarian society. Many, if not most, people accepted this way of life as being the most natural employment for man and possessed of a certain virtue. They would have liked for America to retain this natural and simplistic character indefinitely. They saw no promise or advantage in large cities or in manufacturing industry since they did not complement the agricultural destiny they favored for the country. The most vocal and per-haps the staunchest supporters of this ideology were the Virginia "gentle-men farmers," Thomas Jefferson and James Madison.

Jefferson's background was in farming. His father had owned and oper-ated a farming estate in Virginia. Upon his father's death Jefferson assumed responsibility for the operation of the family estate. He later constructed his own estate in Virginia that he named Monticello. He continued to operate Monticello throughout his life and spent his last days there. Monticello was

---

34 Bell Malcolm, Jr., *Major Butler's Legacy — Five Generations of a Slaveholding Family*, University of Georgia Press, Athens, 1987
35 Ibid., 155 - 156

essentially a self-sufficient estate where Jefferson, with his slave labor, raised and manufactured essentially all that was needed.

From 1785 until 1790 Jefferson lived in Paris as America's emissary to France. During his stay in France he had been won over completely by the spirit of the French Enlightenment. He had acquired a circle of friends among the wealthy, the intellectual and the social sophisticates of Paris. He recognized a commonality of spirit between the French and American peoples in their love of liberty and looked forward to strong diplomatic and commercial ties between the two nations. When he returned to the United States, Jefferson brought with him large amounts of French art, French literature and French wine.

When the French revolution occurred, Jefferson was jubilant. He saw the French Revolution as a reflection of America's struggle for liberty and independence. He was willing to overlook the atrocities that accompanied the French overthrow of their monarchy. When Louis XVI and his wife, Marie Antoinette, were executed by guillotine, an American newspaper financially supported by Jefferson called those executions a great act of justice.

Jefferson's admiration for the French people and their culture was offset by his fierce detestation of the British. In addition to his memory of British oppression of the American colonies, Jefferson had a personal reason for his opposition to all things British. During Cornwallis' scorching of the James River area of Virginia during the Revolution, he plundered Jefferson's Monticello. At that time Jefferson was governor of Virginia and was forced to flee to safety. He was no more likely to forget this personal indignity than he was the personal loss in the damage done to Monticello.

James Madison had earlier agreed with the strong government advocates from his early days as a Virginia Representative to the Confederation Congress and during the Constitutional Convention. As far back as 1782 Madison, in cooperation with Gouverneur Morris, Alexander Hamilton and James Wilson, worked to develop a plan for Congress to have independent taxing authority, based primarily on a 5% impost on imports.[36]

Madison had been an active participant in 1783 in introducing to Congress a measure that would cause the Confederation Congress to assume the justified war expenses of the states as part of the national debt.[37] The measure

---

36 Ketcham, R., *James Madison*, 117-118
37 Ibid.

found insufficient support in Congress, due to objections raised by Rhode Island and New York. Under the Articles of Confederation such a measure would have required unanimous approval by the states for its adoption.

At some point Madison changed his stance and became fully a supporter of Jeffersonian Republicanism. Two possible causes for this philosophical shift seem most likely, either separately or in combination, to have brought about this change. During Jefferson's stay in France his correspondence had impressed Madison with the admirable qualities of the French people and their culture. Jefferson portrayed to Madison the French sophistication in literature and the arts. They fully embraced the American spirit of independence and liberty and sought to spread this spirit contagiously throughout Europe. Both Jefferson and Madison saw advantages to America in continued diplomatic and commercial relations with the French that had been so productive to America during the Revolution.

As a lingering effect of the Revolution both men harbored a strong animosity for Great Britain. Had they had full influence and authority, all relations would have been severed with Britain.

Alexander Hamilton, on the other hand, had taken a more pragmatic approach to relations with those two European countries. Trade with England provided critically needed goods that a growing America needed to sustain its expansion. In addition, England was a ready market for the raw materials that America had for export. Trade with France, on the other hand, could provide America with expensive clothing, artwork, wines and liqueurs but little to advance the growing nation and its economy. Hamilton's financial program was dependent on the income from imposts on imported goods — ninety percent of which were from England. For these reasons Hamilton was open in his enthusiasm for promoting better commercial and diplomatic relations with England.

When Hamilton presented his financial reform plan to Congress the disparity of his views on England and France became alarmingly apparent to Madison, who became a strong opponent to Hamilton's plans.

The second possible cause that had some influence on Madison's politics was a growing sentiment among his Virginian constituents for state sovereignty. While Virginia had ratified the new Constitution by a narrow margin, many influential leaders in that state, continuing to harbor states' rights advocacy, held a strong desire for Virginia to be able to steer its own political course. Although Madison had gone on record as favoring a dominant central government and a vigorous financial system to spur a healthy economy, he could not altogether ignore the opposing views of his constituency.

James Madison had become the most influential member of the House of Representatives as a result of his prominence during the Philadelphia Convention of 1787, his participation in the generation of the *Federalist Papers*, and his being a frequent counselor to President Washington. Madison had been a strong advocate of nationalism and Hamilton relied on his support in the Congressional debates regarding his financial plan. However, Hamilton was shocked to learn that Madison had reversed his position, at least so far as funding of the national debt was concerned. It troubled Madison that the plan was allowing speculators to reap the profit from the appreciation of the value of government securities. He argued that the veterans had not exhibited poor faith in the government when they sold their government notes; rather, they sold them out of an urgent need for money. Madison was further motivated by a strong constituency sympathy for the veteran's position. Despite the ardent objections by that most respected legislator, on February 22 a vote on the discrimination issue defeated Madison's position by thirty-six to thirteen.[38]

Undeterred by this defeat, Madison remained opposed to the plan generally and led the opposition to Hamilton's Plan for assumption of states' debts. Speaking for his state and other southern states (particularly Virginia and North Carolina) that had paid off much of their war debts, he complained that they, "after having done their duty," would be forced, "to contribute to those states who have not equally done their duty." Madison effectively blocked passage of Hamilton's plan of assumption, extending the debates on this issue until the summer.[39]

In defending his plan Hamilton tried to persuade his opponents with arguments based on justice and national honor. He argued that the state's debts had been generated by the Revolution which had benefited all Americans. Accordingly all Americans should bear the burden of the debt in the same sense of unity with which they enjoyed the liberties that it purchased. He had shown earlier that the state debts were in no way proportional either to population or to the individual states' ability to service the debts. It

---

38 Chernow, *Alexander Hamilton*, 304 — 305; Elkins & McKitrick, *The Age of Federalism*, 117

39 Ketcham, R., *James Madison*, 308; Ellis, J., Founding Brothers, Vintage Books, New York, 2002, 55-58

seemed to Hamilton that the real equity came from the assumption by the central government of all of the debts.[40]

On April 12, the House voted down the assumption plan, thirty-one to twenty-nine; and two weeks later voted to discontinue debates on that issue altogether. It seemed that the assumption component of Hamilton's financial reform plan was nearly lost.[41]

Madison's stance on these aspects of Hamilton's Plan seemed to be at odds with his former advocacy of nationalism. A convenient answer to these apparent inconsistencies was that Madison had his own political agenda. For some time there had been a strong sectional rivalry over the selection of the permanent seat of the national government. New York wanted to keep the government in its seat at New York; Pennsylvania vied for it to be located in one of several sites within that state; and the Southern states wanted it situated more conveniently to them. Many Southerners favored a location along the Potomac River which separates Maryland and Virginia. Madison was a forceful advocate for this position. And while Madison opposed Hamilton's assumption plan in principal, he certainly was not going to allow its passage without some form of *quid pro quo*.

In desperation, Hamilton turned to Thomas Jefferson for support. These two men had known of one another by reputation for some time but had met only recently when Jefferson went to New York to assume his post as Secretary of State. Hamilton appealed to him that "the members of the administration ought to act in concert; that although this question was not of my department, yet a common duty should make it a common concern."[42] Jefferson put off Hamilton's request for assistance, saying that he "was really a stranger to the whole subject." In reality, Jefferson had quite closely followed the debate and only recently had written to George Mason urging a compromise on the matter.

Jefferson responded further to Hamilton's plea by hosting what became perhaps the most important dinner in American history, a dinner where Hamilton and Madison could debate their differences in a cordial environment. In an after dinner discussion, James Madison reiterated his opposition to assumption based on the penalty it would impose on Virginia and other states that had already provided for the payment of their debts. He would,

40 McDonald, *Alexander Hamilton*, 167; Syrett, *Papers of Alexander Hamilton, Vol. VI*, 76 - 81
41 Elkins & McKitrick, *Age of Federalism*, 152 - 153 `
42 Jefferson, Thomas, *Anas of Thomas Jefferson*, Da Capo Press, New York, 1970, 32-33

however, desist in blocking the passage of assumption if he were offered something substantial in return. Hamilton agreed to persuade the Representatives from Pennsylvania to vote to move the permanent seat of government to the Potomac in return for a temporary return of the government to Philadelphia for a period of ten years. James Madison and Thomas Jefferson agreed to this compromise.[43]

Even before assuming office at Treasury, Alexander Hamilton knew that duties on imports were the revenue source most acceptable to the country; and this was a revenue source that would grow as America's demand for manufactured goods from abroad grew. Since 90% of the imports of manufactured goods originated in Great Britain, it was essential that trade relations with that country be encouraged.

An unofficial British diplomat, Major George Beckwith was sent by the British government and arrived in New York from London to speak with an influential member of the American government regarding Britain's concern over the Discriminatory Acts that were currently under discussion in the Congress. Since Jefferson had not yet assumed his position as Secretary of State, Hamilton felt justified in holding informal discussions with an unofficial representative of the British government.

As initially drafted by James Madison, the Discriminatory Acts called for higher tariff rates on imports from countries that had no commercial treaty with the United States. According to Beckwith, Britain would feel obliged to retaliate if this legislation were enacted. The discriminatory clause was removed. The Tonnage Act of 1789 set the duties to be imposed on ships entering U. S. ports. If they were made in America and owned by Americans they were to be assessed six cents per ton; if they were made in America but owned by foreign investors they were taxed thirty cents per ton. All other ships were to pay duties of fifty cents per ton.[44]

On the issue of the Revenue and Tonnage bills currently being debated in Congress, Hamilton stated that he personally was opposed to those clauses that discriminated against British shipping. Beckwith replied that he had been surprised to see the name of James Madison listed among those favoring the bill. Hamilton, quick to defend Madison replied, "The truth is, that

43 Pancake, John, *Thomas Jefferson & Alexander Hamilton*, Barron's Educational Series, Woodbury, NY, 1974, 166

44 www.edu/lawweb/avalon/statutesa.html

although this gentleman is a clever man, he is very little acquainted with the world. That he is uncorrupted and incorruptible I have not a doubt; he has the same end in view that I have, and so have those gentlemen who act with him, but their mode of attaining it is very different."[45] In reality, although Alexander Hamilton did not know it, James Madison was opposed to anything British and would have preferred to see a disintegration of all trade with England. Madison was strongly in favor of the discrimination clauses in the Tonnage Bill.

Hamilton described for Beckwith his personal ideas on the foreign trade posture for the United States to take. The manufactured goods available from England were wanted and needed by a growing America, more so than the products of any other nation. Likewise the raw materials offered by America found their highest demand in English ports. Hamilton said that he wished to see a commercial treaty between the two countries, to include improved trade provisions with the West Indies. At that time US trade with the British West Indies, according to British law, had to be carried in British ships. The use of American ships in this trade would provide lower shipping costs for American merchants and provide a spur to the American shipping industry. An often-cited limitation in any proposed relaxation of the trade restrictions with the West Indies was that United States' ships be under a limitation of weight. This restriction was intended to provide Great Britain with assurance that any United States trade with the West Indies would not compete with or otherwise interfere with Great Britain's trade of West Indies products in Europe. Hamilton hoped that eventually improved trade might lead to "political friendship" between the United States and Great Britain. Hamilton assured Beckwith that the opinions he had expressed were those of President Washington as well as most of the Senate.[46]

During these informal discussions, Alexander Hamilton briefly discussed those articles in the Treaty of Peace that still had unfulfilled stipulations. The British were mainly concerned with the return of confiscated Tory property and the removal of impediments in the United States court system to British businesses collecting debts dating from the pre-war era. The United States was concerned over the British retention of forts in the Northwest Territory and over British non-compensation for the confiscation of slaves from the

---

45 Elkins &, McKitrick, *Age of Federalism*, 125
46 Ibid.,

owners in the United States.[47] If Beckwith's account of this discussion is to be taken at face value, and it is the only extant record of it, Hamilton was exceedingly if not excessively accommodating to the British in his discussion of the Western forts and the Negro issues.

At that point in time Hamilton was focused on the need to promote foreign trade, particularly trade with Great Britain, as the single most important factor influencing the financial stability of the government and of the United States economy. Non-trade related issues, however important they were, could not to be permitted to form obstacles to the furtherance of trade with Great Britain. In Hamilton's mind, since improved trade increased the prosperity of both countries, with the formalization of trade relations, each side would be more interested in accommodating those non-trade related issues that were of importance to the other side. Doubtless, Hamilton was aware that his approach to Beckwith in these matters was not consistent with conventional approaches in diplomatic negotiations where each point of interest to either country is discussed in a formal, if not adversarial, manner and concessions are given only as concessions are received. Hamilton and Beckwith were engaged in informal discussions, however, and it was Hamilton's objective to keep their discussions focused on trade related issues.

With the passage of the residence bill in July of 1790 that established Philadelphia as the interim capital, attention shifted to the transition to the new site. On August 12, Congress held its final session in New York. Hamilton moved the Treasury Department, the largest single government department, to Philadelphia during August, having leased a two-story brick building between Chestnut and Walnut Streets on Third Street for this purpose. The Treasury continued its rapid growth until in 1791 it occupied the entire block on Third Street and its employment swelled to 93 in Philadelphia and 122 customs collectors and surveyors scattered across the country.[48] At the time Philadelphia was the largest and most cosmopolitan city in America. The city had ten newspapers published either daily or weekly. The contributions of its favorite son, Benjamin Franklin, were in evidence everywhere; there were theatres, a hospital, and a volunteer fire company, and lightening rods adorned most tall structures.

---

47 Ibid., 126 - 127
48 Chernow, *Alexander Hamilton*, 338 - 339

Throughout much of 1790, as Hamilton's direct involvement in the funding issues and debates waned, he was engaged in a myriad of tasks establishing the Customs Service. Hamilton had to give his personal attention to the execution of contracts for construction, operation and maintenance of these public facilities. By act of Congress, Hamilton was responsible for providing the necessary contracts to assure the correct maintenance and operation of the various lighthouses, beacons, buoys and public piers and in assigning suitable persons to the operation of these facilities. The act required that the President personally approve the various contracts executed by the Treasury Secretary. To both men this must have constituted a most odious task until it was later corrected and made into a more suitable line of responsibility.[49]

Because the large majority of American revenues now were to be generated by duties on imports, Hamilton had to find an effective way of discouraging the smuggling that had been rampant for years. To this end, he requested of Congress, in April of 1790, funding for the construction of a fleet of swift "revenue cutters" that would patrol the coastal waters to intercept ships attempting illegal entry into the United States. Washington signed into law in August the formation of this sea patrol service that would eventually become the Coast Guard.[50]

In Hamilton's first submitted *Report on Public Credit*, in January 1790, he showed that the interest on the foreign and domestic debt of the national government could be met by existing imposts and tonnage revenues and by duties he proposed to be laid on imported beverages, including coffee, tea, wine and distilled spirits, with plans for reducing the principal through the sinking fund. He also listed possible excises on domestic distilled spirits that appear to have been intended for some future application. The funding plan that Congress enacted in June expanded the scope of the duties on imports to include the beverages recommended by Hamilton but excluded any consideration of excises on domestic spirits. The approved funding plan also excluded the issue of assumption of states' war debts.

The battle over assumption, like the contest to win ratification of the Constitution, was a battle over right of taxation. Antifederalists fought to retain some degree of state sovereignty by reserving for the states the right to tax both commerce and the people. They had grudgingly given up the fight

---

49 Syrett, *The Papers of Alexander Hamilton*, Vol. VI, 297
50 Lodge, H. C. (ed.), *The Works of Alexander Hamilton*, Vol. II, 302-304

over taxation of imports and fought valiantly to retain taxation over all domestic products. Federalists, led by Hamilton, fought for federal assumption
of states' war debts with the plan for funding the interest payments on this
debt through the taxation of domestically distilled spirits. The Federalists
saw assumption as the most equitable solution to the uneven distribution of
state war debts, as a way to unite the interest of all public creditors, and as
the means to eliminate competition between state and national governments
for powers of indirect taxation.[51]

As a result of the Compromise of 1790, late in July Congress passed the
Assumption Bill, whereby the war debt of each state was absorbed by the
national government. This created the need for substantial increases in revenue at the national level. When asked by Congress in August 1790 to submit
a *Further Report on Public Credit*, Hamilton presented, in December, a proposal
for taxing all distilled spirits, imported as well as domestic. The rate of taxation was graduated in proportion to the proof of the whiskey, with a 3-way
differentiation between imported and domestic liquor, and that distilled domestically from imported spirits. The first two classes were already taxed as
imports; Hamilton's differentiation was intended to equalize the tax burden
on all three classes. In recognition of the enormous number of distilleries in
remote, rural areas and of the local resentment against the revenue inspectors, Hamilton offered an alternative to those citizens operating distilleries
in any place outside of cities, towns or villages; in lieu of the excise on production they could pay a tax of 60 cents per gallon of distilling capacity.
He proposed an exemption on small stills used exclusively for the domestic
consumption by the proprietors.[52]

In his *Report*, Hamilton took care to point out the resistance that might be
expected to the collection of this excise tax.

> The evasions, which are perceived, or suspected to be practiced by
> some, prompt others to imitations, by the powerful motive of self-defense....
> And thus the laws become sources of discouragement and loss to honest
> industry, and of profit and advantage to perjury and fraud. It is a truth, that
> cannot be kept too constantly in view, that all revenue laws, which are so
> constructed, as to involve a lax and defective execution, are instruments of

51 William & Mary Quarterly Review, *Federal Taxation and the Adoption of the Whiskey Excise*, 3rd
   Series, Vol. 25, No. 1 (January 1968), 72
52 Syrett, *The Papers of Alexander Hamilton*, Vol. VII, 227

oppression to the most meritorious part of those, on whom they immediately operate, and of additional burthens, on the community at large.[53]

Using the experience of the British government in the enforcement of their taxation of distilled spirits, Hamilton cautioned against using expedited judicial means to prosecute offenders in the zeal to collect revenue, and insisted that the right to jury trial was to be maintained. In addition, he said, the inspectors had to be encouraged to be rigorous in their pursuits of attempts to thwart revenue collections. However, they would not be authorized to enter and inspect any warehouses or homes in search of contraband. Rather, the still operators themselves would designate which facilities would be used as storage for the distilled spirits. These designated buildings would be accessible to the inspectors at all times. Of course, search warrants could be obtained for other buildings where illegal storage was suspected and stiff penalties would be imposed when contraband was discovered in these undisclosed locations.

It was Hamilton's position that any organized threat to the collection of this, or any, national revenue was a threat to the nation's economy and to the stability of the monetary system. For this reason he reacted very strenuously to the uprising over the distilled spirit tax known as the Whiskey Rebellion that occurred in 1794.[54]

The day after he submitted his excise tax report to Congress, Hamilton submitted his lengthy *Report on a National Bank*. This proposal formed the keystone of his financial reform plan, tying together his plan to refinance the national debt, including the assumption of the states' war debts, utilization of the funded debt to increase the quantity of money in circulation in the country, and his plan to raise revenues through a comprehensive taxation of imports and the manufacture of distilled spirits domestically.

The National Bank recommended by Hamilton was a bold initiative for his time. He proposed a capital of ten million dollars; some five times larger than the capitalization of the largest domestic bank then in existence. This capital was to be raised by a combination of governmental investment and through subscriptions by individual investors. Each of the twenty-five

53 Syrett, *The Papers of Alexander Hamilton*, Vol. VII, 229; Hamilton, John C., *The Works of Alexander Hamilton*, Vol. III, 99

54 William and Mary Quarterly, 3rd Series, Vol. 25, No. 1 (Jan. 1968), *Federal Taxation and the Adoption of Whiskey Excise*, 60 - 73

thousand shares in the bank was valued at four hundred dollars. Hamilton recommended that Congress grant a charter to incorporate the bank under the name of the *Bank of the United States*, the charter to be for a period of ten years.[55]

It was Hamilton's plan that the government was to invest two million dollars in bank shares so that the public faith in the trust and stability of the United States government would ensure stability in the value of bank notes. At that time the government did not have two million dollars for this investment. Hamilton proposed that the government make a loan on the National Bank for the two million dollars and that loaned amount be invested back into the bank as part of its capital. He proposed a repayment plan where the loan would earn an interest of no more than 5% for the bank and would be reimbursed by ten equal annual payments, or earlier at the convenience of the government. The government, however, was to have nothing to do with the management of the bank; that function was to be performed by a group of twenty-five Directors duly elected by the shareholders. The government was to retain auditing rights whereby the Secretary of the Treasury might examine bank statements as often as he thought necessary to assure the sound and responsible operation of that institution. The bank was to pay dividends every six months in the amounts to be determined as practical by the Directors.[56]

In the purchase of shares, the investor was to make four equal payments, spaced at six-month intervals. The first payment was to be in Gold or Silver coins, the remaining three-fourths to be paid in notes of the public debt.[57]

The proposal for establishing the national bank were based on the advantages offered by such an institution, as had been proved by centuries of experience in European banks, most notably, the Bank of England. Primary among these advantages was what Hamilton termed, "The augmentation of the active or productive capital of a country."[58] To illustrate this principal Hamilton contrasted opposing uses for Gold and Silver coins. In one case where those coins were employed simply as instruments of exchange, they were referred to as dead stock. When these coins are deposited in a bank where they become the specie supporting the circulation of paper currency,

55 Syrett, *The Papers of Alexander Hamilton*, Vol. VII, 292 - 298
56 Ibid., 335 - 336
57 Ibid., 334
58 Ibid., 306

the coins would acquire a of life of their own and generate wealth. Hamilton illustrated this point in a story where a merchant held onto some of his money, awaiting an interesting opportunity for investment. In the first instance, before the money is invested, it yielded the merchant no profit. "Should he, however, deposit it in a bank, or invest it in bank stock, the money provided him a reliable interest and remained available for his future investment opportunity. It also would become part of a fund against which he and others can borrow." Hamilton made the critical point that banks are able to loan far greater amounts than the total amount of the specie invested or deposited in the bank.[59]

Hamilton explained this effect by two considerations. First, "the great majority of the notes issued by the bank which the bank is committed to redeeming for specie, are suspended in circulation over long periods. This is made possible by the community's faith" in the stability of the note. If the bank had an uncertain esteem in the public eye and should the public harbor doubts of the bank's ability to redeem its notes at par value, these notes would depreciate to some lesser value that would be supported by public faith.[60] The second consideration is similar to the first but concerned bank loans. "When a bank grants a loan, the borrower is given credit on the bank's accounting. The bank is then committed to pay to the borrower, in specie, all demands to the limit of the established credit. In actuality, this is seldom required since the borrower, either by check or order, will transfer his borrowed credit to another person for a purchase or the settlement of a debt. The credit, through repeated similar transactions, remains in circulation until some person returns it for a payment he owes to the bank."[61]

The national bank proposed by Hamilton, like all banks, would hold a large quantity of specie available to meet creditors' demands. It is this quantity of specie that establishes public faith in the paper issues of the bank. Because of the public trust in the institution, the bank is able to make commitments for much larger amounts than the specie it holds, being confident that its paper issues would remain almost indefinitely in circulation in the economy.

---

59 Syrett, *The Papers of Alexander Hamilton*, Vol. VI, 307; Hamilton, John C., *The Works of Alexander Hamilton*, Vol. III, 108
60 Ibid.
61 Ibid.

There are two sources of species held by the national bank. The first was the initial payment that bank investors made in specie. The other source is that placed in the bank by depositors to earn interest for themselves and to be readily available when the depositor had a more attractive opportunity for that money.[62]

It was pointed out further in Hamilton's *Report on the Bank* that all banks, as they formed, would establish public confidence through the establishment of well-ordered processes and accounting, assuring that all transactions were secured with real value of one kind or another, whether in specie, auxiliary capital (the notes of public debt which constituted three-fourths of the original assets of the national bank) or collateral offered by borrowers from the bank. In all cases the sum of these assets would not be exceeded by bank commitments.

As an axiom of banking theory, Hamilton described the true wealth of a country as being measured by the amount of money in circulation; his proposed national bank would, in a very short time, significantly increase the wealth of the country and produce the needed spur to its commerce.[63] Hamilton pointed out that, so long as the public trust in the bank was maintained, there was no distinction between the use of paper, gold or silver as the medium of money. The overwhelming convenience of paper money makes a persuasive recommendation for its general use as currency of exchange.

The scheme in the design of the National Bank was that, once fully capitalized, the bank would print paper currency and introduce it into the economy through bank loans. This increased currency in circulation would, in addition to other benefits, make the payment of taxes easier in the future. As the government received the revenues, they would be funneled into the bank to pay the interest due on national debt notes invested in the bank.

The Bank of the United States was chartered by Congress in 1791 for a period of twenty years. During that period it did successfully create a much larger amount of currency in circulation, and provided a net of sound credit practices in the major cities in which it operated. The main facility of the bank was located in Philadelphia with branch operations located in major cities across the country. The bank satisfied the government's needs by serving as the center for tax collection; it was the transactional institution for

---

62 Syrett, *The Papers of Alexander Hamilton*, Vol. VI, 308
63 Ibid., 308 - 309

government fiscal policy and was available to advance loans to the government in time of war.

As the national prosperity grew due to the government fiscal policies initiated in the early 1790s and due to the increased currency created by the Bank of the United States, the need for additional banks grew in every community of any size. The states chartered these banks to serve the growing and expanding economy. Soon the state-chartered banks felt constrained in their growth by the existence of the larger branches of the Bank of the United States. Charges surfaced that the Bank of the United States and its branches represented unfair competition to the smaller state banks. The fact that the US currency was stable as a result of the government investment in the Bank of the United States seemed to be a forgotten consideration.

When 1811 came and the charter for the national bank was up for renewal, the opposition of the state banks and the fear that foreign investment in the Bank of the United States would somehow undermine the economy of the country caused President Madison to allow the bank charter to expire. When the War of 1812 occurred, the country did not have the Bank of the United States to depend on for needed loans and nearly suffered financial collapse. This error in closing the national bank, along with the decision not to maintain a standing army in peacetime, were decisions that cost the country dearly.[64]

With this report as its recommendation, Hamilton submitted to Congress for their consideration a bill to grant a charter of incorporation of a National Bank.

By February 16, President Washington had the enacted bill on his desk for signature. He was aware that there existed some significant concern that the bill would not pass a test of its constitutionality. To better prepare himself with arguments of its constitutionality, Washington asked both Edmund Randolph, the Attorney-General, and Thomas Jefferson, the Secretary of State, for their written opinions. Both men replied that the bill was not consistent with the Constitution; both agreed that the principal offensive article was the erection of a corporation for the formation of the bank. Washington then directed a letter to Alexander Hamilton in which he said,

---

64 Remini, Robert V., *Andrew Jackson and he Bank War*, W. W. Norton & Co., New York, 1967, 21-26

"I now require, in like manner, yours on the validity and propriety of the above recited Act."[65]

Alexander Hamilton turned out a comprehensive and closely argued response in record time. The Constitution required the President to sign or to veto a bill within ten days of its receipt. Hamilton answered in seven days with a report that covers forty printed pages. At the beginning of his report, Hamilton summarized his reason for responding so strenuously, emphasizing "The sense ... of the great importance of such an institution to the successful administration of the department under his particular care; and an expectation of serious ill consequences to result from a failure of the measure.... But the chief solicitude arises from a firm persuasion, that principles of construction like those espoused by the Secretary of State and the Attorney General would be fatal to the just and indispensable authority of the United States."[66]

Hamilton then proceeded to present a brilliant and forcefully persuasive case. Not only did he win Washington's approval of the bill but also he established a precedent to define the correct interpretation of the Constitution; a precedent that set the course for the United States government to function as a strong and sovereign central government, over the objections of the remaining states' rights advocates. He began by re-stating the focus of the objections given by Jefferson and Randolph, "that the objections of the Secretary of State and Attorney General are founded on a general denial of the authority of the United States to erect corporations. Now it appeared to the Secretary of the Treasury that *this general principle is inherent* in the very *definition of Government* and *essential* to every step of the progress to be made by that of the United States, namely — that every power vested in a Government is in its nature *sovereign*, and includes by *force* of the *term*, a right to employ all the *means* requisite, and fairly *applicable* to the attainment of the *ends* of such power; and which are not precluded by restriction & exceptions specified in the constitution, or not immoral or not contrary to the essential ends of political society. The circumstances that the powers of sovereignty are in this country divided between the national and state governments does not afford the distinction required. It does not follow from this that each of the *portions* of powers delegated to the one or the other is not sovereign *with*

65 Ibid., Vol. VIII, 50
66 Syrett, *The Papers of Alexander Hamilton*, Vol. VIII, 97; Hamilton, John C., *The Works of Alexander Hamilton*, Vol. IV, 104

regard to its proper objects. It will only *follow* from it, that each has sovereign power as to *certain things*, and not as to *other things*."

To conclude the argument for the constitutionality of the bank bill, Hamilton identified and explained the article of the Constitution that applied to the power to form corporations. "It is that which declares, that the Constitution and the laws of the United States made in pursuance of it, and all treaties made or which shall be made under their authority shall be the supreme law of the land. The power which can create the *Supreme law* of the land, in any case, is doubtless sovereign *as to such case*. For it is unquestionably incident to *sovereign power* to erect corporations, and consequently to that of the United States, in *relation to the objects* entrusted to the management of the government. The difference is this — where the authority of the government is general, it can create corporations in *all cases*; where it is confined to certain branches of legislation, it can create corporations only in those cases."[67] Washington accepted Hamilton's reasoning and signed into law the Bank corporation act.

The mode of investing in subscriptions of the Bank of the United States, as originally envisioned and promoted by Hamilton, was for the buyer to purchase any number of shares for $400 each, one fourth in specie and three fourths in public debt notes. The $100 investment in specie was to be required initially. Opponents were not few in number and arose from rural, agricultural interests who feared that the monied men with the national bank would eventually enslave farmers. Responding to these interests, Congress enacted legislation to modify the mode of investing in bank subscriptions. According to the new regulations, investors could secure the right to purchase stock for an initial investment of twenty-five dollars. For this sum an investor received "scrip" which authorized him to purchase a subscription at par by depositing a balance of $75 to complete the initial investment requirement of the subscription by January 1792. The initial demand was so strong and so frenzied that 4000 shares were over-subscribed in less than an hour. This strong demand continued and resulted in an escalation of the value for the scrip. By August 10 the scrip purchased on July 4 for $25 sold for $325 dollars.[68]

---

67 Syrett, *The Papers of Alexander Hamilton*, Vol. VIII, 97-99; Hamilton, John C., *The Works of Alexander Hamilton*, Vol. IV, 105-106
68 McDonald, *Alexander Hamilton — A Biography*, 222

The speculative buying of the scrip drove its price beyond reasonable limits, and essentially paralyzed everyday business activity. In each of the cities where scrip was available, ordinary people joined in the rush for wealth that they supposed scrip speculation represented. In New York, Rufus King reported, "The business was going on in a most alarming manner, mechanicks deserting their shops, Shop keepers sending their goods to auction, and not a few of our merchants neglecting the regular and profitable commerce of the City."[69] Thomas Jefferson said that in Philadelphia, "Ships are lying idle at the wharfs, buildings are stopped, capitals withdrawn from commerce, manufactures, arts and agriculture, to be employed in gambling.[70]

This bubble of speculative buying worried Hamilton; he commented that "These extravagant sullies of speculation do injury to the government and to the whole system of public credit."[71] The upward spiral in the price of scrip peaked on August 11. When holders of the scrip realized that its price had topped out, they tried to sell to at least recover their investment. Those investors who had cash responded slowly to the desperate offers of scrip, allowing its price to plummet. Hamilton stated in a letter to Rufus King that, "When I saw this I thought it advisable to speak out, for a bubble connected with my operation is of all the enemies I have to fear, in my judgment, the most formidable — and not only to promote but as far as depends on me, to counteract delusions, appears to me to be the only secure foundation on which to stand."[72]

In a letter to William Seton of the Bank of New York, Hamilton revealed his concern over the falling price of scrip, "And yet I do not know what effect the imprudent speculation in Bank Script may produce. A principal object with me is to keep the Stock from falling too low.[73] He arranged for a loan of $150,000 from the Bank of New York and he directed Seton to purchase $150,000 worth of government securities in an effort to stem the tide of falling prices and investor desperation. Hamilton's strategy worked and the money market regained stability. Scrip prices fell to a low of $110 and

---

69 Syrett, *The Papers of Alexander Hamilton*, Vol. IX, 60

70 McDonald, *Alexander Hamilton — A Biography*, 223

71 *New York Historical Society Quarterly*, October 1948, "Hamilton's Neglected Essays," 287

72 Syrett, *The Papers of Alexander Hamilton*, Vol. IX, 75 - 76; Hamilton, John C., *The Works of Alexander Hamilton*, Vol. V, 476

73 Syrett, *The Papers of Alexander Hamilton*, Vol. IX , 71 — 72; Hamilton, John C., *The Works of Alexander Hamilton*, Vol. V, 477

recovered in September to $145 per share.[74] Hamilton demonstrated, by this maneuver of redeeming government securities, the power of the government to exercise a stabilizing influence in the financial world through judicious manipulation of government paper.

Objections to the formation of the Bank of the United States were raised by those states' rights advocates who viewed in the institution yet another intrusion by the federal government into the rights and prerogatives of the states.

On January 28, 1791, Hamilton submitted to Congress his report on *The Establishment of a Mint* in response to a congressional directive to him on this subject, transmitted on Aril 15, 1790. In this lengthy report on such an arcane subject, Hamilton discussed in great detail the consideration for setting the quantity of gold and silver in the unit monetary system, selected as the dollar. The dollar was proposed as the basic unit of currency because "it is certain that nothing can be more simple or convenient than the decimal subdivisions."[75]

In the end Hamilton recommended that both gold and silver dollars be coined. As to the denomination of coins, he recommended a gold piece equivalent to ten dollars, both a silver and gold one-dollar coin, a silver piece equal to a tenth (or disme) of a dollar, a copper piece equal to one-hundredth of a dollar and a second copper coin to be set at half the value of the first copper.[76]

In the first seventeen months that Hamilton served as Secretary of the Treasury, the credit of the United States rose from essentially non-existent to roughly equal to that of the most stable and long established countries in the world. Through his proposal that the federal government assume the debts of the states and that the federal government be given the sole right of taxation of imports, major obstacles to the unity of the country were removed. The disparity between those states that had well-established commercial seaports and others that did not had been contributing to a rich state/poor state division. Likewise the onerous war debt of some states seriously retarded their economic growth. The financial plan proposed by Hamilton and enacted by Congress not only strengthened the central government but dramatically improved the popular support of the government and thereby

---

74 Syrett, *The Papers of Alexander Hamilton, Vol. IX,* 71-72
75 Syrett, *The Papers of Alexander Hamilton,* Vol. VII, 462, 600
76 Ibid.

strengthened the Union. The effect of the Bank of the United States being chartered increased the flow of money in circulation, and made more money available for investments and commercial enterprises, powering a growing economy.

CHAPTER 6. CHALLENGES FOREIGN AND DOMESTIC

The Treaty of Paris that concluded the Revolutionary War, requiring that Britain recognize the independence of America and cede to the United States land as far west as the Mississippi River with the northern border similar to that on modern day maps. Other articles gave assurance that no lawful impediment would be presented to British merchants in the recovery of debts incurred prior to the hostilities. It was agreed that Congress would recommend to the states that estates and properties originally owned by Loyalists and confiscated following evacuation of British forces be returned to their rightful owners. The British agreed to grant to the United States liberal fishing rights in the northwest Atlantic, to withdraw their military forces from American soil, and to refrain from carrying away Negroes belonging to American citizens. The two countries agreed to perpetual, mutual and free use of the Mississippi River from its source to the mouth.

The British realized as soon as the treaty was agreed upon that the article requiring them to withdraw their military forces from American soil posed a grave and potentially dangerous disadvantage to them. During the war they had occupied frontier posts on American soil from northern Lake Champlain in Vermont to what today is the City of Detroit. These posts were important to the British in that they provided military protection to Canada against American invasion or Indian attacks, and served as trading posts with the Indians through which the large and lucrative fur trade was carried on. At the conclusion of the Revolutionary War the fur trade in the interior of North America was channeled mainly through Montreal and had a volume of some £200,000 annually.[1] Through this trade the British established a relationship with the Indians, in which the British cast themselves as the guardians and protectors of the Indians and Americans as hostile aggressors into rightful Indian territory. Settlers on lands west of the Alleghenies and north of the Ohio River lived in constant danger of attacks from Indians who were equipped and motivated by the British housed within the forts. The British foreign office knew that relinquishing these posts would cost them the profitable fur trade, expose Canada to threats of invasion and would forever shut Britain off from the possibility of acquiring other North American territory south of Canada. They searched for a diplomatic excuse for retaining the forts and found them in legal technicalities in Articles 4,5 and 6 of the Peace Treaty.

The American settlers beyond the mountains asked two things of the government; peace from the Indians and unobstructed use of the Mississippi in shipping their farm produce to market. So long as the British maintained their forts, the settlers were denied peace from the Indians and, with the Spanish control of New Orleans, free use of the Mississippi. In 1786 John Jay had proposed to the Confederation Congress that the United States grant to Spain the exclusive rights of use of the Mississippi River for a period of twenty-five years in exchange for trading rights in some European ports.[2] While it was never enacted, the fact that such a move was considered illustrates the little regard that the government had for the welfare of the frontier farmer in the post-war era. This apparent lack of concern and support caused the people settled in western lands to vacillate in their support of the government and even to consider seceding from the union, forming their own political unit and instituting those alliances that best served their needs.

The British government held hope that the final resolution of their various interests in North American would be the political dissolution of the American government. Should this occur, and there were signs that it might, even as late as the ratification of the Constitution in 1788, the states could be expected to form smaller confederations or to remain singly independent. In the Virginia ratification convention, delegates from Kentucky were wary

1 Bemis, S., *Jay's Treaty*, Yale University Press New Haven, 1962, 6 - 7
2 Ibid., 24

of casting their lot with the new government; that they finally did vote for ratification indicated more their meager options rather than enthusiastic support. In any event these smaller political units, should they be formed as a result of the failure of the national government, would be in no position to assist or in any way utilize the western lands. In case of national dissolution, the individual states likely would gradually turn back to the British Crown for unity and protection.

In direct trade between the United States and Great Britain, there were other problems. Hamilton's plan for financial reform fixed the major source of governmental revenue as taxes on imports. Since 90% of manufactured goods entering the United States were from England, continued trade with this country was imperative. The manufactured products offered by Great Britain were essential materials in the growth of America and the luxury items were of a quality that Americans who could afford them had grown to desire. Conveniently, England remained a ready market for the raw materials that America exported. Britain continued, however, to manipulate the commerce with America, as she had done prior to the Revolution. American trade with the British West Indies was restricted to the goods being carried in British ships, requiring shipping charges to be paid that were dictated by the British. The growth of America's shipping industry was retarded by British domination of the commerce between the two countries. American envoys to London were discreetly ignored so that no progress could be made toward negotiating a commercial treaty. American raw materials were accepted into British ports on equal terms with those from any other country because of Great Britain's need for these materials, not because America enjoyed a most-favored trading status in England.[3]

The revenue on American imports from England was contributing largely to funding the public debt and providing revenues necessary for the operation of the government. Commercially, trade with England was important as it provided the manufactured goods necessary to sustain a growing economy in this country. Hamilton would soon work to lessen America's dependence on foreign manufactured goods: a subject that will be more thoroughly discussed later in this chapter. America was eager to pursue two opportunities for commercial expansion; the lifting of restrictions to American trade with the West Indies, and easing of obstacles to shipping through the Mississippi

---

3 Ibid., 28 - 34

River, which was prohibited by Spanish control of New Orleans. Overland travel in that era was so difficult and dangerous that farmers in the western lands found it cheaper, safer and more expeditious to ship their produce down the Mississippi and by sea to eastern markets as opposed to shipping by wagon across the mountains. It was Alexander Hamilton's position that a commercial treaty with Great Britain could secure trade between the two countries to open the British West Indies to some level of direct trade by American shipping. Further, a commercial treaty between the United States and England could be used to leverage an accommodation by Spain to open the Mississippi River to American shipping passing through New Orleans. Improved and less costly commerce on the Mississippi would provide an important spur to further expansion of the American population into the western lands and help to solidify relations between the western lands and the central government. Britain would benefit from a commercial treaty because it would be assured of American raw material exports in the future, securing British dominance on the growing American marketplace and the possibility of negotiating more favorable terms for British shipping carrying goods to the United States.[4]

On October 7, 1789, shortly after Hamilton took office as Secretary of the Treasury and prior to the arrival of Thomas Jefferson to his post as Secretary of State, President Washington met with Hamilton and John Jay to discuss the considerations of sending an informal representative to London to explore the questions of a commercial treaty and the British maintenance of the western forts. All were in agreement that such an informal mission was both advisable and timely. Alexander Hamilton proposed that Gouverneur Morris be selected as the American representative. It turned out that Morris was at that time in Paris on a matter of personal business. Gouverneur Morris was a brilliant man. He had demonstrated his understanding of the principles of political science during the Constitutional Convention and his adroitness in stylizing the final form of the Constitution gave him the stature of a leader among the founding fathers. He was a wealthy man whose business interests took him to the various capitals of Europe. From 1789 until 1796 he spent most of his time abroad. He was personally known in principal government circles in Europe as well as in the United States.[5]

4 Ibid., 35 - 50
5 Ibid., 65 - 66

Morris accepted Washington's commission to represent the United States with the British Foreign Minister, the Duke of Leeds. When first arriving in London, Morris took the opportunity to call upon the French Ambassador, La Luzerne, who was a personal friend. Unfortunately, Morris committed the indiscretion of sharing with La Luzerne his instructions from Washington even before meeting with the British. This diplomatic error was interpreted by the British ministry as a sign of arrogance that made constructive discussions between them and Gouverneur Morris difficult when they first met on March 26, 1790.[6] According to Washington's instructions, Morris was to inquire of Leeds the reason for the British continuing to retain the posts in the American northwest and also to ask what action the British government planned regarding the large number of Negroes whom they took from their indentured labor in America. Prior to the end of hostilities in the Revolution, the British forces in the South had let it be known that any slaves who made their way to British lines would be granted their freedom. Many slaves took advantage of this offer and were transported away from America when the British evacuated their forts in the South. Finally, Morris had been directed to determine the acceptability to the British of the idea of exchanging diplomatic representatives. While Morris described his meeting with the British ministry as warm, he was unable to extract anything from Leeds more definitive than a commitment to give the questions serious consideration and to give him an appropriate response as timely as possible. Morris was to wait a month until he received a terse reply restating England's position that their occupation of the western posts was to ensure America's fulfillment of their unsatisfied treaty obligations. In regards to the idea of a commercial treaty, the note expressed, "a sincere wish...to cultivate a real and bona fide system of friendly intercourse." Morris correctly interpreted this to say that Britain desired no more formal arrangement than currently existed in the trade between the United States and England. Britain had what they desired in commercial interest with the America and saw no purpose in extending any additional advantages to the United States.[7]

At the time of Morris' mission Britain had become engaged in some sword-rattling diplomacy with Spain over what became known as the Nootka Incident. Spanish ships had attacked and captured some British merchant

6 Ibid., 68
7 Ibid., 68 - 70

ships on the American Pacific coast in Nootka Sound, which is an inlet on the west coast of modern day Vancouver Island. The British protested this unprovoked measure of force, which Madrid ignored. The British government threatened retaliatory action that would surely create a general state of war in Europe. Finally, in response to an ultimatum issued by the British, Spain agreed to pay compensation for British losses and to recognize Britain's right to free trade and settlement on unoccupied lands along America's Pacific coast, concluding the Nootka Incident. Apparently Spain's capitulation resulted from a lack of confidence in the support of her ally, the Revolutionary Forces of France.[8]

During the diplomatic crisis of the Nootka Incident, England was concerned over a possible American reaction should war with Spain occur. Following resolution of the Nootka affair, Britain began to more seriously pursue deliberations on the exchange of diplomats with the United States. The British again made use of Major George Beckwith to informally explore America's readiness for more formalized relations with Great Britain.[9]

When Major Beckwith returned to the United States, he went immediately to visit Alexander Hamilton for he felt both comfortable and confident in the forthrightness and utility of conversations they had previously held. On the subject of exchanging diplomatic representatives, Hamilton advised Beckwith that any formal representative of the government of Great Britain must be prepared to work directly with the newly installed Secretary of State. Of this cabinet officer Hamilton said, "Mr. Jefferson is a gentleman of honor and zealously desirous of promoting the interests of his country...but for some opinions which he has given respecting your Government, and possible predilections elsewhere, there may be difficulties which may possibly frustrate the whole, and which might be readily explained away." As to the existing grounds for supporting a commercial treaty between the two countries, Hamilton argued, "You have a great commercial capital and an immense trade, we have comparatively no commercial capital, and are an agricultural people, but we are a rising country, shall be great consumers, have a preference for your manufactures." [10]

Regarding those points which divided the nations, Hamilton presented an overview intended to show the American view as eminently reasonable,

8 Ibid., 70 - 73
9 Ibid., 83 - 86
10 Ibid., 104 - 106

"You have considerable American and West India possessions, our friendship or enmity may soon become important with respect to their security, and I cannot foresee any solid ground of national difference between us, I do not think that the posts are to be considered in this light, and we have no desire to possess anything to the northward of our present boundaries as regulated by the peace; but the navigation of the river Mississippi we must have, and shortly, and I do not think the bare navigation will be sufficient, we must be able to secure it by having a post at the mouth of the river, either in New Orleans or somewhere near it." Hamilton added that the time was right for a commercial relationship, "You know we have two parties with us; there are gentlemen who think we ought to be connected with France in the most intimate terms...there are others who are at least as numerous, and influential, who evidently prefer an English connection, but the present condition of Great Britain and the States is favorable to the former party, and they are zealous to improve it, the present therefore, is the moment to take up the matter seriously and dispassionately, and I wish it done without loss of time."[11]

Hamilton anticipated a concern that the British could rightfully entertain, that of the United States commitment to France resulting from their assistance during the War for Independence. He stressed that America would always take seriously its treaty obligations; however, this did not mean taking the part of France in a contest where the French participation was supportive of their ally (Spain). Even in those cases where France was engaged in a conflict as a major participant, "Certain points have occurred since the peace which leave us perfectly free with respect to France." Hamilton was referring to the extent of the excesses of the French Revolution. The American obligation was to the government of King Louis XVI. When he and his wife were so ignominiously executed, Hamilton held that the new government did not automatically inherit the treaty commitments of the slain monarch.[12]

Late in 1791 the British government selected George Hammond for the diplomatic appointment to the United States. Because of the coarse treatment that the British had afforded to John Adams when he was sent to England shortly after the Peace Treaty had been executed, America chose to take no action on selecting a diplomat to send to England until the British sent

11 Ibid., 106 - 107
12 Ibid., 108

their appointee to America. The degree of sincerity on the part of the British government in establishing either constructive political or commercial relations with the Untied States can be gauged by a review of the instructions Hammond was given prior to sailing for America. First, he was authorized to negotiate a commercial treaty on the basis of the proposals made by the Privy Council Committee for Trade. These proposals required that the United States guaranty that no discrimination in tariff laws would be enacted in the future against British goods and never to raise the existing tariff on British manufactures. Hammond was authorized to offer nothing to the United States in reciprocity for these concessions.[13]

Hammond was permitted to speak with the United States government on matters of outstanding obligations from the Peace Treaty but to make no agreements committing Great Britain to any action or concession. Britain took the position that the posts in America's western territory were essential to British control of the Great Lakes and the continued monopoly of the fur trade was to be retained. Although it was well known that America felt that direct trade with the West Indies was, because of its geographical proximity, a more natural and desirable commercial objective, Hammond was prohibited from giving any concessions from the existing requirement that trade between the United States and the British West Indies was to be carried by British shipping. He was directed to urge the United States to provide a schedule for their completion of Articles 4, 5 and 6 in any conversation on the unfulfilled obligations of the Peace Treaty. Should Hammond meet with an agreeable and accommodating attitude regarding these articles of the Peace Treaty, he was authorized to assure the United States government of, "His Majesty's disposition to contribute on His part towards removing the Grounds of future difficulties by some practical and reasonable Arrangement on the Subject of the Posts."[14]

Upon arrival in the United States, Hammond was obligated to await the nomination by the United States of a diplomatic appointee to the British post prior to tendering his credentials. In due course Thomas Pinckney of South Carolina was nominated as American envoy to Britain and on November 9, 1791 Hammond presented his credentials.[15]

---

13 Ibid., 122 - 126
14 Ibid., 126, 128 - 130
15 Ibid., 130

The British took the position in regard to the forts occupied on American soil in the western territories that any proposition for the removal of British forces from these forts had to include British mediation of a zone dedicated as Indian Territory. This territory, as proposed by the British, would extend from the northern boundary of the United States to the Ohio River on the south and generally to be bounded by the Mississippi River on the west. Under this thinly disguised diplomatic stratagem the United States would have ceded sovereignty of its mid-western territory forever; first to the Indians and, following their sure and certain demise to a British Protectorate, constructed purely to regain for the British Crown part of the territory lost by the War for Independence.[16]

The history of the management of Indian affairs subsequent to the Peace Treaty had met with mixed success. The Treaty of 1768 had given the Indians title to the lands north of the Ohio River and along a line running irregularly through the middle of Pennsylvania and dividing New York roughly in half. This treaty was the last that had been ratified by the confederacy of Indian tribes under the able leadership of Mohawk chief Joseph Brant. Because the lifestyle of the Indian was primitive and nomadic, they required a much larger per capita acreage than did man in western civilization. The premium that western man placed on each acre of land, due to its potential productivity, created a sociological pressure that increasingly displaced the Indian away from the advancing frontier. The United States government made repeated attempts at negotiating new boundaries with the Indians; however, since these negotiations were with single tribes, they were not universally accepted. The encroachment of settlers on lands the Indians felt were theirs and the repeated atrocities by the Indians created an air of hostility between the two factions. It was this animosity that the British sought to exploit to their own advantage in proposing the mediation zone.[17]

The position of the Washington Administration with respect to the western lands was that it was fundamentally an American possession and, while they would like to accommodate the needs of the Indians, those needs were of a scale and indeterminacy that precluded any possibility of accommodation. Washington turned to military intervention to stop the atrocities committed by the Indians on western settlers. The ineffective campaign led

16 Ibid., 147 - 148
17 Ibid., 148 - 150

by Colonel Harmar in 1790 followed by the disastrous defeat of General St. Clair in 1791 embarrassed the American government and further discouraged the settlers who already had been uncertain regarding their best political interests.[18] They were formally within the United States and would be eligible for statehood once they acquired sufficient population. Alternatively, they considered seceding from the Union and seeking political alliances either with Spain or Great Britain.

The defeat of St. Clair was painfully reminiscent of that suffered by Edward Braddock in 1755 in the French and Indian War. Both had been guilty of underestimating the capabilities of their Indian foes and of being overly confident in their own abilities and tactics. In the case of St. Clair, the defeat was also the result of being poorly equipped and staffed by incompetent officers. Accusations of profiteering involving Hamilton's friend, William Duer, cost the government severely in their stock of public trust. Lack of confidence in the government resulting from this defeat shackled Washington's Administration for years.[19] The next step in the solution of the Indian problem occurred as part of the settlement of the Jay Treaty. This important treaty negotiated with Great Britain would provide an important impetus to the developing American economy, freed the northwest territory of English occupation and lead to the liberating of the Mississippi waterway.

During the summer of 1791, Hamilton had become engaged in an extramarital affair that cost him seriously in reputation and domestic tranquility. In mid-May of 1791, Hamilton's father-in-law Philip Schuyler wrote to his daughter, Elizabeth Hamilton, inviting her and the four Hamilton children to spend the summer at the family home in Albany. Eliza looked forward to the summer in the relative coolness of Albany; she and the children left Philadelphia in early July.[20]

Prior to the family's departure Hamilton received a visit at his home from a woman who introduced herself as Maria Reynolds. She was married to a James Reynolds who, according to her, had been abusive toward her for some time. She said she went to Hamilton, knowing he was a citizen of New York, to request only sufficient money to allow her to return to her friends

---

18 Ibid., 153 - 154
19 Elkins & McKitrick, *The Age of Federalism*, 271 - 273
20 Mitchell, B. *Alexander Hamilton — The National Adventure (1788-1804)*, The Macmillan Company, New York, 1962, 400

in New York. Later that same evening, he took a $30 note and went to the address she had given him. As Hamilton described events in the ensuing conversation, Maria gave him to understand that "other than pecuniary consolation would be acceptable." Hamilton later wrote, "After this, I had frequent meetings with her, most of them at my own house; Mrs. Hamilton with her children being absent on a visit to her father."[21]

According to a disclosure document that Hamilton published under duress years later, at some point he was inclined to terminate his relationship with Maria. During a meeting between Hamilton and James Reynolds, the latter accused Hamilton of taking undue advantage of his wife. However, Reynolds agreed to forget the incident for a consideration of one thousand dollars. Hamilton agreed, and paid. Several more letters to Hamilton from both Reynolds and his wife, which encouraged a continuation of the affair, provided proof of a collusion between the pair to ensnare Hamilton for their personal gain. Later, Reynolds again wrote Hamilton requesting a three hundred dollar loan for a subscription on the Lancaster Turnpike, which Hamilton refused. On June 23 Reynolds again requested a loan, this time for fifty dollars. Hamilton acceded to this request. Additional requests stretching out through August 1792 obtained an additional two hundred dollars for Reynolds in coerced loans from Hamilton.[22]

Eventually James Reynolds was incarcerated on a charge of subornation of perjury. He confided to a friend, Jacob Clingman, that he had it in his power to destroy the Secretary of the Treasury and asked Clingman to contact Speaker Muhlenberg, requesting his assistance to free Reynolds in consideration for the damaging information he had against Hamilton. When Muhlenberg obtained the damaging evidence, he consulted his colleagues, James Monroe and Abraham Venable. They determined that the information was sufficiently serious that it was incumbent upon them to refer the matter to the President. Out of personal respect for Alexander Hamilton they agreed to first approach him on the matter to see what information he could provide on the subject. When the three men visited Alexander Hamilton at his office, Hamilton replied that he "always stood ready to meet fair inquiry with frank communication — that it happened, in this present instance, to be in (his)

21 Syrett, *The Papers of Alexander Hamilton*, Vol. XXI, 250 - 251; Lodge, Henry C., *The Works of Alexander Hamilton, Vol. VII*, 388

22 Syrett, *The Papers of Alexander Hamilton*, Vol. XXI, 251-255, Lodge, Henry C., *The Works of Alexander Hamilton, Vol. V II*, 369-423

power by written documents to remove all doubt as to the real nature of the business."[23] As the documents in question were at Mr. Hamilton's home, he invited the three Congressmen to meet with him there on that evening.

At the meeting that evening, Hamilton discussed with them his indiscretion with Maria Reynolds, the correspondence and meetings between himself and James Reynolds and the documents showing the money that had passed from Hamilton to Reynolds along with the nature of the payments. Afterwards the three men acknowledged their entire satisfaction with Hamilton's explanation and expressed regret for having put him to the "trouble and embarrassment."[24] Before they departed Hamilton requested that he be permitted to copy the documents that Muhlenberg had been given by Reynolds and Clingman.

The issue of Alexander Hamilton's improper conduct in the office of Secretary of the Treasury having been thus cleared, the matter lay dormant for more than four years. In June and July 1797 pamphlets were published by James Callender accusing Hamilton of collaboration with James Reynolds in "a series of speculative ventures that were at best improper and at worst illegal."[25] These pamphlets contained copies of the documents that Muhlenberg, Monroe and Venables had in their possession when they approached Hamilton in 1792 and which James Monroe had retained. To acquit himself of any accusations of impropriety in his role as Secretary of the Treasury, Alexander Hamilton published a lengthy report known as *The Reynolds Pamphlet*. In this pamphlet Hamilton decried the accusations in the Callender pamphlet as false and libelous. Alexander Hamilton accused the Callender pamphlets and those who provided the false documents as being, "Incessantly busied in undermining all the props of public security and private happiness, it seems to threaten the political and moral world with a complete overthrow."[26] After defending himself against accusations of pecuniary impropriety, Hamilton made a candid and complete confession of his intimate affair with Maria Reynolds, of his experience of blackmail by James

---

23 Syrett, *The Papers of Alexander Hamilton*, Vol. XXI, 257-258; Lodge, Henry C., The Works of *Alexander Hamilton, Vol. VII, 399*

24 Syrett, *The Papers of Alexander Hamilton*, Vol. XXI, 258; Lodge, Henry C., *The Works of Alexander Hamilton, Vol. VII, 399*

25 Syrett, *The Papers of Alexander Hamilton*, Vol. XXI, 121(note)

26 Syrett, *The Papers of Alexander Hamilton*, Vol. XXI, 238; Lodge, Henry C., *The Works of Alexander Hamilton, Vol. VII, 370*

Reynolds and the discussion that these relationships led to with Muhlenberg, Monroe and Venables.

Contemporary Hamiltonian opponents were critical that he had overdone the *Reynolds Pamphlet*, giving excessive detail in his forty-seven printed page self-defense. Those critics and some modern historians as well argued that offering his confession of the adulterous conduct as an alibi to prove his innocence of the fiscal misconduct charges was both cheeky and an unconvincing argument for his personal integrity. In Hamilton's defense, however, the depth of detail that he gave of the affair was not intended to hurt or embarrass his wife, or as his own *mea culpa* for his transgressions, but to show that the affair was instigated and prolonged by collusion between James Reynolds and his wife, albeit made possible by Hamilton's personal weakness. He showed that the Reynolds' motives were personal financial gain, which they partially accomplished through the nearly $1300 given to them by Hamilton. He wanted to make the point that people who would indulge in so sordid an affair for personal gain would not hesitate to make the false accusations Reynolds and Clingman did to disparage Hamilton's integrity.

His affair with Maria Reynolds was not done in a moment of weakness but was pursued over a nine-month period. Hamilton knew that Maria's husband was aware of, and likely was manipulating, the meetings between Hamilton and his wife. James Reynolds extorted some $1300 from Hamilton in exchange for his consent to their liaisons and for his silence. And the affair continued. On the subject of how Hamilton confessed and reconciled his behavior with his wife and family, history has nothing to say.

This incident again highlights certain features of Hamilton's personality. He was an enterprising man, full of life and ready to seize opportunities, on occasion demonstrating poor judgment and offending even those whose respect and good opinion he valued most. He also seems to have cared more for accuracy, objective fact and practical realities than certain questions of tact, feelings and diplomacy. This quality made him a major contributor to the structure of the fledgling nation, but it did not always win him friends.

In responding to the Callender pamphlet Hamilton could not have ignored his affair since it was contained in the accusing pamphlet. But there is a much deeper aspect to Hamilton's response that only incidentally relates to the Reynolds incident. At the time the Callender pamphlet was published in 1797, Hamilton had been retired from government employment for two years.

During his early years at Treasury, Hamilton had made many major contributions to the government in his financial reform package. A significant faction within the government, led by Thomas Jefferson and James Madison, sought to undermine and reverse numerous aspects of Hamilton's Plan through personal attacks on the integrity of Alexander Hamilton. When the Callender pamphlet was published, Hamilton's opponents claimed it as validation of their accusations. In this renewed attack Hamilton's professional reputation was at stake as were the contributions he had made to the government structure. His response in *The Reynolds Pamphlet* was intended to set the record straight on the Reynolds incident, and also to highlight for the public the calumny of his opponents as well as to defend his professional integrity and the institutions he had created.

In another display of anger that earned him the reputation for being petulant, Hamilton accused James Monroe of providing Callender with the information regarding his affairs with the Reynolds family. Monroe had been entrusted with the documents provided to himself, Muhlenberg and Venable, so Hamilton assumed that either he had collaborated with Callender or he knew who did. A series of accusation and denial letters were exchanged.

Since the enactment of his financial plan, Hamilton had found himself increasingly under attack from opponents of his fiscal reforms. His antagonists would never criticize his plans on their merits; they knew he had schooled himself too well on their advantages to be vulnerable to an open debate. Rather, they resorted to personal attacks caricaturizing Hamilton as an avaricious pawn of the monied class and insensitive to the cares and needs of the agrarian segment of society. Thomas Jefferson wrote in his Anas (diary or journal), "Hamilton's financial system had two objects; 1st, as a puzzle, to exclude popular understanding and inquiry; 2nd, as a machine for the corruption of the Legislature."[27] Jefferson was fully intelligent and sufficiently well read to understand Hamilton's financial plan. He knew, however, that the average American was not and he used that fact to his political advantage by presenting a distorted view of Hamilton and his plan to the American public.

In a personal letter to Edward Carrington, a man who had been prominent in Virginia politics for years, Hamilton said that he reluctantly accepted

---

27 Jefferson, *The Anas of Thomas Jefferson*, 30

as truth, "That Mr. Madison cooperating with Mr. Jefferson is at the head of a faction decidedly hostile to me and to my administration, and actuated by views in my judgment subversive of the principles of good government and dangerous to the union, peace and happiness of the country."[28]

By the spring of 1791 Hamilton had seen his plan for financial reform enacted into law. He shifted his attention to the national need, as he saw it, to supplement the agricultural productions of the country with manufacturing industry. Congress directed him to prepare a report proposing and justifying government involvement in the development of domestic manufacturing technology.

Hamilton had joined forces with Tench Coxe, a Philadelphia businessman and well-known advocate of manufactures and enticed Coxe to accept the position earlier vacated by the resignation of William Duer, that of Assistant Secretary of the Treasury.[29] Coxe had been Secretary of the Pennsylvania Manufacturing Society and had communicated with similar organizations in other states to the extent that he was well known and understood the technologies and special needs of manufacturing industry. He numbered among his acquaintances Philadelphia's leading merchants and the leading advocates of manufacturing developments throughout the country.

On January 15, 1790, Congress had directed the Secretary of the Treasury to prepare a report containing a plan for "the encouragement and promotion of such manufactories necessary to make the United States independent of other nations for essential, particularly military, supplies."[30] In the same manner that Hamilton's financial *Reports* were based on concepts he had derived from extensive readings and matured through the workings of his genius, his *Report on Manufactures* was to be the culmination of study and active participation in promoting the acquisition of manufacturing technologies by the United States.

Hamilton's recognition of the importance of manufacturing industry to the economic life as well as the political independence of a country dated from his King's College days when he published his pamphlet, *The Farmer Refuted*, in response to Samuel Seabury's pro-British writings. In this pam-

---

28 Syrett, *The Papers of Alexander Hamilton*, Vol. XI, 429

29 William & Mary Quarterly Review, July, 1975, *Coxe, Hamilton & The Encouragement of American Manufactures*, 370 — 1

30 Syrett, *The Papers of Alexander Hamilton* Vol. X, 230; Hamilton, John C., *The Works of Alexander Hamilton*, Vol. III, 192

phlet Hamilton presented his idea that manufacturing countries would always be politically dominant over agricultural countries. Being a voracious reader on any topic that touched on the welfare of nations, Hamilton surely kept himself informed on the mechanical developments of the 18th century. He saw the utility of Watt's steam engine that had been first demonstrated in Britain in the 1760s and understood that the introduction of the manufacturing concept of interchangeable parts in the 1790s would extend the life of manufacturing machines. When Sir Richard Arkwright developed a machine that transformed the energy of rapid water movement into a useful form that he used to power multiple thread spinning devices, it was easy to recognize the potential it had for the textile industry. By 1789 Arkwright's machine was in use in Scotland and provided employment for 1300 people.[31] Britain led the way in the developments that spurred this industrial revolution and was careful to guard and protect their interests. It was unlawful to export textile machinery, and England went so far as to stop merchant ships on the high seas if they carried such contraband. Mechanics and technicians that were key to the development and maintenance of these machines were forbidden to emigrate.[32]

Following the end of the American Revolution, Lord Sheffield published, in England, a pamphlet in which he described the economic policies he thought Great Britain should pursue with the United States. The content of these policies showed a stark contempt for the new nation as an economic entity. He promoted an English policy that would deny to the United States a commercial treaty; American products could be obtained elsewhere. Sheffield quite arrogantly argued that the superiority of British manufactured goods would continue to find eager consumers in the American markets without the need for a formalized treaty.[33] Hamilton and others in America resented the attitude reflected in Sheffield's pamphlet and sought means of circumventing this British position.

Hamilton participated in a gathering of investors at Rawson's Tavern in January 1789 when the New York Manufacturing Society was dedicated. He participated in a financial venture in a woolen factory in Manhattan, which due to an inadequate supply of waterpower failed but Hamilton's interest never flagged. About this same time a young immigrant from England, Sam-

---

31 Chernow, *Alexander Hamilton*, 370
32 Ibid.
33 Syrett, *The Papers of Alexander Hamilton*, Vol. X, 5

uel Slater, had managed to elude the British prohibition on emigration of skilled workers in the textile industry. Once in the United States, Slater contacted a Quaker investor and oversaw the construction of a reproduction of Arkwright's spinning machine in Rhode Island. Once the mill was operating, the investor told Hamilton with pride "mills and machines may be erected in different places, in one year, to make all the cotton yarn that may be wanted in the United States."[34]

No one in America was more captivated by the industrial advancements taking place in England than was Hamilton. He understood that the industrialization of America would not only strengthen its independence but also would power its economic growth and give to the United States a preeminence that agricultural production never could. Unavailable a few short years before, the new capital provided by his funding of the national debt could help to finance the expansion of America's manufacturing.

Tench Coxe played a major role in helping Hamilton to assemble the information necessary to support his *Report on Manufacturing*, prepared a draft of his own version of the report that significantly influenced Hamilton's final draft. Perhaps just as important was Coxe's influence in engaging Hamilton's interest in establishing a manufacturing society. This organization, conceived, constructed and operated as a private enterprise and funded with investment capital, was intended as a pilot project for the transfer, development and advancement of manufacturing technologies. The *Society for Establishing Useful Manufactures (SEUM)* envisioned the construction of a town of manufacturing industries. The prospectus, which Hamilton drafted, planned a host of industries for the manufacture of such products as paper, sailcloth, cottons and linens, shoes, thread, worsted stockings, hats, ribbons, blankets, carpets and beer. A site was selected for the construction of the town at the falls of the Passaic River in New Jersey. Of this site Hamilton recalled one stolen moment during the Revolution when he, General Washington and Lafayette had enjoyed a 'modest repast' of cold ham, tongue and biscuits. Once the site for the town was selected, it was named after the current governor of New Jersey, William Paterson.[35]

Tench Coxe had managed to acquire much of the critically needed manufacturing technology prior to joining the Treasury Department. He had paid

---

34 Chernow, *Alexander Hamilton*, 371
35 *W&MQR, Tench Coxe, Alexander Hamilton and the Encouragement of American Manufactures*, July 1975

Andrew Mitchell to travel to England to observe the operations of British mills and covertly learn the machine designs and processes that made British manufacturing so successful. Coxe had also brought an English weaver, George Parkinson, to the United States to construct a replica of one of Arkwright's flax mills. Parkinson was granted a patent for his flax mill even though his application stated that the process included improvements upon the mill or machinery used in Great Britain.[36]

These covert means of acquiring the basic technologies of manufacturing industries may be viewed as industrial espionage; some historians write critically, attaching to it some degree of wrongdoing. When analyzed objectively, however, the involvement of one country in the protection of the proprietary rights and intellectual property of another country is properly seen as an appropriate and reciprocal article of a commercial treaty. The United States had shown repeated interest in negotiating such a treaty with Great Britain but the British took the position that they already had the trade advantages they desired with the United States and saw no further motive for formalizing the commercial relationship. Viewed in this light, the protection of their industrial interests was entirely a British responsibility. Any profit another country could gain by acquiring British manufacturing technologies was as valid as the British maritime regulations that protected British shipping by restricting shipments of British products to America by other than British or American vessels. Or as valid as Britain's prohibition of American ships from dealing directly with British West Indies possessions and certainly more valid than the British monopoly of the fur trade in the American northwest by force of maintaining their forts on American soil.

Hamilton submitted his *Report on the Subject of Manufactures* to Congress on December 5, 1791. His *Report on Manufactures* addresses two basic topics. In the first section Hamilton presented a case arguing that manufacturing industries can compete favorably with agriculture in terms of the productive use of land. In this section he drew heavily from Adam Smith's, *Wealth of Nations* to justify his pro-manufacturing stance. In this section Hamilton acknowledged the common arguments used by opponents of manufacturing to advance the merits and utility of agrarian productivity. One such argument, very much of a prejudicial nature, stated, "That in the productions of the soil, nature co-operates with man; and that the effect of their joint labour must be

---

36 Ibid.

greater than that of the labour of man alone." In his response Hamilton was more tentative and less forceful than normal and thereby lends more authority to the argument than its merits deserve. He stated, "It is very conceivable that the labor of man alone laid out upon a work, requiring great skill and art to bring it to perfection, may be more productive, *in value*, than the labour of nature's and man's combined, when directed towards more simple operations and objects."[37] Early in his report Hamilton paused to define the singular importance that agriculture plays in a society. It is the one essential industry; with it the society can survive, which it cannot do in its absence. Hamilton concedes, "That the cultivation of the earth — as the primary and most certain source of natural supply — as the immediate and chief source of the sustenance of men — as the principal source of those materials which constitute the nutriment of other kinds of labor — as including a state most favorable to the freedom and independence of the human mind — one, perhaps most conducive to the multiplication of the human species — has *intrinsically a stronger claim to pre-eminence over every other kind of industry*."[38]

After conceding the importance of agricultural industry, Hamilton challenged the more generalized claim, "It has been maintained, that Agriculture is not only the most productive but the only productive species. The reality of this suggestion in either aspect has, however, not been verified by any accurate detail of facts and calculations."[39]

The second topic addressed by Hamilton's report was the means by which the government could encourage manufacturing. Given that American manufacturing industry at the time was in its infancy and had not matured sufficiently to be capable of competing with established foreign manufacturing (especially Great Britain's), it could grow most rapidly and become more expert and efficient if it were provided a temporary cost advantage over foreign products. Hamilton proposed the establishment of additional duties on selected foreign goods to temporarily raise their cost to the point that American goods could compete. He proposed that the revenue from these duties be provided to selected American industry in the form of bounties to spur the capital investment necessary to enhance the productivity of Ameri-

---

37 Syrett, *The Papers of Alexander Hamilton*, Vol. X, 240; Hamilton, John C., *The Works of Alexander Hamilton*, Vol. III, 198

38 Syrett, *The Papers of Alexander Hamilton*, Vol. X, 236; Hamilton, John C., *The Works of Alexander Hamilton*, Vol. III, 195

39 Ibid.

can manufacturers so that they could compete with foreign products. He drew attention to the national defense benefit to be derived from industries engaged in the manufacture of fire arms and other military weapons, gun powder and lead shot.[40]

Unlike Hamilton's earlier financial reports, his *Report on Manufactures* did not gain congressional acceptance. This report was never transformed into legislation and simply died for want of support. The failure of the *Report* to gain acceptance by Congress was due mainly to an uncharacteristic lack of effectiveness in Hamilton's presentation. In place of his normal forceful persuasiveness, this report was written with a tone of academic abstraction. Hamilton should have had the information to show how much more productive one worker could be in manufacturing than in agriculture but chose not to be emphatic on that point; rather, he was vague and tentative in comparing the potential productivity of the two kinds of labor. He commented that, "It is not known that the comparison (of productivity between manufacturing and agriculture) has ever yet been made upon sufficient data properly ascertained and analised."[41] On his proposal for a system of duties and bounties, he was unconvincing. Foreign manufactured goods introduced into the American economy inherently carried a cost penalty due to the trans-oceanic transportation expense. Hamilton failed to show why a further duty was required to make domestic products competitive and how his proposed bounty would be used to cause the cost of the domestic product to become more competitive without further governmental assistance. Whether it was because he fashioned his report too much after Smith's, *Wealth of Nations*, or if he was unduly distracted by the attacks from his opponents, this report was not one of Hamilton's more effective efforts. That Congress did not act on this report to enact legislation that would have encouraged the growth of manufacturing industries definitely slowed the growth of the American economy and prolonged the national vulnerability to commercial and military pressures of foreign powers.

With the failure of Hamilton's plan for the system of duties and bounties to promote the rapid expansion of America's manufacturing industries, the grand scheme for the *Society for the Establishment of Useful Manufactures* also ran into serious trouble. Hamilton's former friend and associate, William Duer,

---

40 Syrett, *The Papers of Alexander Hamilton*, Vol. X, 293 - 340
41 Syrett, *The Papers of Alexander Hamilton*, Vol. X, 244; Hamilton, John C., *The Works of Alexander Hamilton*, Vol. III, 200

had participated in the wild speculations over the value of bank scrip, borrowing heavily from the cash reserves of the SEUM and from any banks and private friends that he could entice. When the scrip investment bubble burst and Duer found himself unable to meet his debt obligations, he found himself faced with debtors' prison where he remained for the rest of his life. The loss of capital from Duer's extravagance placed the SEUM in a precarious financial position. The employment of Pierre Charles L'Enfant to design the manufacturing city at Paterson, New Jersey, a grossly ill-advised decision, further threatened the financial solvency of this venture. The absence of any solid management of the combined industries and the incompetence of the employed technicians and artisans combined to affect the slow but certain demise of this grand plan to bring America into the midst of the Industrial Revolution.[42] Effective execution of Hamilton's vision of a manufacturing dimension to America's economy was to wait a full generation for fulfillment.

In the spring of 1792 Phillip Freneau came to Philadelphia and began to publish the *National Gazette*. Freneau had been born in New York during 1752. He studied theology at Princeton, responding his parents' wish that he turn to the ministry. He was more drawn to literature and began writing poetry, eventually earning the title of the Poet of the American Revolution. Freneau married rather late in life and settled into an assistant editor's position in New York in 1790. His friends, Thomas Jefferson and Jame Madison, convinced him to move to Philadelphia and set up a newspaper to counter the Federalist paper, *The Gazette of the United States.* He was also hired by Thomas Jefferson to do publishing for the State Department; there was speculation that Freneau was brought to Philadelphia by Jefferson so that his newspaper could be the howitzer through which Jefferson and Madison could launch their verbal attacks on Alexander Hamilton and his Treasury Department edifice. The printing contract with the State Department was seen as an enticement to Freneau. In mid-March the first volley was fired wherein Freneau, under the pseudonym "Brutus," accused the Treasury Department of creating the speculative fury over bank scrip to "aggrandize the few and the wealthy, by oppressing the great body of the people."[43] Hamilton was accused of attempting to corrupt the American government by an outrageous system of excises, of plotting to replace the American Republican govern-

---

42 Elkins & McKitrick, *The Age of Federalism*, 278 - 280
43 Elkins & McKitrick, *The Age of Federalism*, 283

ment with a hereditary monarchy and of pandering to the wealthy and to Great Britain.

By the summer of 1792, Hamilton remained silent as long as he was able in the war of words waged by his Jeffersonian Republican opponents. He began to publish articles under various pseudonyms in the newspaper owned by John Fenno, *Gazette of the United States*. In his letters Hamilton first attacked Freneau for his "publications to vilify those to whom the voice of the people has committed the administration of our public affairs-to oppose the measures of government, and, by false insinuations, to disturb the public peace. In common life it is thought ungrateful for a man to bite the hand that puts bread in his mouth; but if the man is hired to do it, the case is altered."[44] Hamilton soon turned his invective against Jefferson, charging that Jefferson, though "the head of a principal department of the Government" was "the declared opponent of almost all the important measures which had been devised by the government."[45] Hamilton felt sharply the attacks on his person and the persecution of the measures of the Treasury Department by Jefferson and Madison and continued his retaliatory strikes through the end of 1792.

In July 1792 Hamilton wrote to Washington encouraging him to sacrifice his own interests and tranquility once more for the benefit of the country and to permit his name to be entered as eligible for re-election to the Presidency. Hamilton said that "The impression (of the country) is uniform — that your declining would be deplored as the greatest evil, that could befall the country at the present juncture, and as critically hazardous to your own reputation-that your continuance will be justified in the mind of every friend to his country by the evident necessity for it.[46] Washington was persuaded and Hamilton worked energetically to secure his re-election and the re-election of John Adams to the office of Vice President, particularly since it became clear that opponents to Adams's candidacy included his nemesis George Clinton and Aaron Burr, a man Hamilton had come to view as motivated entirely by his self interest. The electors met on December 5, 1792 and again elected George Washington as President by unanimous vote. John Ad-

---

44 Syrett, *The Papers of Alexander Hamilton*, Vol. XII, 107

45 Elkins & McKitrick, *The Age of Federalism*, 284 - 285

46 Syrett, *The Papers of Alexander Hamilton*, Vol. XII, 137 - 139; Hamilton, John C., *The Works of Alexander Hamilton*, Vol. IV, 235-236

---

ams was also returned to office by a respectable margin, although Governor George Clinton did receive a very impressive fifty votes.[47]

Hamilton continued to be despondent over the bitter attacks of his opponents. In a letter to John Jay shortly before Christmas Hamilton remarked, "'Tis not the extra attention I am obliged to pay to the course of legislative manoeuvers that alone add to my burthen and perplexity. 'Tis the malicious intrigues to stab me in the dark, against which I am too often obliged to guard myself, that distract and harass me." Of the results of the recent election he observes, "The success of the Vice President is as great a source of satisfaction as that of Mr. Clinton would have been of mortification & pain to me. Willingly however would I relinquish my share of the command, to the Antifederalists if I thought they were to be trusted —but I have so many proofs of the contrary as to make me dread the experience of their preponderancy."[48]

The faction led by Madison and Jefferson, as Hamilton described to Edward Carrington, was not content to soil Hamilton's public reputation; their ultimate objectives of disassembling Hamilton's programs could only be accomplished through his professional destruction. To accomplish their deeds from the safety of anonymity, Madison and Jefferson chose, as their spokesperson, a fiery Virginia congressman named William Giles. As was the vogue among Virginia politicians, Giles opposed all of Hamilton's financial reform programs; especially he hated banks and financial systems that contained the obscure concepts proposed by Hamilton such as creating capital through funding the national debt. Giles was dispatched to discredit Hamilton's management of the manipulation of federal funds at the Treasury.[49]

Hamilton had wanted to use the money from a foreign loan to repay the debt owed by the government to the National Bank. This debt constituted the government's subscription of twenty per cent of the capital of that bank. Many of the short-term foreign loans made at that time were contracted from banks or governments of countries in the United Netherlands. Hamilton had acknowledged that he had previously used foreign loans to meet government payments of the national debt while awaiting the receipt of tax revenues. While this was technically a violation of the law, it was done with Washington's concurrence as an expedient against missing a scheduled debt payment

47 Jefferson, *The Anas of Thomas Jefferson*, 186
48 Syrett, *The Papers of Alexander Hamilton*, Vol. XIII, 338
49 Miller, John C., *Alexander Hamilton and the Growth of the New Nation*, Harper Torchbooks, New York, 1959, 325 - 329

that would have severely injured the public credit. Prodded by Giles, the House demanded an accounting from Hamilton of all foreign loans during December 1792. Hamilton responded by January 3 with a full accounting of all foreign loan transactions. This accounting satisfied the Congress. Giles, however, initiated five resolutions calling for more detailed accounting of essentially all transactions by the Treasury Department. This new congres-sional requirement, issued on January 23, gave Hamilton until March 3 to respond. On February 19 Hamilton submitted to Congress a massive report explaining in detail the authority for each loan made by the Treasury De-partment, the considerations that were pertinent to each and the manner in which the government had utilized the funds made available by the loans. As a body Congress accepted Hamilton's reports, exonerating Hamilton of any wrongdoing. Still, his opponents were neither satisfied nor defeated. In less than a month Giles had filed a number of resolutions censuring Hamilton for improperly mixing foreign and domestic loans. Each of Giles's resolutions was defeated by Congress, formally vindicating Hamilton. These attacks on Hamilton in his role as Secretary of the Treasury as well as on his personal reputation by the Jeffersonian faction were not to cease. The charges and in-nuendos followed him for the remainder of his life and have cast an unjustifi-able pall over his memory throughout most of the intervening two hundred years since his death.[50]

---

50 Ibid., 327 - 332

Chapter 7. The French Revolution in America

The second term of the presidency of George Washington was to involve some very critical diplomatic challenges with old friends and old adversaries alike. The French Revolution, begun in late 1789 when Jefferson was still minister to France, had been praised in the United States where it was seen as a child of the American Revolution, an expression of man's innate desire for personal liberty. The Revolution began as an expression of resentment of the bourgeoisie's discontent with the existing political structure in France that suppressed opportunities for them to rise above their middle class status. Americans rejoiced when the French National Assembly gave recognition and honorary citizenship to "Georges Washington, N. Madison and Jean Hamilton."[1]

This diplomatic *faux pas* was overshadowed by the terror of the guillotine near the Tuileries where 1400 political prisoners were "sacrificed" in a bloody September massacre. Jefferson and his supporters, long friendly to the French, at first denied the horrors of the slaughter that had occurred in France. When finally faced with its reality Jefferson said, "Rather than it [the Revolution] should have failed, I would have seen half the earth desolated."[2] On January 21, 1793 the Jacobins, a radical anti-monarchial party, executed Louis XVI and his wife and buried them ignominiously. In early February the new French government declared war on England and the Netherlands

1 Elkins & McKitrick, *The Age of Federalism*, 311 - 312
2 McCullough, D., *John Adams*, Simon & Schuster, New York, 2001, 438

in their ardor to rid Europe of monarchies and in March they extended the war to include Spain. When Louis XVI was still in power he had been enticed into declaring war on Austria and Prussia so that by March of 1793 the European war was spread over most of the Continent.

In America the news of King Louis's execution met with mixed reaction. The Jeffersonians who had long expressed a preference for alliances with France rather than with England, based principally on the supposed moral superiority of the French, said, through Freneau's *National Gazette*, that the King's execution was a great act of justice.

Four American government figures who had held diplomatic posts in France contributed to the widely share American view of the French Revolution. These men were John Adams, who had spent two of his ten years of diplomatic missions in Paris; Dr. Benjamin Franklin, who spent nearly the entire period of the American Revolution in Paris negotiating for French support; Thomas Jefferson, who had relieved Benjamin Franklin and served four years as the United States Minister to France, leaving in 1789; and Gouverneur Morris, who went to France on private business and was subsequently appointed minister there in 1789. Of these three men Morris most directly observed the Revolution, remaining in France through the Terrors of 1793 and attempted to offer his counsel and advice to the French nobles and to King Louis XVI. Morris kept official Philadelphia informed on the actions and effectiveness of the French Revolution, even through the horrors of the Reign of Terror. During 1791 as the new French Constitution was being debated in the National Assembly, Morris was offering his counsel to French aristocrats and royalty alike. In a conversation with the Comte de Luxembourg, Morris wrote in his diary that Luxembourg stated his intention to give the king advice on the best conduct for the king during the period of intrigue. Morris replied "that the aristocratic party must be quiet unless they wish to be hanged."[3] Later Morris violated his own advice and counseled the King and Queen that it would be advisable for them to forbid anyone from discussing with them the impending constitution, giving as their rationale, "We do not wish in any way to influence or prejudice the question, as it is a solemn convention between the Nation and its Head."[4]

3 Morris, G., *Diary of the French Revolution*, Vol. II, Greenwood Press, Westport Ct., 1939, 53
4 Ibid., 230

Morris's counsel extended to practical matters of administration as well as to political posturing. In a letter to Comte Montmorin of September 24, 1791 and subsequently referenced in a letter to the King, Morris pointed out that, due to the activities of the Revolution, it was more than likely that in the spring there would be an extreme shortage of bread in Paris. As it remained the responsibility of the King to anticipate and supply the needs of his people, this vital need should be recognized and dealt with. Morris offered a specific plan for the King to purchase flour from America, and have it shipped to and stored in England until the need manifested itself. Morris volunteered his services as the King's agent to arrange for the flour purchase and shipment and to have provisions made for its storage and eventual shipment to France.[5]

Neither Morris' advice nor his plan to avoid a bread famine were taken or acted upon by the French. Apparently the counsels and plans offered by Morris were inconsistent with the realities and priorities of the French Revolution. The government, formed under the new constitution, did not hold Morris in high regard due to his former association with royalty and the ruling aristocratic party. Morris was essentially isolated from his diplomatic role. The government did not consult him in their selection of a new minister to be sent to the United States, nor did they advise him of the instructions that had been given to the new minister. The French government failed to avail themselves of the advice that Morris could have given them regarding the likely reception that their new minister would receive in the United States, given the instructions that he carried. Certainly much difficulty in the strained relations between France and the United States could have been avoided.

The new French minister, Edmond Charles Genet, arrived in Charleston, South Carolina on April 8, 1793. He was only thirty years old but highly intelligent and unusually experienced in government for a man of his years. Genet had received his diplomatic experience at the Court of Catherine II of Russia where he served in a number of ascending appointments from 1787 to 1792. Genet was a genial, gregarious personality, although somewhat self-indulgent. Genet had been selected to succeed Jean Baptiste Ternant as French minister to the United States at the encouragement of the ruling Girondins; the *americaniste* Brissot was his most likely sponsor. At the time of Genet's

---

5 Ibid., Vol. I, 276, 278, 290

appointment, the King was on trial; it was generally assumed that he would be allowed to go into self-imposed exile to America and that Genet would accompany the royal family on that journey. Events transpired rapidly and the King was executed late in January 1793. Genet left for America a month later aboard the frigate *Embuscade*.[6] The party that emerged as dominant in the French government from early 1792 until mid-1793 were the Gironde. They maintained the majority of seats in the Legislative Assembly during this period. They brought to the French government an extreme love of liberty, an enthusiasm for spreading liberty throughout the world and little else in the form of credentials for administering the government. Their inspirational leader was Jacques Pierre Brissot de Warville. Brissot gained prominence as a journalist and motivational leader although he had little in the way of substantial political experience or real leadership skills.[7]

The instructions that Genet received prior to leaving France were, like much else that controlled France during the revolution, full of a hearty enthusiasm but totally devoid of any fundamental diplomatic plan for the furtherance of Franco-American relations. The first objective Genet was to pursue was to enflame the people of Louisiana, Florida and Canada with the fervor of liberty by agitation, propaganda, privateering and by underwriting military expeditions against the Spanish in Florida and Louisiana. His second objective was to negotiate a treaty with the United States, based on the Treaty of 1778, which was viewed by the French as still being in force. The new treaty would embrace a renewal and consolidation of the Franco-American commercial ties and would commit the two countries to joining their commercial and political interests to promote the growth of the "empires of liberty," mutually guarantying the sovereignty of both countries and to invoke a commercial punishment of those powers that continue to hold colonial interests — prohibiting those countries access to the ports of both signature countries. To the French interpretation, the treaty of 1778 permitted French privateers to arm and equip in American ports and required the United States to impose discriminating tonnage duties, favoring France and penalizing British vessels. The third and final objective Genet had was to acquire the full liquidation of the American war debt owed to France, which, at that time amounted to approximately $5.6 million. Genet was authorized

6 Elkins & McKitrick, *The Age of Federalism*, 330 - 331
7 Ibid., 331

to use these funds to finance his planned operations in America, including outfitting privateers, to fund the expenses of his de-stabilizing activities in Florida, Louisiana and Canada, and the purchase of provisions for the French army and colonies.[8]

On April 8, Alexander Hamilton received a reliable report that France had declared war against England, Russia and Holland as of February 8, 1793 and relayed this intelligence to President Washington.[9] At that time Washington was at Mt. Vernon, since Congress was not in session. While he awaited Washington's response, Hamilton addressed two letters to John Jay in which he asked Jay's opinion on the proper reception for Genet. Should it be an unqualified acceptance, implying the Treaty of 1778 was still in force; or should his reception be qualified, considering the unsettled state of the French government? In the second letter Hamilton requested Jay to draft a neutrality proclamation, including those considerations which he thought most important, allowing the United States to remain neutral in the European conflict and to maintain friendly relations with all combatant countries, without prejudicing relationships with any of them. Jay responded quickly to this request with a short, incisive draft of a proclamation of neutrality, along with his qualification that he would like to devote more time and thought to this proclamation.[10]

President Washington responded to Hamilton on April 12, advising that he would return to Philadelphia around April 24. Washington stated that the position of America should be to prevent its involvement in the general European war. He was aware that privateering vessels were outfitting in American ports, an action that should be terminated. He directed that the Cabinet officers consider how America could maintain strict neutrality and that they be prepared to present their thoughts to him as soon as he returned to Philadelphia. Washington managed to arrive in Philadelphia on April 17 and the following day met with his cabinet. In that meeting Washington presented a list of thirteen questions regarding the proper way the United States should respond to the new French minister; should the United States issue a Neutrality Proclamation and what is the correct status of the Franco-American Treaty of 1778? The President requested his cabinet to study the

---

8 Ibid., 333
9 Syrett, *The Papers of Alexander Hamilton*, Vol. XIV, 291
10 Ibid., 307 - 310

list of questions and to be prepared to meet and discuss them on the following day at Washington's house.[11]

Jefferson wrote that night in his diary that, while the questions listed for consideration had been written in Washington's hand, it was clear from the wording ("their ingenious tissue and suite"), that Alexander Hamilton had drafted them. Edmund Randolph confirmed Jefferson's suspicions, saying that on the day preceding Washington's original meeting that Alexander Hamilton had reviewed with Randolph the reasoning behind these questions. Randolph said that he recognized their source as soon as he had read the questions.[12]

The questions generally applied to the applicability of the treaty with France of 1778. The first question asked, should the United States issue a neutrality proclamation? The next two questions pertained to receiving the new minister from France; should he be received with or without qualifications? The next eight questions investigated how the 1778 treaty applied to the circumstances of 1793. The final question asked whether Congress, not then in session, should be convened to consider the state of war among the European powers.[13]

In the debate that ensued at the meeting called by President Washington, all cabinet offices agreed that a proclamation should be issued stating that the United States was to remain friendly and impartial with all warring parties and that United States citizens were forbidden to take any part in the hostilities. On April 22, 1793 Washington issued his Proclamation of Neutrality. This important policy decision was a clear victory for Hamilton. He had argued that American foreign policy should be dictated by self-interest; that the appearance of altruism by foreign powers often merely shadowed baser, more self-serving motives. Jefferson, on the other hand, managed to keep the word "neutrality" out of the proclamation. France, he felt, would interpret this term as indicating a disavowal of the Treaty of 1778.[14]

On the question of receiving the new French minister, all agreed that he should be received. On the question of receiving him with or without qualifications, Jefferson and Randolph rook the position that the 1778 treaty remained in force so there was no basis for a qualified reception of the minister;

---

11 Ibid., 326 - 327
12 Jefferson, *The ANAS of Thomas Jefferson*, 118 - 119
13 Elkins & McKitrick, *The Age of Federalism*, 337 - 341
14 Ibid., 338 - 339

Hamilton and Knox felt that it was not clear that the treaty remained in force and, accordingly, he should be received with qualifications. Hamilton was concerned that, while we may recognize the new government of France, the situation there was far from being stable so that, it remained unclear what final form the government of France would take. If it were to be agreed that the 1778 treaty remained in force and subsequently the French government radically changed into a form that the United States could not recognize, it would be very difficult to declare the treaty void at that time without risking giving offense to France. Hamilton reasoned that, "To elect to continue them is equivalent to the making of a new treaty at the time in the same form; that is to say, with a clause of guarantee (of mutual defense); but to make a treaty with a clause of guarantee, during a war, is a departure from neutrality, and would make us associates in the war. To renounce or suspend the treaties therefore is a necessary act of neutrality."[15]

It was clear to all those involved in the decision-making process that strict neutrality was the only course that the country could take at that time. The new government was only beginning to take firm effect in the country. Hamilton's financial systems were working and the public credit was strong; however, with the burden of debt that still existed, it was doubtful that any country would have advanced the United States loans of the size necessary to enter a war. Even should loans be arranged they would represent, in combination with those currently in existence, a crushing burden to the country's economy. The country had purposefully avoided creating a navy or standing army of any substantial size; so, therefore, it was in no position to counter an armed conflict, particularly one in support of an ally who had not even consulted America prior to initiating its conflict.

On the questions relating to the status of the Treaty of 1788, Washington asked his cabinet officers to respond in writing. Hamilton, Jefferson and Randolph responded to this request. Hamilton argued for the suspension of the treaty in order to see the final form that the government of France would assume and to assess how the warring parties would react to the neutrality of America. Jefferson and Randolph each wrote arguments supporting the continuation of the treaty. Henry Knox, it may fairly be assumed, sided with Hamilton. On May 6, Washington decided, this time accepting Jefferson's perspective that the treaty remained in full effect and that Genet was to be

---

15 Syrett, *The Papers of Alexander Hamilton*, Vol. XIV, 329 (note)

received without qualifications. All three officers had couched their arguments in terms of the accepted authorities on international law and treaties, Vattel, Pufendorf, Grotius and Wolf. They had written that sovereign nations have the right to change their form of government any time they see as appropriate. Treaties made between nations remain valid when one of the parties chose to alter or change their form of government.

Certainly, with respect to the Treaty of 1778, the United States had changed its government with the adoption of the new constitution in 1788. These authorities agreed that valid causes to revoke national commitments to treaties do exist, including the inability of one nation to fulfill its guarantee of mutual defense to the other. Hamilton extracted from Vattel the exception that when the change in form of government of one party to a treaty renders the treaty *useless*, *dangerous* or *disagreeable* to the other nation, that nation may validly terminate the treaty. Hamilton argued that, while he had no tangible evidence that the new republican government in France produced any of these deleterious effects on the treaty, the fact that the politics in France remained in such a state of transition caused an unqualified continuance of the treaty to be irresponsible. He said,

> Prudence at least seems to dictate the course of *reserving* the question, in order that further reflection and a more complete development of circumstances may enable us to make a decision both *right* and *safe*. It does not appear necessary to precipitate the fixing of our relations to France beyond the possibility of retraction. It is putting too suddenly too much to hazard.[16]

Had George Washington been aware, in early May, of the mischief that Genet was planning and actually already had engaged in, respecting the outfitting of privateers in Charleston harbor and of forming military incursions into Louisiana and Florida from United States territories, one would wonder whether his decision relative to the treaty would have been the same.

At the time Genet had landed in South Carolina, much of America continued in a state of euphoria over the success of the French Revolution and the establishment of a republican form of government there. This enthusiasm was expressed in a lavish welcoming of the new French Minister. Local dignitaries and state politicians formally greeted him. Governor William Moultrie met with Genet and welcomed him with assurances of America's

---

16 Syrett, *The Papers of Alexander Hamilton*, Vol. XIV, 393; Hamilton, John C., *The Works of Alexander Hamilton*, Vol. IV, 379

friendship and commitment to France. Genet discussed his plan of sending disruptive expeditions into Spanish territory and was encouraged by Moultrie's assurances that he would meet with no governmental resistance. He recommended to Genet the names of men who could be instrumental in the outfitting of privateers in the Charleston harbor.[17]

Genet traveled by land to Philadelphia to acquaint himself with the American people and to solicit their support for the causes he would espouse as the French minister to America. During Genet's travel, a British ship, the *Grange*, was captured by a French frigate and taken as prize into Philadelphia. Thomas Jefferson's total support of the French Revolutionary cause is exemplified in his letter to James Madison describing the scene when the captive British vessel was brought into port in the national capital. "Upon her coming into sight, thousands and thousands...crowded and covered the wharves. Never before was such a crowd seen as these, and when the British colours were seen *reversed* & the French flag above them they burst into peals of exultation."[18] By contrast, to the proud capture of the *Grange*, "Hamilton," he says, was "panic struck if we refuse our breach to every kick which Gr. Brit. May chuse to give it."[19]

Before Genet had arrived in Philadelphia, his activities had prompted a strong protest from George Hammond to Thomas Jefferson over the French harassment of British shipping in American waters. Jefferson had responded by transmitting a letter to the retiring French Minister Ternant, citing the illegality of the French act of outfitting privateers in American ports and of the capture of English ships in American waters — both acts that could be interpreted as violations of the American Neutrality Proclamation. Ternant had forwarded this letter to Genet. Genet responded in a letter to Jefferson that he was to restore the *Grange* as a gift, "to convince the American government of our deference and friendship." He made no mention of Jefferson's statement that arming or outfitting of vessels in American ports was offensive to America.[20]

Genet arrived in Philadelphia on May 16. Two days later he presented his credentials to the President. During this introductory meeting, Genet stated, "We know, that under present circumstances we have a right to call upon

---

17 Elkins & McKitrick, *The Age of Federalism*, 335
18 Ibid., 357
19 Ford, *Writings of Thomas Jefferson*, Vol. VI, G. P. Putnam, New York, 1896, 238
20 Elkins & McKitrick, *The Age of Federalism*, 342 - 343

you for the guarantee of our islands. But we do not desire it. We wish you nothing but what is for your own good, and we will do all in our power to promote it....We see you the only person on earth who can love us sincerely & merit to be so loved."[21] Doubtless Washington received Genet courteously and formally, for that was his style. Jefferson, who was also present at the meeting, observed to James Madison, "It is impossible for anything to be more affectionate, more magnanimous than the purport of his mission....In short he offers everything and asks nothing."[22]

Washington held discussions in cabinet meetings over the matter of any of the belligerent powers in the war using American ports for outfitting privateering ships. Hamilton and Knox were opposed to the practice, which they viewed as a violation of American sovereignty, and Jefferson felt that the existing treaty permitted the practice with regards to France. In an uncharacteristic move, Edmund Randolph disagreed with Jefferson and sided with Hamilton and Knox. President Washington also felt that American neutrality could not permit that practice. Jefferson was directed to inform the belligerent powers of the American policy, which he did on June 5. On June 17 Jefferson had occasion to send another letter to Genet, detailing for him the position of the United States government forbidding either belligerent arming or fitting out of privateering ships in American ports to be used against another nation in friendly relations to the United States.[23]

To this communication Genet responded with what Hamilton referred to as "the most offensive paper, perhaps, that ever was offered by a foreign Minister to a friendly power, with which he resided."[24] In his letter Genet accuses Jefferson, "You oppose to my complaints, to my just reclamations, upon the footing of right, the private and public opinions of the President of the United States; and this aegis not appearing to you sufficient, you bring forward aphorisms of Vattel, to justify or excuse infractions committed on positive treaties." He goes on as if to shame and chastise the American government, "If you cannot protect our commerce, and our colonies, which will, in the future, contribute much more to your prosperity than to our own, at

---

21 Ford, Writings of Thomas Jefferson, Vol. VI, 260 - 261
22 Ibid.
23 Elkins & McKitrick, *Age of Federalism*, 345, 347
24 Syrett, *The Papers of Alexander Hamilton*, Vol. XV, 75

least do not arrest the civism of our own citizens; do not expose them to a certain loss, by obliging them to go out of your ports unarmed."[25]

In an affront to the American government, Genet began to outfit, as a privateer, the captured British merchant ship *Little Sarah*, right in the harbor at Philadelphia, "under the immediate eye of the government."[26] At that particular time President Washington was enjoying a rest at Mt. Vernon, Congress being not in session. Jefferson pressed Genet for assurance that the *Little Sarah* would not sail before President Washington's return to Philadelphia, and Genet indicated that it would not leave that soon. When Washington was briefed on the escalating furor over foreign privateers operating from American ports, he decided to have the legality and treaty implications of the American position reviewed by the Supreme Court and requested that privateers currently in American ports remain there until the American position was clarified. Although the *Little Sarah* did not sail until after Washington's return, it eventually did sail in defiance of Washington's request that such privateers remain in port while the question was clarified.[27]

Upon Washington's return, Thomas Jefferson briefed him on the *Little Sarah* incident. When he fully understood the extent of Genet's disrespect to the government, Washington became quite angry. "What must the world think of such conduct, and of the Government of the U. States in submitting to it?[28] Washington set a cabinet meeting for the following day, July 12. Jefferson wrote a distressed letter to James Madison, describing his disappointment with Genet. "Never in my opinion, was so calamitous an appointment made...hot-headed, all imagination, no judgment, passionate, disrespectful & even indecent towards the P(resident) in his written as well as verbal communications, talking of appeals from him to the Congress, from them to the people."[29] Jefferson had finally seen the crassness of Genet's ministry and had changed his assessment of him.

At the cabinet meeting of July 12, the President and the Heads of the Department discussed at length the issue raised by the actions and positions taken by the new French minister. It was readily agreed that his recall was to be requested from France. In the end the Secretary of State was directed to

25 *American State Papers: Foreign Relations*, Vol. I, 155 — 156 (http://memory.loc.gov/ammem/am/aw/lwsp.html)

26 Syrett, *The Papers of Alexander Hamilton*, Vol. XV, 75

27 Elkins & McKitrick, *The Age of Federalism*, 350 - 352

28 Ibid., 350 - 352

29 Ford, *Writings of Thomas Jefferson*, Vol. VI, 338 - 9

draft the letter requesting his recall. The letter would be transmitted to the American minister in Paris for delivery to the French government. But they did not know, prior to mid-August, that the Gironde government in Paris had fallen and been replaced by the Jacobins, headed by Maximilien Robespierre. Under this government and mainly through the actions of the Committee of Public Safety, most of the leading Girondins were sent to the guillotine. The new Jacobin government was more than happy to recall Genet, "since he had offended France's friend, America." Now, Alexander Hamilton realized that Genet's fate back in France would likely be the guillotine. Hamilton urged Washington to allow Genet to remain in the United States, lest the Republicans accuse Washington of having Genet sent to his death. Washington gave Genet asylum and Genet subsequently became an American citizen. He married Cornelia Clinton, daughter of New York governor George Clinton, a longtime adversary of Alexander Hamilton. Genet and his wife spent the rest of their lives in upstate New York.[30]

Washington decided that an additional stipulation required definition as part of America's neutrality; that of the extent of ocean declared as United States waters. This need had been brought about by French privateering activities in waters close to America. In November 1793 Washington established this limit as three miles or one league.[31] During 1793 the United States also defined a uniform set of policies governing the jurisdiction over prizes. It had been held that foreign consulars presuming to establish admiralty courts for condemning prizes on American soil was a violation of United States sovereignty. The Neutrality Act of 1794 embodied most of these provisions that had been generated by Washington's cabinet officers. This act was considered to be so effective and so far reaching that it remained the basis for American neutrality into the twentieth century.[32]

The settlers in the western portion of the states of Pennsylvania, Virginia and North Carolina were separated from the main body of the country by the Appalachian Mountains and by attitudes and perspectives that created an even sharper divide. These people, mostly farmers, had crossed the mountains in search of land that they could till and own, but they found that eastern speculators had bought all of the better farming acreage without

---

30 Elkins & McKitrick, *The Age of Federalism*, 365 - 372
31 *American State Papers: Foreign Relations*, Vol. I, 183
32 Elkins & McKitrick, *Age of Federalism*, 353 - 354

lifting a finger to improve it. When they did settle, either on poor land that they could purchase or on good land where they tenant farmed, moving their produce to market was an almost insurmountable obstacle. Roads across the mountains to eastern markets were so bad as to be essentially impassable. It was far easier to take their products down the Ohio River to the Mississippi and out to the Gulf of Mexico and from there, around Florida to eastern ports of America. The problem with this solution was that Spain owned New Orleans and would often close the river to commercial traffic. There was also the continuing threat of Indian attacks to concern them.

The challenge of transporting their produce to market was often solved by raising grain and converting it into whiskey that could be easily transported. These bottled spirits could be packaged and carried across the mountains on horseback to eastern markets. Their distilled whiskey was such a staple of life in those mountain communities that it often served to barter for other necessities of life. Distilleries were ubiquitous; if the product wasn't shipped to the east to market or down the Mississippi, despite Spanish prohibitions, it was traded to neighbors for food or clothing or consumed in the home as the one available release from their impoverished and stressful lives.

As a result of Hamilton's excise taxes of 1791, the western settlers reviled the government, which had consistently refused assistance to their life-threatening problems and now demanded subsidies from their one profitable industry, distilling of spirits. The perceived inequity of the excise infected the State Legislatures and, particularly in Pennsylvania, resulted in the Legislature passing resolutions condemning that tax as unjust and unnecessary. Encouraged by this support from their state government the people of western Pennsylvania became more resentful and looked for ways to avoid the tax. As a follow-up to the resolutions, public town meetings were held in protest and resolutions made for both passive and aggressive measures to defeat the collection of these excises. In Washington county a resolution called for citizens to treat the excise collectors "with that contempt they deserve, and [recommended] that they absolutely refuse all kinds of communication or intercourse with them, and that they will withhold all aid, support or comfort from such officer or officers."[33]

In Alexander Hamilton's communication to the President of August 3, 1794, describing the Pennsylvania uprising (to become known as the Whis-

---

[33] Syrett, *The Papers of Alexander Hamilton*, Vol. XVII, 29 (note)

key Rebellion), he stated that the opposition had been in progress for the three years since the enactment of the excise taxes and had been both steady and violent.[34] In fact, several cases were recorded where the excise men and those working with them had been tarred and feathered.

Early in the insurrection Hamilton had taken a decisive and hard-line position. In September of 1792 he had written to Washington, promoting military intervention and arguing that if it were not firmly suppressed, "the spirit of disobedience will naturally extend and the authority of the government will be prostrate."[35] Based on the experience of Shay's Rebellion, Hamilton must have thought that the most effective response to an organized civil disobedience, particularly one that involved violence, was first to determine if the rebellion was based on any valid complaints. If there was no evidence of justifiable objections, the uprising had to be squelched both firmly and rapidly to prevent it spreading and encouraging similar actions elsewhere. Because of the continuing threat of violence as well as ongoing resistance to the collection of whiskey excises, the government resolved to put an end to the insurrection. Hamilton recommended to Washington that a militia formed from New Jersey, Virginia and Maryland as well as Pennsylvania be assembled, twelve thousand strong, to suppress the rebellion by force.[36]

Washington's proclamation of August 7 summarized the extent of the rebellion as given in Hamilton's letter to him of August 5. Washington directed that the militia as proposed by Hamilton be formed and warned the insurgents that, unless they cease all forms of opposition to the excise by September 1 the militia would be employed to suppress the violence of their opposition. Washington stated that he would dispatch Commissioners to the area that would be authorized to extend amnesty to all who would pledge the cessation of protest and submit to the collection of excise duties on stills and the production of whiskey in accordance with the Excise Act. On August 17 the commissioners determined that the insurgents were both "numerous and violent" and were determined to resist the excise "at all hazards." Washington's commissioners returned to Philadelphia on September 24 and reported to Washington their conclusion that "there is no probability that the act for raising a revenue on distilled spirits and stills can at present be enforced by the usual course of civil authority; and that some more com-

34 Ibid., 15 - 19
35 Ibid., Vol. XII, 311 - 312
36 Ibid., Vol. XVII, 18 - 19

petent force is necessary to cause the laws to be duly executed, and to ensure to the officers and well-disposed citizens that protection which it is the duty of Government to afford."[37]

Washington called on Hamilton to fill in for the absent Secretary of War and to prepare for the supply of the militia. The combined militia marched on September 25. President Washington and Hamilton set forth on September 30 to join the troops in Carlisle. At the end of October, Washington determined that the command of the militia, between Virginia Governor Henry Lee and Alexander Hamilton, was in good hands, and he returned to Philadelphia. When the military reached its destination there was little evidence of existing protest. Some distillers were arrested for not paying the excise, some voluntarily surrendered, some fled into the mountains. The soldiers presented greater disciplinary problems than did the rebels. At least two civilians were killed by militia who themselves were drunk on local whiskey. The guilty militiamen were tried in civilian courts for the murders.[38]

When Hamilton returned to Philadelphia, he felt that it was time that his family stopped having to suffer a lack of material advantages so that he could grapple with the problems of forming and developing the government of the new republic. The position of Secretary of the Treasury simply did not compensate him nearly as well as being an attorney in New York and he felt that his family deserved better than he had been providing for them. He told Washington of his decision and finally left government service in mid-February, 1795.[39]

37 Elkins & McKitrick, *Age of Federalism*, 482; Chernow, *Alexander Hamilton*, 471
38 Syrett, *The Papers of Alexander Hamilton, Vol. XVII*, 338, 348-352
39 Hamilton, *The Intimate Life of Alexander Hamilton*, 164

CHAPTER 8. FOREIGN DIPLOMACY

At the beginning of 1792 the balance of the Anglo-American commercial relations leaned decidedly in favor of Great Britain. They enjoyed a profitable and increasingly voluminous trade with the United States on terms very advantageous to them, if not actually dictated by them. The tonnage and impost duties paid by British ships were as favorable as those paid by countries that had commercial treaties with the United States. Britain was aware that the United States revenue system established by Hamilton was critically dependent upon British trade so they had this leverage to promote British trade interests. Britain continued to deny America trading rights to the West Indies in American bottoms although America had made it known through the unofficial diplomatic channel of Hamilton and George Beckwith that the acquisition of these trading rights was a high priority to this country. If these rights were important to America, Britain would withhold them until there was an interest of equal importance to them that could be traded.

The situation to the west of the Appalachians appeared to be moving in the direction of British interests also. The territories of Kentucky and Franklin (later to become Tennessee) were becoming increasingly frustrated in their lack of support from the Federal government relative to the Indian problem and the Spanish blockade of the Mississippi River. These territories were considering secession from the United States to seek independent alliances that would better serve their interests. Both Spain and England were cautiously courting these territories toward this initiative. The British continued to use their occupation of the posts in the American northwest, contrary to the provisions of the Peace Treaty, to incite Indian uprisings against settlers, particularly those north of the Ohio River.

In the Treaty of 1783, Britain and the United States shared the right of usage of the Mississippi River from its source to the mouth in the Gulf of Mexico. Britain soon discovered that it had no direct access to the Mississippi at its northern extremity. There remained differences between the two countries concerning the outstanding, unresolved issues of the Peace Treaty. As was earlier discussed, England claimed that the United States had not fulfilled its treaty obligations relative to the restitution of property owned by Loyalists and confiscated by the several States following the evacuation by the British. The second area of American delinquency claimed by Britain concerned the impartial functioning of the United States judicial system in requiring the repayment of debts owed by Americans to British merchants from pre-war transactions. For their part, America pointed to the British retention of the forts in her northwest territory, in defiance of the treaty, and the final issue of the return of many Negroes that had been taken by the British during their evacuation. These issues had been the subject of repeated charge and counter-charge for nine years since the Treaty had been ratified with no significant progress having been made.

During the war between England and France, England acknowledged that the United States execution of its Neutrality Proclamation was consistent, equitable and honest. America's conduct as a neutral party in that conflict was, in fact, noted by a member of the British government as an ideal model for neutrality when a war existed between two countries with which one has significant relations. However, this did not deter Britain from enacting, as a British Order of Council, a directive that authorized British ships to stop ships of all other nations carrying grain or flour to French ports, either in France or in their West Indies possessions. This order, passed on June 8, 1793, was intended to weaken the ability of France to conduct war and, in fact, nearly did cripple the nation. Since it was impossible to differentiate between grain and flour intended for the French army from that intended for the populace, the latter suffered greatly in order to ensure that the army was fed. Any ship that Britain intercepted and seized the cargo of was fully compensated by the British. As a neutral power America abided by an embargo to ship materials that in wartime would normally be considered as contraband, but this British act of prohibition on common foodstuffs was viewed in America as being unwarranted.[1]

During this same time period the British Foreign Office made a moderately obscure appointment in Canada of Colonel John Graves Simcoe to the post of first Lieutenant Governor of Upper Canada when that province was created on May 16, 1791. In addition to this civil post, Col. Simcoe was made at his own request, military commander of the new province. In this post he was subordinate to Major General Alured Clarke at Quebec.[2] Simcoe's father had been in the military and had lost his life on the Plains of Abraham in the Battle for Quebec, along with the renowned General Wolfe. During the American Revolution the younger Simcoe had commanded a regiment of light horse known as the Queen's Rangers. In Benedict Arnold's treasonous plan of collusion with the enemy, General Henry Clinton had assigned Simcoe to take command of West Point until the discovery of Major John Andre thwarted the entire scheme. Col. Simcoe publicly shared contempt with other inexperienced British officers for George Washington as a military commander.

Yet another event that threatened the Anglo-American relations was General Anthony Wayne's war on the Indians during the summer of 1794. When the Congress originally passed the bill to strengthen the country's armed forces for the purpose of putting down the Indians, the British foresaw a military calamity for the United States similar to the fate encountered by Col. Harmar and General St. Clair, and they saw the current action in February of 1792 as constituting no threat to their status in the American northwest. Nor did they view the subsequent appointment of General Anthony Wayne as having any ominous potential for them. Wayne was equipping and training his army of 5000 men when Washington appointed a three-man peace commission to try one last time to peaceably negotiate a new boundary that would both give the Indians ample lands east of the Mississippi to pursue their life style and to meet the demands of white settlers for adequate farm land beyond the Appalachians. When these negotiations failed, Wayne was commanded to "pacify" the Indians by force. General Wayne and his

---

1 Elkins & McKitrick, *Age of Federalism*, 377 - 378
2 Bemis, *Jay's Treaty*, 168

army spent the winter of 1793–94 at Fort Recovery, located approximately fifty miles north of present day Dayton, Ohio.

Lord Dorchester felt that Wayne could possibly have as his ultimate mission the forceful removal of the British army from the forts they occupied in the American northwest. Knowing the location of Wayne's winter quarters, he projected that Wayne's primary target might be the fort at Detroit. To better protect Detroit, Dorchester ordered Col. Simcoe to occupy and re-fortify the abandoned Fort Miamis, located at the Rapids of the Maumee. This positive act of British aggression, taking and occupying an additional fort over and above those that had been occupied since the Treaty of parties, on American soil, constituted the most flagrant violation of the Peace Treaty of 1783 and of American sovereignty; but that did not seem to be a consideration to Lord Dorchester. By April of 1794, Simcoe had completed his fortification of Fort Miamis. In addition, he had installed some guns on Turtle Island, at the mouth of the Maumee River. This defensive buildup would both protect Detroit from attack and prevent General Wayne from establishing a naval force at Presque Isle on Lake Erie, from which an attack on Detroit might be launched.[3]

General Wayne began his offensive in July 1794. He worked his way north on the Maumee. At every opportunity Wayne attempted to negotiate for an Indian pullback but met only with obstinate resistance as the American forces cautiously advanced downriver. When they were within a few miles of Fort Miamis, he met a stronghold of Indian resistance. The Indians had established their defensive position behind a thicket of tornado-felled trees intertwined with newer growth, forming a nearly impenetrable barrier. Wayne sent a detachment of mounted infantry around the thicket to out-flank the Indians. The ensuing charge by the army overwhelmed and panicked the Indians. Wayne's victory at *Fallen Timbers* on August 20, 1794 was decisive and ended the Indian problem that had long been a major impediment to the western expansion of the United States.[4]

Following the Battle of Fallen Timbers the British were extremely tense; they felt confident now that Wayne, flush with victory over the Indians, would march toward Detroit to free the American post of British occupation. Indeed, when Wayne found the bodies of white men among his victims,

---

3 Ibid., 240 - 241
4 Ibid., 242 - 246

he was indignant that British aid to the Indians could take such an obvious form. An angry exchange issued between General Anthony Wayne and Col. Campbell, the British commander of the illegal Fort Miamis. The British position was that Wayne was threatening the security of the fort while Wayne was outraged at the blatant evidence in the vicinity of British collusion with the Indians and of their inciting the Indians to hostility toward the Americans. Anthony Wayne remained in the area for several days, destroying cornfields and Indian storehouses. Subsequently, Wayne fell back to Fort Defiance, strengthened the fortifications there and remained in place to put down any subsequent Indian hostility.[5] With this victory General Wayne put an end to British aspirations to mediate a neutral zone for the Indians, and to British hopes for access to the headwaters of the Mississippi; the British position occupying forts on American soil became quite precarious.

In December of 1793 word was received in Philadelphia that Britain had mediated a truce between Portugal and Algiers. The objective of Great Britain in this intervention had been to win the support of Portugal's navy in their current war against revolutionary France. Since the Portuguese navy had previously been engaged in restraining the movement of the Algerian pirates in the Mediterranean, America saw the new truce as a British ploy to release a flood of Algerian pirates against American merchant vessels engaging in commerce in the Mediterranean.[6]

In November of 1793 Britain enacted an Order in Council authorizing the seizure of any and all ships bound for the French West Indies. Under this order the British had captured over 250 American ships. If a British captain suspected a ship of planning to trade with a French possession in the Caribbean, he was authorized to take the ship as a prize. American ships were stripped of their sails; the possessions of American sailors would be confiscated and the sailors themselves were often left stranded. American consuls in the Caribbean had to expend all of their assets to assist those hapless sailors so that they would not need to enlist in some foreign service. President Washington learned of these malicious acts in late March. About the same time he learned from New York Governor Clinton of continued Indian hostilities and of continued British incitement of Indian aggression. It was

---

5 Ibid., 247 - 248
6 Elkins & McKitrick, *The Age of Federalism*, 378

then he sent word to Anthony Wayne to proceed with the planned offensive against the Indians.[7]

Alexander Hamilton quickly assessed this new British aggression as having the potential to lead to armed conflict. He wrote to Washington March 8, 1794 that the potential for conflict with Great Britain was, in his opinion, critical and required that the United States take defensive measures. He itemized those actions he thought appropriate, including establishing defensive measures in several states, enlisting an army of 20,000 men and arming them against the possibility of British invasion.[8] Thomas Pinckney, then the American ambassador to England, wrote that he, too, thought the outbreak of war with Great Britain was only a matter of time and requested permission to move his family to France for protection in the event of war. Several members of Congress met to decide on a course of action they would recommend to President Washington. As their spokesman, Oliver Ellsworth presented to Washington a plan of action, not unlike that offered by Hamilton.[9]

On March 28, an urgent message was received that Great Britain had rescinded the November 6 Order of Council and replaced it with one dated January 8. This new order authorized the resumption of trade with French islands excepting for contraband materials and any direct trade between the West Indies and ports of France. In early April a dispatch was received from Thomas Pinckney explaining the January 8 Order of Council and containing as well an explanation by Grenville that the November 6 order had been intended as a temporary measure aimed at a specific objective. The British claimed that, in the West Indies trade, American ships were transporting French cargo under the guise of its being American material. This was the infraction of international law that the November 6 Order of Council was intended to correct. He added that full compensation would be made to American ships and sailors not involved in the suspected illicit trade.[10] These were the influences that drove Great Britain and the United States to the brink of a war in late 1794 that neither country wanted, nor could afford.

Washington decided that he must send a special envoy to England to express the regret and disappointment of the United States over the aggressive behavior of the British navy toward America. There was much debate over

7 Ibid., 391
8 Syrett, *The Papers of Alexander Hamilton*, Vol. XVI, 134 - 136
9 Ibid., 130 — 133 (note)
10 Elkins & McKitrick, *The Age of Federalism*, 392 - 393

the selection of the envoy; many people expected that it would be Alexander Hamilton. Rufus King, in his personal notes, stated that, "Every effort has been made through Randolph, the Secretary of State, to defeat Hamilton's appointment."[11] In the end, Washington selected John Jay as his special envoy on April 15. On May 12, the embargo on British imports that had been in place for thirty days was discontinued so that no oppressive measures would be in force to impede Jay's progress in his negotiations.

When Washington discussed this decision with Robert Morris, he listed the names of individuals he was considering, including John Adams, John Jay, Alexander Hamilton and Thomas Jefferson. Morris replied that he would not consider either Adams or Jefferson, and between Jay and Hamilton he would select Hamilton. But Washington stated that he would not send Hamilton, saying, "Col. Hamilton does not possess the confidence of the country."[12] Many historians have viewed this as a very surprising statement, given Hamilton's role in promoting the ratification of the Constitution through his authoring of most of *The Federalist Papers* and in the creation of a stable financial system for the country that had spawned a thriving economy. They see this statement of Washington's as an olive branch extended to the Jeffersonian Republicans, who were strenuous opponents of Alexander Hamilton; they, it is true, would likely have opposed any treaty Hamilton would negotiate with the British.

On April 14, Hamilton wrote a letter in which he offered the chief executive his thought on the nature of the crisis, the spectrum of opinions of the people concerning how the matter should be handled, and his own analysis of the proper treatment of the matter. Hamilton argued against war, if it is avoidable. "Wars oftener proceed from angry and perverse passions than from cool calculations of Interest. This position is admitted without difficulty when we are judging of the hostile appearances in the measures of Great Britain towards this country."[13] Later, he summarized his recommended strategy by saying, "At no moment were the indications on the part of Great Britain to go to War with us sufficiently decisive to preclude the hope of averting it by a negotiation conducted with prudent energy and seconded by such military preparations as should be demonstrative of a Reso-

11 Syrett, *The Papers of Alexander Hamilton*, Vol. XVI, 262 (note)
12 Ibid., 262 (note)
13 Syrett, *The Papers of Alexander Hamilton*, Vol. XVI, 267; Hamilton, John C., *The Works of Alexander Hamilton*, Vol. IV, 521

lution eventually to vindicate our rights."[14] In the letter Hamilton showed that war would dent the prosperity that America was currently enjoying and pointed out to Washington that, "It is unnecessary to urge the extreme precariousness of the events of War. The inference to be drawn is too manifest to escape your penetration. This Country ought not to set itself afloat upon an ocean so fluctuating so dangerous and so uncertain but in a case of absolute necessity."[15] Hamilton concluded the letter by asking Washington to withdraw his name from consideration for this envoy position. "I am not unapprised of what has been the byass of your opinion on the subject. I am well aware of all the collateral obstacles which exist and I assure you in the utmost sincerity that I shall be completely and intirely satisfied with the selection of another."[16] In closing, Hamilton proposed that John Jay be selected as the special envoy.

As soon as the Senate approved the appointment of John Jay as special envoy, Hamilton engaged himself in drafting his thoughts as to the appropriate content of Jay's instructions for the negotiations. As early as April 23 Hamilton sent to President Washington an outline of the subjects that Jay should endeavor to cover in his talks with the British Foreign Secretary, along with his ideas pertinent to each negotiation topic. At the top of the list, of course, was the matter of "Indemnification for the depredations upon our Commerces." Under this topic Hamilton anticipated a British argument to justify their actions based upon the nature of the cargoes being carried by the intercepted and confiscated ships. Hamilton offered the United States' position that "seizures and confiscations of ships belonging to neutral nations could be justified, only under the law of Nations, when such ships are carrying contraband materials, or in cases of actual blockade or embargoes, any materials." He offered a criterion for fair compensation based on the actual cost of the cargo, at point of exportation, plus a percentage increase for cost of shipment, loss of profit, etc., the percentage add-on to be negotiated. Hamilton promoted the position that once an accord was reached on compensation, the accord should be made permanent in the form of a treaty or other such document to guide both nations in the future.

---

14 Syrett, *The Papers of Alexander Hamilton*, Vol. XVI, 269; Hamilton, John C., *The Works of Alexander Hamilton*, Vol. IV, 523

15 Syrett, *The Papers of Alexander Hamilton*, Vol. XVI, 271; Hamilton, John C., *The Works of Alexander Hamilton*, Vol. IV, 524

16 Syrett, *The Papers of Alexander Hamilton*, Vol. XVI, 278

Hamilton suggested that the negotiations be expanded to include the resolution of unfulfilled articles from the 1783 Peace Treaty. Beyond this, Hamilton pressed for exploration of a formalized Commercial Treaty to include "most favored nation" status for the United States in British and Irish ports, opening of the British West Indies islands to trade in American bottoms, and the fixing of duties and tonnage taxes on British vessels in American ports — a point in which Great Britain had expressed interest in earlier negotiations. The official instructions given to John Jay were signed by Edmund Randolph and contained the same scope of topics as proposed by Alexander Hamilton.[17]

On May 6, prior to Jay's departure, Hamilton drafted a letter to Jay giving his viewpoints on the potential that could come of these negotiations. On the primary purpose of Jay's trip, Hamilton offered, "The object of indemnification for the depredations committed on our Trade in consequence of the instructions of the November 6 is very near the hearts and feelings of the people of this country. It would not answer in this particular to make any arrangement on the *mere appearance* of indemnification. I am however still of opinion that substantial indemnification on the principles of the instructions of January 8th may in the last resort be admissible."[18] In the ensuing paragraph, Hamilton gave away his priorities on the potential accomplishments of the upcoming negotiations. "What I have said goes upon the Idea of the affair of indemnification standing alone. If you can effect solid arrangements with regard to the points unexecuted of the treaty of peace, the question of indemnification may be managed with less rigor and may be still more laxly dealt with if a truly beneficial treaty of Commerce (embracing privileges in the West Indies Islands) can be established. It will be worth the while of the Government of this Country, in such case, to satisfy itself & its own citizens, who have suffered."[19]

Hamilton proceeded to give Jay information showing that Britain had a vital interest in continuing and expanding its trade relations with the United States — information that would prepare Jay to understand British interests even if they remained hidden for the purpose of negotiations. Ham-

---

17 Ibid., 319 - 323

18 Syrett, *The Papers of Alexander Hamilton*, Vol. XVI, 381-382; Hamilton, John C., *The Works of Alexander Hamilton, Vol. IV*, 552

19 Syrett, *The Papers of Alexander Hamilton*, Vol. XVI, 381-382; Hamilton, John C., *The Works of Alexander Hamilton, Vol. IV*, 550

ilton showed that the United States was in a commercial sense more important to Great Britain than any other country. The United States consumed £1,500,000 more of British products than any other nation. While trade levels with other nations were nearly stagnant, trade with America was rapidly increasing and would do so for many years. It would be quite unwise for Britain to hazard this important element of commerce by denying to the United States a formalized commercial relationship. Hamilton opened the issue of free commerce on the Mississippi River to Jay, but with caution. It would be helpful to have British assistance in permanently opening the Mississippi to the western territories for shipment of their produce to market. Hamilton cautioned Jay on this subject because negotiations were currently in progress between the United States and Spain on this topic and it would be unwise to strike an accord in London that conflicted with agreements previously reached with Spain.[20]

Jay arrived in London on June 12, 1794. At this time Lord Grenville was engaged in other pressing business relative to the ongoing war with France, so it was some time before Jay was able to present his credentials and to begin negotiations. The treaty that he did negotiate with the British foreign secretary aroused much adverse reaction in America and has been heatedly debated ever since. To Jay's credit he did succeed in defining a legitimate course of action for American merchants to recover their valid losses in the Caribbean privateering incidents relative to the November 8 Order in Council. He won British agreement to evacuate the posts in America's northwest. The matter of the definition of the boundary between the United States and Canada was slightly redefined with respect to that portion of the boundary running along western New York. However, trading rights were made reciprocal so that each nation could trade on any part of each lake.[21]

He won access for American ships to trading privileges in the British West Indies and East Indies as well. The Senate subsequently voted to reject the West Indies trade, however, because it contained a provision that prohibited the United States from the re-exportation of any West Indian product except rum. It was feared that a prohibition on the re-exportation of West Indian cotton would likewise prejudice the export of American cotton.

---

20 Syrett, *The Papers of Alexander Hamilton*, Vol. XVI, 383 - 385
21 Elkins & McKitrick, *The Age of Federalism*, 408 - 410

Jay failed to obtain any concession from the British on their carrying off of Negro slaves following their evacuation after the Revolution.[22] This failure was felt and strongly reacted to in the South where it was perceived as another attempt by Federalists to undermine and eventually to destroy the slave trade. The issue of pre-war debts owed to British merchants was assigned to a five-man commission to decide on a case-by-case basis.

Jay had acquiesced in the matters pertaining to the British system of maritime law. The Treaty allowed the continued practice of British ships taking property from the ships of neutral nations. The fact that this agreement had its only effect only during the existing British-French war did little to assuage America's sense of damaged sovereignty. The reality was, however, that at that time Britain enjoyed unchallenged mastery of the sea and America had no respectable naval force. It made more sense to Jay to concentrate on those articles of the Treaty that he had a fair chance of prevailing over.

Jay was unable to get Grenville to agree to an article that prohibited either power from influencing Indians within the territory of the other power. In this event, however, General Wayne had solved the issue by his decisive defeat of the Indians at Fallen Timbers.[23]

It must be accredited to Jay that he steadfastly denied Grenville's insistence that Britain be granted a relief from the 1783 boundary and to allow them direct access to the navigable headwaters of the Mississippi River. The Peace Treaty proclaimed that mutual use was to be enjoyed of the Mississippi, from its source to the mouth. Britain claimed that the intent of the Treaty was to define the international boundary so as to include the headwaters of this important waterway in Canadian territory. Jay refused to accept this reasoning, stating that the Treaty was clear on the location of the boundary and that Britain was free to use the river as detailed by the Treaty.[24]

It remains an open question whether another person could have negotiated a better treaty with Grenville under the conditions prevailing in 1794. There is a temptation to think that the quick wit and analytical reasoning of Alexander Hamilton might have leveraged some additional advantages in the negotiations. Hamilton had been so determined that West Indies trade must be a part of any commercial treaty that he likely would have anticipated the Senate's objection to the re-exportation prohibition and perhaps been able

---

22 *American State Papers: Foreign Relations*, Vol. I, 486 - 487
23 Bemis, *Jay's Treaty*, 361 - 362
24 Ibid., 329 - 331

to negotiate definitions of that prohibition that would have been acceptable to the Senate. It is not altogether certain that the opponents of Hamilton's appointment as special envoy for this negotiation did not, in fact, provide a substantial disservice to the country by their opposition.

Historians generally agree that Jay's Treaty was not a particularly advantageous one for the United States. Henry Adams, a renowned American historian, said that, "There has been no moment since 1810 when the United States would have hesitated to prefer war rather than peace on such terms."[25] While that may have been true after 1810, in 1794 the United States was not in a position to conduct war with a power like Great Britain. The greatest needs America had at that time were to be internationally respected as a neutral power, to secure formalized trade relations, particularly with England, and to secure its sovereignty over its western territory to make it more attractive and secure to settlers.

As a minimum accomplishment, Jay's Treaty extended the period of peace that allowed the American political and economic system to solidify and to mature; it provided a formalized commercial relationship with Great Britain, and won the British withdrawal from the western territory.

Continued negotiation with the Indians produced the Greenville Treaty of 1795 that ceded to the United States the land constituting most of the present State of Ohio. The Indians retained a strip of land on the shore of Lake Erie from the Maumee to the Cuyahoga River. Over the succeeding fifteen years from the Greenville Treaty, the Indians were progressively displaced, by treaty, from nearly all of the Northwest Territory, opening the lands of Indiana, Illinois, Wisconsin and Michigan to settlement by the white man.[26]

The Catholic monarchy of Spain found itself increasingly uncomfortable with its interests in the New World. In Europe, the successes of France and the unsteady alliance with England caused Spain to reassess its alliances and to seek a means of realigning itself with France. When Spain learned that the United States was sending a special envoy to London, the chief minister, Manuel de Godoy, feared that a treaty between England and the United States might include a consideration unfavorable to her possession of Louisiana. Godoy decided that its alliance with Britain was as much a cause for fear as was its current enmity with France. It was time to reinstate its tra-

---

25 Ibid., 370
26 Ibid., 361

ditional alliance with France and to reach an accord with the United States over the Mississippi River. In response to a request from Spain, Washington sent Thomas Pinckney to Madrid from England to conduct negotiations on a treaty to resolve the differences between Spain and the United States over the free use of the Mississippi. Godoy agreed to give the United States the right of navigation of the River and tariff free storage of farm produce in New Orleans. Pinckney agreed to this and the Treaty of San Lorenzo was signed on October 27, 1795.[27]

With the opening of the Mississippi River to commerce, the British evacuation of the forts in the northwest by Jay's Treaty and the pacifying of the Indians by Anthony Wayne, the American West was fully opened to settlement. Further, the war in Europe produced a boon market for American shipbuilding and for farm produce. Migrations to America and to the excellent farming country west of the Appalachians were to provide this needed food source as the population of these territories rose rapidly. The political settlements of 1794 and 1795 produced an explosive growth in the American economy that was supported by the Hamiltonian financial systems put in place Congress several years earlier.[28]

To maintain the country's policy of neutrality and to complement the Jay Treaty made with England, Washington set out to negotiate a new treaty with France. American objectives in this treaty were to negotiate an end to attacks on American shipping by French privateers and to seek compensation for the justifiable losses previously sustained by America's commercial fleet. To this end Washington sent James Monroe, an avowed Republican and staunch supporter of improved Franco-American relations. The French National Convention on August 14, 1794 belatedly received Monroe. In his remarks during his reception Monroe lost the restraint which the decorum of his office demanded and praised the valor of the French army in their battle with Great Britain. Monroe seemed to have forgotten that his diplomatic colleague, John Jay was, at that moment, in Great Britain on a mission very similar to his own. Upon receiving Monroe's report on his reception, Washington directed Secretary of State, Edmund Randolph, to issue a reprimand to Monroe to recompose himself, to limit his personal enthusiasm for the French Government and to recall that, as his instructions directed him, he

27 Elkins & McKitrick, *Age of Federalism*, 440
28 Ibid., 432

was to always regard the best interest of his country with regard to all foreign countries.[29]

Monroe seemed to have forgotten or disregarded his instructions from Edmund Randolph when he anxiously gave to the Committee of Public Safety information that indicated that American relations with England and Spain were at low ebb. He reported to Randolph, "Finding that my idea of our situation with Britain and Spain was correct, I was extremely happy that I had given that representation of it."[30] He went on in the same letter to Randolph to report that he "told them I had received a dispatch from you since our last conference, and that our dilemma with those two Powers was even more critical than I had before intimated." It would seem that Monroe assumed it to be his duty to establish as intimate relations with France as possible, to the exclusion, if necessary, of all other powers. Nothing in his formal instructions from Randolph or subsequent admonitions from Randolph could have encouraged Monroe to this position. He had to have been certain of his moral justification to stray so far from his instructions and convinced that events in the near future would vindicate his judgment to have taken such steps as these. Subsequent events proved Monroe wrong on both counts. In the end he embarrassed his government to the extent that subsequent United States ministers to France were rejected. Strained diplomatic relations and the incompetence of Monroe's ministry moved the United States and France to the brink of war with one another.

Monroe's ministry to France ended in abject failure when, on numerous occasions, Monroe displayed an unbridled favoritism for France's interests, even over the interests of the United States. At Washington's direction, Monroe was recalled.[31]

Monroe's replacement was Charles Cotesworth Pinckney, a Federalist from South Carolina. Pinckney was chosen because of his friendliness toward France and in the hopes that his higher standards of professionalism would be recognized and appreciated by the French and that, in an improved atmosphere of diplomatic relationship, Franco-American relations would be improved. However, the French rejected Pinckney and expelled him from

29 Ibid., 498 - 499
30 *American State Papers: Foreign Relation*, Vol. I, 688
31 Elkins & McKitrick, *Age of Federalism*, 498 - 503

their country. The French recalled their minister Pierre Adet and for a while there were no diplomatic relations between France and the United States.[32]

The third United States presidential election was scheduled for December of 1796. Early that year Washington had determined that his service to his country was at an end. He was sixty-four years of age, had spent a large portion of his life in the service of his country and yearned for the tranquil life at Mt. Vernon. Washington had been the country's chief executive for eight years, during which time a degree of political stability had been achieved. Washington listed among his reasons for seeking retirement his "disinclination to be longer buffitted [sic] in the public prints by a set of infamous scribblers." He judged that it was time for other political leaders to be selected. President Washington met with Alexander Hamilton and asked for his assistance in preparing a farewell address as a way of publicly stating that he was making himself ineligible for re-election. Hamilton acceded to this request, as he had all of Washington's requests since his years as aide-de-camp. On May 15, Washington sent Hamilton a first draft of his address consisting of an earlier draft by James Madison, augmented with some notes of his own. Hamilton was offered the option to use this first draft as a basis or to draft an entirely new address. Hamilton did both. Both drafts were sent to Washington by July 30. Of the two, Washington chose the one Hamilton had originated.[33] Washington contacted the publisher of the Claypoole's *American Daily Advertiser* to have his Farewell Address included in the September 19, 1796 issue.[34]

In the Address, Washington described "Unity of Government" as the principal pillar upon which stands the independence enjoyed by the people. Beware, he cautioned, of any and all attacks on that unity, domestic as well as foreign. "Efforts would be made, various artifices employed to weaken your conviction of the importance of our unity. Watch for its preservation with jealous anxiety."[35]

Washington advised the country on the importance of public credit. "One method of preserving it is to use it as sparingly as possible.[36] On international relations, Washington's guideline was, "Observe good faith and

32 Ibid., 510

33 Syrett, *The Papers of Alexander Hamilton*, Vol. XX, 169 - 170

34 Syrett, *The papers of Alexander Hamilton, Vol. XX,* 239

35 Fitzpatrick, *Writings of George Washington,* Vol. 35, 218 - 219

36 Ibid., 230

justice tow(ar)ds all Nations. Cultivate peace and harmony with all. In the execution of such a plan nothing is more essential than that permanent in-veterate antipathies against particular Nations and passionate attachments for others should be excluded."[37] He also said,

> Of all dispositions and habits, which lead to political prosperity, re-ligion and morality are indispensable supports. In vain would men claim the tribute of Patriotism, who shall labor to subvert the great Pillars of human happiness, these firmest props of the duties of Man and citizens... Whatever may be conceded to the influence of refined education on minds of peculiar structure, reason and experience both forbid us to expect that National morality can prevail in exclusion of religious principle.[38]

As Washington's Vice President for two terms, John Adams was clearly his heir apparent. The Republicans were anxious to promote the name of Thomas Jefferson as his opponent. Thomas Jefferson was a more reluctant candidate. He was not at all sure that he wished to follow directly behind George Washington as the country's chief Executive. Since his early tenure as minister to France, Jefferson had been an outspoken friend to Revolution-ary France. In 1796 the uncertainties and instabilities in the French Revolu-tionary government and its roughshod treatment of America in its foreign policies must have exerted a restraint to any enthusiasm Jefferson may have had for the office of President. The success of the *Jay Treaty* had improved commerce with Great Britain and, along with the *San Lorenzo Treaty*, had thrown open the doors to western expansion. It was clear that the best thing the next President could do was to force France's hand in fair treatment of American merchant shipping and to force fair compensation to American merchants for losses suffered at the hands of the French fleet. With his his-tory of softness for France, Jefferson was poorly positioned to wrest these concessions from them.[39]

Although the final vote tally would not be known until February 1797, it became accepted knowledge in Philadelphia, in early December 1796, that John Adams would be the new President and Thomas Jefferson the Vice President. Adams received seventy-one electoral votes; Jefferson won the of-fice of Vice President with just three fewer votes.[40]

---

37 Ibid., 231
38 Ibid., 229
39 Elkins & McKitrick, *The Age of Federalism*, 537 - 546
40 Elkins & McKitrick, *The Age of Federalism*, 528

Of the affairs of state that Adams inherited from the Washington admin-istration, the most pressing problem was very clearly that of the relationship with France. The French were outraged at the provisions of the American *Jay Treaty* with Great Britain although the provisions of France's 1778 Treaty with America were explicitly protected in it. Despite the provisions encour-aging free trade in the 1778 Treaty between the United States and France, France had encouraged their privateers to confiscate the cargo of neutral ships bound for enemy ports ever since the outbreak of hostilities in Europe in 1793.[41]

On January 27 of 1797 Alexander Hamilton published a series of articles in the *Gazette of the United States* and the *Philadelphia Daily Advertiser*, entitled *Warning No. I through VI*, in which he addressed various aspects of the French disruption of American shipping. In his *Warning No. IV*, Hamilton cited the French justification of their abuse of neutral shipping in which they said that they had treated American shipping no more harshly than had the British prior to the implementation of the *Jay Treaty*. Hamilton responded to this argument with clear and incisive logic,

> If this apology were founded in fact it would still be a miserable sub-terfuge. For what excuse is it to France, or what consolation to us, that she, our boasted friend and benefactress, treats us only not worse, than a Power which is stigmatized as an envious rival and an implacable foe?[42]

When John Adams had been in office no longer than three weeks, he received notification that the French had refused to receive Charles Cotes-worth Pinckney. On the strength of this insult to American sovereignty, Ad-ams issued a recall to Congress on March 15, 1797, requiring Congress to con-vene on May 15. On May 16 President Adams delivered a speech to Congress in which he censured the French for their treatment of Pinckney, claiming they showed the ultimate disrespect to America by their treatment of its ap-pointed diplomat.[43]

Adams did gain Congressional support for an incremental increase in naval power to the extent of authorizing the completion of three frigates that were already being built. Adams named a three-man commission, El-bridge Gerry, Charles Cotesworth Pinckney and John Marshall, to travel to

---

41 Elkins & McKitrick, *The Age of Federalism*, 529, 537 -538

42 Syrett, *The Papers of Alexander Hamilton*, Vol. XX, 524; Lodge, Henry C., *The Works of Alexander Hamilton*, Vol. VI, 245

43 Elkins & McKitrick, *The Age of Federalism*, 550 - 551

France in an effort to re-establish diplomatic relations with that country. The instructions given the trio before their departure were constructive and conservative. Similar to the instructions given to John Jay in preparation for his negotiations with the British, this commission's brief instructed them to work for reparation of American losses at the hands of the French privateers but to avoid directly blaming the French government and to "terminate our differences in such a manner, as with out referring to the merits of our respective complaints and pretensions, may be the best calculated to produce mutual satisfaction and good understanding."[44]

By the time the American commission arrived in France, the ruling oligarchy, the French Directory, had replaced foreign minister Charles Delacroix, who had dealt so harshly with Pinckney, with Charles Maurice Tallyrand.[45] Tallyrand was a defrocked bishop in the Roman Church and saw in the French Revolution an opportunity for personal career growth and the accumulation of wealth through graft.

During May 1797 Vice President Thomas Jefferson had begun unofficial and personal meetings with Alexandre Hauterive, the former French consul at New York, and with Consul General Letombe, encouraging the following approach to the Adams administration. "Mr. Adams is vain, suspicious, and stubborn, of an excessive self-regard, taking counsel with nobody....But his presidency will only last five years; he is only President by three votes and the system of the United States will change with him." In regard to Adams's American envoys, he advised that France "should receive them and hear them, drag out the negotiations at length and mollify them by the urbanity of the proceedings."[46] Had this subterfuge of Jefferson's been public knowledge at the time it most likely would have brought about an end to his political career.

When Gerry, Pinckney and Marshall arrived in Paris in October 1797, they were optimistic that their mission held a strong likelihood of success. After some understandable delays, the commissioners gained access to Tallyrand, who accepted their credentials. Tallyrand informed the Americans that he was currently preparing a report for the Directory "relative to the situation of the United States with regard to France." In four or five days

44 *American State Papers: Foreign Relations*, Vol. II, 157: Elkins & McKitrick, *Age of Federalism*, 562 - 563
45 Elkins & McKitrick, *Age of Federalism*, 562
46 Ibid., 566

the report would have been given to the Directory, at which time Tallyrand would receive instructions for what was to follow. Beginning in mid-October, the American envoy team was visited by unofficial representatives of the French government who shrouded their identities in secrecy, referring to themselves only as Mr. X, Y and Z. These men informed Pinckney, Gerry and Marshall that the Directory had been offended at the remarks made by President Adams in his May 16 address to Congress. The reparations required by the Directory for these offensive remarks included an apology, a "douceur" amounting to fifty thousand pounds sterling to be used as pocket money by the Directory, and a sizable loan to the French government by the United States. They insisted that Tallyrand would not be authorized to negotiate with them until this matter of affront was resolved. In the end Charles Pinckney and John Marshall were resigned that the negotiations with France would not proceed and decided to return to America, ostensibly to refer the matter of reparations to the government. Elbridge Gerry thought further progress was possible and remained in France for some time until ordered by his government to return to America.[47]

Early in March the first of the dispatches sent by the commissioners arrived in Philadelphia. It immediately became clear that the diplomatic mission to France had so far failed even to gain recognition of the special envoys President Adams had sent. It was also learned that the French Executive Directory had issued a new and sweeping proclamation that any neutral vessel carrying anything of English manufacture, or manufactured in any English possession, was declared to be good prize. The new decree also stated that French ports would be closed to any neutral ship that had visited any English port. This decree obviously affected all American ships since they all carried some British product. All American ships were subject to seizure and confiscation by the French.[48]

It was clear to President Adams, even before the remaining documents had been decoded, that this French action was unacceptable. However, what his appropriate reaction should be was anything but clear. The Republican stance in America remained as firmly in support of France as ever. Jefferson had set the standard for Republican thinking when he had said, "war would be the ultimate calamity, to be avoided at almost any cost."[49]

---

47 Ibid., 569 - 580
48 Ibid., 582
49 Ibid., 583

Alexander Hamilton communicated in a letter to Secretary of War James McHenry a clear and cogent plan for dealing with the new crisis. He proposed a course of action of "A mitigated hostility," arguing that it remained important to keep the door open for further negotiation in case the French chose a moderate course. Hamilton recognized that a sizable faction in the country would oppose open hostility in any event and that there was little of commercial value to the United States to be gained through war with France, so that declaring such a war did not make sense. He recommended leaving one or more of the commissioners in Europe, perhaps in Holland, to be available to meet any opportunity for negotiation.[50]

Hamilton proposed a course of action that included an immediate increase in naval power, authorizing merchant vessels to equip themselves for defense against French privateers, expediting the completion of the frigates then under construction and acquiring a number of sloops of war carrying between ten and twenty guns apiece. To prepare the country for defense against a possible French invasion, Hamilton proposed forming a standing army of 20,000 men, with an additional 30,000 on stand-by status. He recommended an increase of the tax base and the authorization of a loan to finance the military measures he proposed. He further recommended that the Executive communicate the nature of the crisis "to Congress with *manly* but *calm* and *sedate* firmness & without strut."[51] The Executive should maintain the hope that continuing discussion with France might yield some positive results and should be continued. Congress should be advised that the French, in their seizures of American shipping had violated the Treaty of 1778 and the United States should, accordingly, consider that treaty, for the time being, to be suspended.[52]

McHenry paraphrased Hamilton's advice and presented it to Adams. The ideas were eventually accepted by the President and formed the basis of the policy he chose to follow. On March 19 President Adams transmitted to Congress a memorandum that had been drafted for him by Oliver Wolcott announcing the failure of the three-man commission intended to resolve the differences that existed with France. He said, "It is incumbent on me to declare that I perceive no ground of expectation that the objects of their mission can be accomplished on terms compatible with the safety, the honor,

---

50 Ibid., 584
51 Syrett, *The Papers of Alexander Hamilton*, Vol. XXI, 344
52 Ibid., 341 - 346

or the essential interests of the nation."[53] Adams requested Congress for authorization and funding to strengthen the Navy, fortify the nation's defenses and to establish foundries and other industry for the manufacture of military supplies.

In the message Wolcott and Adams fairly captured Hamilton's recommended presentation style of *manly, calm* and *sedate*. Still, Jefferson, caught up in the unalterable emotional alliance with France, called it an "insane message." He used every means and tactic to cause delay in those actions Adams had hoped would be prompt and unanimous. On April 2, Congress formally requested to see the documents sent by the trio of American envoys to France. Although he feared a possible extreme reaction to the treatment received by the American envoys, President Adams acceded to the request. After Congress had had an opportunity to digest the detailed documents of the exchange with France, the Republican opposition to Adams's recommendations collapsed. Congress essentially authorized everything that President Adams had requested. Expedition of the completion of the frigates under construction was authorized; twelve sloops of war were funded along with fifteen additional ships of war. Funds were authorized to fortify the harbors and to establish foundries for the production of cannon. Trade with France was frozen by an embargo and all treaties with France were annulled. American warships were authorized to use force to resist the seizure of American merchant vessels and to forcefully reclaim any American vessels already taken.[54]

President Adams recalled George Washington to active command as Commanding General of all of America's armies. On May 19 Alexander Hamilton wrote to Washington to encourage him to accept the certain offer of the primary command position, saying, "There is no certain great probability that we may have to enter into a very serious struggle with France; and it is more certain that the powerful faction which has for years opposed the government is determined to go every length with France....You ought also to be aware, my Dear Sir, that in the event of an open rupture with France, the public voice will again call you to command the armies of your Country...yet

---

53 *American State Papers, Foreign Relations*: Vol. II, 152
54 Elkins & McKitrick, *Age of Federalism*, 586 - 590

it is the opinion of all those with whom I converse that you will be compelled to make the sacrifice."[55]

Washington's response was an agreement with the seriousness of the situation with France and a willingness to accede to the call of the country. On a personal note, Washington said, "I should like, precisely, to know whether you would be disposed to take an active part, if arms are to be resorted to."[56]

Hamilton responded in respect to Washington's question, "If I am invited to a station in which the services I may render may be proportioned to the sacrifice I am to make — I shall be willing to go into the army."[57]

As Washington's first order of business, President Adams directed that he was to recommend the names of the three men directly under his command who were to be commissioned at the rank of Major General. There had already been considerable controversy over this list, principally because John Adams, in his detestation and perhaps some fear of the man, did not want the name of Alexander Hamilton to appear on this list. Despite Adams's wishes, the three men nominated for the rank of Major General were Charles Cotesworth Pinckney, Henry Knox and Alexander Hamilton. These three men were particularly important because Washington's age and physical condition would permit him to be little more than a figurehead. Of these candidates, the man who would be named as the first Major General would become the Inspector General and would, in fact, assume the role of the commander of the armies.[58]

To the idea of Alexander Hamilton as the second man, Adams said, "Oh no, it is not his turn by a great deal."[59] Washington took matters into his own hand and sent Adams a letter at his home at Quincy, Massachusetts on October 8. "In the arrangements made by me with the Secretary of War, the three Major Generals stand, Hamilton, Pinckney and Knox...but you have been pleased to order the last to be first and the first to be last."[60] Adams replied to Washington that he supposed the Commander-in-Chief had been

55 Syrett, *The Papers of Alexander Hamilton*, Vol. XXI, 466 - 468; Hamilton, John C., *The Works of Alexander Hamilton, Vol. VVI*, 290
56 Syrett, *The Papers of Alexander Hamilton*, Vol. XXI, 470-474
57 Syrett, *The Papers of Alexander Hamilton*, Vol. XXI, 479; Hamilton, John C., *The Works of Alexander Hamilton, Vol. VI*, 294
58 Elkins & McKitrick, *Age of Federalism*, 604
59 Ibid., 603
60 Fitzpatrick, *Writings of George Washington*, Vol. 36, 453 - 462

informed of the commissions and said that any further controversies, "will of course, be submitted to you...and if, after all, any one should be so obstinate as to appeal to me, from the judgment of the Commander-in-Chief, I was determined to confirm that judgment." [61] President Adams lost the exchange and, in his mind, some of his dignity in the process.

With his normal single-mindedness, Hamilton flung himself into the task of Inspector General. During November and December he worked in Philadelphia, side by side with General Washington, planning the new American army. General Washington had once again made a splendid appearance when he returned to Philadelphia, greeted by government dignitaries and citizens alike. For five weeks Washington, Hamilton, Pinckney and McHenry worked closely to define the structure of the army and its organization, reviewing candidate commanders for all echelons and dividing functional responsibilities between Major General Hamilton and Major General Charles Cotesworth Pinckney.

Alexander Hamilton proved to be a master administrator. He laid out the organization of the army in minute detail. He specified the rank and number of officers and men to constitute each organizational echelon. He laid out details of their respective uniforms, headpieces and boots. He designed the housing for officers and men in the field. He generated texts on drills to be used in the training of soldiers; he specified the etiquette to be followed in addressing superiors and inferiors. He enlisted the help of German-born John De Barth Wallbach to evaluate the cavalry systems used by England, France and Prussia to determine which would best serve America's needs.[62]

One of Hamilton favorite ideas was the establishment of a military academy. Hamilton envisioned the curriculum at the military academy as consisting of five separate schools of "Fundamental School (Military Science), Engineering and Artillerists, Cavalry, Infantry and the Navy. He went so far as to outline the curriculum for each of the schools; he envisioned that each Cadet would study for two years in the Fundamental School to gain a solid background in tactics, surveying and topography along with introductory mathematics and engineering courses. The second two years of a Cadet's career at the academy would be focused in one of the remaining four schools to provide a specialty in Engineering, Cavalry, Infantry or the Navy. Hamilton

---

61 Taylor, R., *Papers of John Adams*, Vol. VIII, Harvard University Press, Cambridge, 1977, 600 - 601

62 Syrett, *The Papers of Alexander Hamilton*, Vol. XXIII, 493; Vol. XXIV, 143-153

and James McHenry proposed to the House of Representatives the establishment of such a Military Academy, and the idea eventually came to fruition with the establishment of the academy at West Point — under the unlikely presidency of Thomas Jefferson.[63]

Congress approved the establishment of a new cabinet position, Secretary of the Navy, during the summer of 1798. Benjamin Stoddert became the country's first Secretary of the Navy on June 24, 1798. Stoddert had been a successful shipping merchant in Maryland and enjoyed the reputation of being a very capable man with sound judgment. In June and July the three frigates, the *Constellation*, the *United States* and the *Constitution*, became operational. These frigates, sporting forty-four guns, proved to be more than a match for any ship having fewer than sixty-four guns. In legislative reaction to the XYZ disclosures, Congress had authorized not only the completion of these frigates but also the construction of an additional three. They also approved the acquisition by gift or purchase of six more plus the acquisition of forty more ships, including sloops, brigs, schooners and galleys.[64]

Emboldened by America's lack of naval power, French cruisers had taken to patrolling US territorial waters looking for unarmed merchant shipping. When the first three frigates became operational and as a significant number of merchant ships armed themselves, the business of piracy in American waters would soon become prohibitively expensive for the French. With the addition of a growing number of war ships available to him, Stoddert distributed the new fleet strategically throughout the Caribbean to thwart the French privateering raids on American commercial shipping. Very soon the success of the American navy in stopping seizures by the French began to be reflected by declining insurance rates and by a dramatic increase in the number of American merchant vessels willing to chance the Caribbean waters that had been so hazardous just a year or two earlier.[65]

In his characteristically solitary style, Adams decided that another attempt at diplomacy with the French was worthwhile and, without advising anyone or consulting with his cabinet, he took the decisive, if controversial,

63 Syrett, *The Papers of Alexander Hamilton*, Vol. XXIV, 69 — 75; Chernow, *Alexander Hamilton*, 565
64 Elkins & McKitrick, *Age of Federalism*, 644 - 645
65 Ibid., 644 - 647

step of nominating William Vans Murray, the current American minister at The Hague, as his new minister plenipotentiary to France.[66]

The Senate countered Adams's appointment by raising the idea of creating a commission to include Murray along with other, more seasoned diplomats. Before this idea could be further advanced, President Adams changed his mind once again and proposed a three-man commission consisting of Murray, Oliver Ellsworth of Connecticut, then Chief Justice of the Supreme Court, and Patrick Henry of Virginia. The Senate confirmed this commission on February 27, 1799. Before this envoy team could be sent to France, Patrick Henry declined his appointment to the commission on the basis of advanced age and poor health. Adams named Governor William R. Davie of North Carolina as his replacement. The three ministers sailed aboard the *United States* about November 1, 1799.[67]

The American ministers met Napoleon Bonaparte on March 8, 1800 and formal negotiations began shortly thereafter. After months of difficult negotiations, a compromise agreement was reached that contained a provision for a lasting peace between the countries, the restoration of public ships that had not yet been condemned, debt recovery, agreements for the prevention of any further illegal seizure and confiscation of ships and cargoes and the establishment of procedures for the resolution of disputes in cases of any future capture. The French were given most of the port privileges they had enjoyed as part of the Treaty of 1778. There was an establishment of mutual most-favored nation status in the alignment of import duties. It was concluded that the agreements reached would be called a "convention" as opposed to a treaty. That document of agreement was signed at *Mortefontaine*, Joseph Bonaparte's country estate, on October 3, 1800.[68]

President Adams received copies of this Convention on December 11 and submitted it to the Senate on December 16. The Senate gave a majority vote to ratify the Convention but was well short of the two-thirds needed for ratification. Alexander Hamilton, convinced that Thomas Jefferson would eventually win the Presidency, advised his friends in the Senate that it would be better to ratify the Convention in its imperfect state than to leave it to a "Jacobin Administration" to negotiate a worse agreement. A second vote

66 McCullough, *John Adams*, 523
67 Elkins & McKitrick, *The Age of Federalism*, 618 — 619, 639
68 *American State Papers: Foreign Relations*, Vol. II, 339 - 343

on February 3, 1801 ratified the Convention with an amendment limiting its term to eight years.[69]

George Washington died on December 14, 1799 from a fever he contracted following exposure to a snowstorm. In his will Washington specified that, upon the death of his wife Martha, his slaves were to be freed; and he made provisions for those slaves who were either too young or too old to provide for themselves. Washington was the only president of the nine who owned slaves to have set all of them free.[70]

The death of George Washington, in confluence with the Convention with France, spelled the end of the army that Alexander Hamilton was attempting to build and organize. In February 1800 Congress terminated enlistments in the army, signaling the end of Hamilton's efforts to construct a homeland defense force. News was received from France that Napoleon had designated himself as his country's first Consul, ridding France of the tyranny of the Directory. This move by Napoleon ended the French Revolution and, with it, America's perceived need to maintain a standing army. This decision was called into question twelve short years later, with the sacking and burning of the new capital city in Washington, DC by the British. On May 22 Hamilton reviewed his troops in a final ceremony before the army was disbanded in June. Early in July Hamilton closed his New York headquarters and put a permanent end to his military career. He was, ever after, referred to by his friends as General Hamilton.[71]

69 Elkins & McKitrick, *The Age of Federalism*, 687
70 Ford, W. C. (ed.), *The Writings of George Washington*, Vol. XIV, G. T. Putnam's & Sons, New York, 1893, 245-267, 271-298
71 Adams, A., *New Letters of Abigail Adams*, Greenwood Press, Westport Conn.,252

CHAPTER 9. THE FINAL YEARS

At the time that the government was relocating to its permanent seat in Washington, DC in 1800, the pressing issue commanding attention was the upcoming fourth election of the President and Vice President. The Federalists were promoting the re-election of John Adams; they favored the Southerner Charles Cotesworth Pinckney for Vice President. The Republican Party was overwhelmingly supportive of Thomas Jefferson for President and Aaron Burr as Vice President. Burr's candidacy was based on his having delivered a Republican majority in the New York legislature, assuring the appointment of Republican electors. At that time most states selected their electors through their legislature; only Rhode Island, Maryland, Virginia, North Carolina and Kentucky had a form of popular election of electors.

Among the Federalists there was a burning sense of dissatisfaction with the first Adams administration. His go-it-alone approach had bred a feeling of disenfranchisement among many good and capable men in the cabinet and in the Congress, as their ideas and council had so often been disregarded. His handling of the crisis with France had alienated more people than it won over; while some did admire him for avoiding war with France, many others felt he was far too liberal with the French government, given their abusive treatment of the American ministers.

On the issue of defensive preparations for the potential armed conflict with France, Adams supported the establishment of a strong navy to combat the French privateers and to provide protection for convoys of merchant vessels. Adams, however, never supported the formation of a standing army to protect against possible French aggression. He felt coerced into the establishment of the army with Washington as its Commander-in-Chief and was humiliated by being forced to name Alexander Hamilton as Inspector General, second in command to George Washington. Adams's longtime distrust and dislike for Hamilton was manifest when Adams failed to lend his support to Hamilton's efforts to organize and enlist the authorized force. Without presidential support, funds were not made available as required by the army; as a result the soldiers and officers went unpaid for months at a time, reminiscent of the Revolutionary War period. The rate of enlistments never approached the anticipated rates; again, the prestige of the presidency could have been employed to encourage enlistments but it was not. When General Washington died suddenly in late 1799, it might have been expected that Hamilton would have been promoted and raised to the post of Commander-in-Chief, but this, too, failed to materialize.

These negative aspects of John Adams's first term of office combined to limit Federalist support for his re-election. Oliver Wolcott, who had replaced Hamilton as Secretary of the Treasury in 1795, confirmed to Alexander Hamilton, "the poor old Man is sufficiently successful in undermining his own credit and influence."[1] Alexander Hamilton suffered his own quandary. He, more than any other individual with the possible exception of George Washington, had been responsible for the formation of Federalism; he had been the key architect in building the federal structure of government during Washington's administration, and had been a major contributor to the foreign policy that was based on cordial relations with all foreign countries, entertaining commercial interaction with all but no entangling alliances with any. Hamilton had influenced the instructions given to John Jay to negotiate a treaty with Great Britain and broadly promoted the ratification of the treaty he brought home that was so important in opening up the western territory to expansion. Hamilton was concerned that the Republicans would undo many of the institutions that he and his colleagues in the Washington administration had successfully implanted in the government. On a personal level, Alexander Hamilton had suffered affronts by John Adams, who characterized him as pandering to the moneymen and who had derogated his

---

1 Syrett, *The Papers of Alexander Hamilton*, Vol. XXV, 107

foreign birth and the meanness of his heritage. Adams's open resistance to the appointment of Hamilton as second in command to Washington struck at Hamilton's capability, dedication and personal dignity.

Alexander Hamilton was desperate. If the Republicans were successful in their election of Thomas Jefferson as Chief Executive, as seemed probable in the summer and fall of 1800, Hamilton could foresee a decentralization of the power of the central government. A shift of power from the federal government to the states would threaten the system of taxation he had worked to create, and would alter the government oversight of foreign commerce that had served the national interest to one focused more on the parochial interests of individual states. More importantly, Hamilton viewed the decentralization of power as a threat to the popular faith in national sovereignty; those state sovereignty advocates that still existed in Congress would be quick to exploit that opportunity. Hamilton concluded, after consultation with Federalist leaders across the country, that the best hope of preserving Federalist domination of the executive would be to shift Federalist support from Adams to General Pinckney. Hamilton hoped that support for Pinckney could be encouraged, either through the first or second vote of a sufficient number of electors, to give him the Presidency.[2]

This was indubitably Hamilton's thinking as early as the spring of 1800. He thought that the best thing he could do for the Federalists and for General Pinckney was to circulate a letter critical of John Adams and his shortcomings as President. He aired this thought with a number of friends and advisers. In September, Oliver Wolcott agreed, and advised Hamilton that he believed that it is "perfectly proper & a duty to make known those defects & errors which disqualify Mr. Adams for the great trust with which he is now invested."[3] He went on, however, to caution Hamilton against publishing any such letter under his own name.[4]

Unfortunately, Hamilton was not much known for taking the advice of friends. He had a burning desire to reverse the tide of Republican supremacy, and by sharing his private views of Adams as president with selected electors and friends of electors he hoped to withhold from Adams enough votes to enable Pinckney to win. It had been Hamilton's plan from the start to circulate his letter only to those interested and influential readers in South Carolina.

2 Chernow, *Alexander Hamilton*, 616
3 Syrett, *The Papers of Alexander Hamilton*, Vol. XXV, 104
4 Ibid., 106

There was no need to address the attributes of Pinckney that were so well known to Hamilton's intended audience. The letter that Hamilton authored was typically lengthy, devoted nearly in its entirety to a litany of examples and characteristics intended to persuade that Adams was not a suitable candidate to represent the Federalists as the Chief Executive. "Not denying to Mr. Adams patriotism, integrity, and even talents of a certain kind, I should be deficient in candor were I to conceal the conviction that he does not possess the talents adapted to the *Administration of* Government, and that there are great and intrinsic defects in his character which unfit him for the office of Chief Magistrate."[5]

This was undoubtedly the poorest and the most ill-advised letter that Alexander Hamilton ever wrote. Gone was the incisive analytical reasoning which is so characteristic of his literary style. Hamilton had been well advised by friends not to publish anything under his own name for fear of the advantage the opposition would take from it. It is difficult to imagine the constructive good that Hamilton supposed that he, the Federalists, or General Pinckney would realize from the letter.

When it reached the public press, Hamilton's *Letter* was a shock to the political apparatus of the Federalists and Republicans alike. The effect on the Federalists was to split that camp into separate and distinct sides, one supporting John Adams, the other General Pinckney. The Republicans were overjoyed. Their archenemy, Alexander Hamilton, had, in practical terms, assured Thomas Jefferson of victory and had destroyed his own political life in the process.

When the electoral votes were finally tallied, Jefferson and Burr were tied with 73 votes apiece. John Adams had 65 votes and General Pinckney was one behind Adams with 64 votes.[6] According to the Constitution, the tie between Jefferson and Burr would be resolved by the House of Representatives. Each state would have one vote that was to be determined by the majority of votes of the representatives of that state. The man having a majority of the state's votes was to be President; the other man would be Vice President. Voting began in Congress on February 11, 1801.[7]

---

5 Syrett, *The Papers of Alexander Hamilton*, Vol. XXV, 186; Lodge, Henry C., *The Works of Alexander Hamilton*, Vol. VII, 310-311
6 McDonald, Forrest, *Alexander Hamilton*, 352
7 Elkins & McKitrick, *Age of Federalism*, 746 - 747

Alexander Hamilton was horror-struck at the prospect that Aaron Burr could conceivably become President. In a letter to Gouverneur Morris, he revealed his distress.

> The latter in my judgment has no principle public or private — could be bound by no agreement — will listen to no monitor but his ambition; & for this purpose will use the worst part of the community as a ladder to climb to perman(en)t power & an instrument to crush the better part. He is bankrupt beyond redemption. From the elevation of such a man heaven preserve the Country![8]

Aaron Burr had graduated from Princeton College while Alexander Hamilton was still on the island of St. Croix working for Nicholas Cruger, and he had served admirably as both a staff officer and commander of combat units in the Revolution. He studied law and was admitted to the New York Bar six months prior to Alexander Hamilton. In his New York law practice, Burr often had professional contact with Hamilton, even, on occasion, the two men cooperated on some high profile law cases.

Following the untimely death of Burr's wife, he was widely known to have had amorous relations with many women, essentially wherever his travels took him.

Aaron Burr was an accomplished, wily politician. He worked tirelessly and cleverly to promote Republican candidates for offices in New York State. In the election of 1800 for the New York Assembly seats, Burr secretly assembled a list of high-recognition names to run as Republican candidates. He put together a list of all voters in New York City, their political affiliation and how much money they might be willing to contribute to the Republican campaign. His opponent, managing the Federalists, Alexander Hamilton, had great difficulty in assembling a list of Federalist candidates willing to run for office. The state capital having recently been moved to Albany, delegates would have to spend several months each year in Albany and away from their business or employments in New York City to attend the sessions of the Assembly. He found few notable Federalists willing to make this sacrifice.[9]

New York had a requirement that to be eligible to vote, a citizen must own property having a minimum value of $50. Burr promoted the idea of several voters investing together in a small property and each of them claim-

8 Syrett, *The Papers of Alexander Hamilton*, Vol. XXV, 272; Hamilton, John C., *The Works of Alexander Hamilton*, Vol. VI, 497
9 Fleming, *Duel*, 88-89

ing that property as their qualification for voting. Burr also endorsed giving suffrage to freed slaves.[10] His personal friends, Edward Livingstone of New York, Samuel Smith of Maryland and James Linn of New Jersey, all Republican supporters of Jefferson's, each had a swing vote for their state. Fearful of appearing too ambitious of his own interests, Burr did not ask any man for support in winning the Presidency.[11]

The election was decided by narrow margins for each seat but the Republicans won each race. The effect of this stunning victory ensured that the New York legislature would have a Republican majority and therefore the electors of that state would be Republicans. This victory almost certainly gave the Jefferson-Burr team the 1800 election over the incumbent John Adams and General Pinckney.[12]

Nowhere is Burr's dedication to scheming and manipulation more evident than in his conduct in influencing the run-off balloting between himself and Thomas Jefferson. Burr had publicly, if disingenuously, stated his support for Jefferson as President; but he took no action to swing his votes to Jefferson to achieve that end. He told Samuel Smith of Maryland that, while he did not promote himself for the office of President, neither would he refuse it if it were offered to him.[13]

Most of Burr's supporters in the House of Representatives, voting to decide the winner out of this deadlock, were Federalists. Burr continued to walk the fence, striving to offend neither Republicans nor Federalists, and he didn't ask a single swing vote from either party to give his vote to Jefferson to decide the election.

The deadlock continued through thirty-six ballots cast over six days. Eventually, James Bayard of Delaware, appalled at Burr's style, changed his vote from Burr to Jefferson, ending the deadlock. Bayard later stated that the manner in which Burr conducted himself during the run-off "gives me but a humble opinion of the talents of this unprincipled man."[14]

The transfer of power took place peaceably on March 4, 1801. Jefferson began his inaugural address with appropriate modesty "to declare a sincere consciousness that the task is above my talents." Jefferson sought to

---

10 Ibid., 89
11 Fleming, *Duel*, 94
12 Ibid.
13 Chernow, *Alexander Hamilton*, 634
14 Syrett, *The Papers of Alexander Hamilton*, Vol. XII, 487; Vol. XXV, 345

reunify the country that had been polarized by the struggle to elect its Chief Executive,

> We have called by different names brethren of the same principle. We are all Republicans, we are all Federalists. If there be any among us who would wish to dissolve this Union or to change its republican form, let them stand undisturbed as monuments of the safety with which error of opinion may be tolerated where reason is left free to combat it.[15]

To disclose the foreign policy he intended to pursue, he said, "honest friendship with all nations, entangling alliances with none." He gave perhaps the greatest cause for concern for his policies when he evoked, "the support of State governments in all their rights, as the most competent administration of our domestic concerns and the surest bulwark against anti-republican tendencies." This clearly implied an intention to lessen the sovereignty of the central government in favor of making the states more autonomous.

The election of 1800 is often described as marking the ascendancy of the Republican and the demise of the Federalist Party in the political system of the United States. Certainly there are abundant reasons for this viewpoint. Thomas Jefferson had long been recognized as the leader of the Republican interests. He favored a decentralization of power in the Federal Government with a return to the States of a greater degree of autonomy and sovereignty. George Washington had been the standard bearer for the Federalist for two terms as the Chief Magistrate during which period the American government matured from the indefinitely defined organizational concept of the Constitution into a fully functioning and respected governing structure.

The election of 1800 marked not so much the triumph of one political party over another as the beginning of a new phase in the life of the republican government in America. The Republican Party of 1800 was truly a political party in every sense of the word. It drew its strength principally from one geographical area of the country, the South. With the admission of three states into the Union, Vermont in 1791, and Kentucky in 1792, and Tennessee in 1796, the party had received seven additional electoral votes to four for the Federalists. Its advocates did promote a reduction in the power of the central government with more influence to be given to the individual states. The Republicans wanted to see the government take more action to promote the welfare of farming interests and less to the advantage of money interests.

---

15 Jefferson, *The Anas of Thomas Jefferson*, 279

It is difficult to characterize the Federalist collaboration as clearly. In 1786 when they advocated the Constitutional Convention, George Washington, Alexander Hamilton and James Madison knew that the primary deficiency of the Confederation was the weakness of the central government. That Convention endowed the central government with those powers that Alexander Hamilton had broadly defined in a letter to James Duane in 1780, including absolute sovereignty, a public credit respected throughout the world, an undisputed system for raising needed revenues, and a stable financial system. Hamilton, Madison and John Jay had defined the operation of the republican system of government established by the new Constitution in *The Federalist Papers*. During the eight years of the Washington Administration and, to a lesser extent, in the four years of Adams's Presidency, the Federalists had worked to create the structure of government within the constraints of balance defined by the Constitution, to provide unity, strength and permanence to the republic. The Federalists did not draw their advocates from any one section of the country, nor did they cater to any special interest group, although there certainly were accusations to the contrary. In this sense the Federalists were not so much a political party as they were a collaboration of architects intent on fashioning the process of a workable government based on the Constitution. This fundamental task had been, for the most part, completed prior to 1800. Viewed in this light the election of 1800 can be seen as the transition from a constructionist to a politically operated government. The Republicans were to retain the White House for the next twenty-four years, whereas the Federalists, except for a one-term Presidency of John Quincy Adams, were not to resurface as a political entity.

With the ascendancy of the Republican Administration in 1801, Alexander Hamilton realized a further diminishing of his political influence. He remained active in his law practice in New York and in the construction and embellishment of a country house that he named the *Grange*. His estate was situated on thirty-five acres of land on Harlem Heights on the northern end of Manhattan. The vantage point of this elevated property offered a panoramic view of the Hudson River to the west and the Harlem and East Rivers to the east. The name *Grange* recalled the ancestral Hamilton home in Scotland and the sugar plantation owned and operated by his uncle, James Litton, on St. Croix during Hamilton's youth. Hamilton was fully engaged in the design and planning of this estate, as documented in his various letters to Eliza while he was out of town tending to his legal business. There are numerous directions to Eliza including the installation of cedar shingles on the icehouse, and suggestions about the selection of trees for the orchard, borders and decorative purposes. The *Grange* was located nine miles from New York City, so that he could conveniently commute to and from his law office daily.[16]

Although Hamilton was devoted to each of his eight children, he was particularly fond and proud of his eldest son, Philip. Born in 1782, Philip was following in his father's footsteps. He had graduated in 1800 from Columbia College and had gone on to study the law. During a 4th of July celebration he became engaged in an altercation with a Captain Eacker over the honor of Philip's father. A duel challenge was made to settle the issue. In the duel Philip was mortally wounded and was taken back to the city, where he was attended by a physician. Eliza and Alexander came to their son's side, staying with him all night. Philip died at five in the morning. Both parents were beyond consoling. At the funeral Alexander had to be physically supported. Eliza gave birth to their last child, a boy, on June 2, 1802. They named this child Philip, also, and he was called "Little Phil."[17]

As busy as Hamilton was with his law practice and the construction and improvements at the *Grange*, he maintained his life-long interest in politics. Predictably, he approved of little that President Jefferson was doing. Under the pseudonym *Lucius Crassus*, he wrote eighteen papers, entitled *The Examination*, critical of an address to Congress given by Jefferson in December of 1801. The *New York Post* published these articles from December until April 1802. In this speech Jefferson had proposed sweeping changes in the government, consistent with the fears expressed by the Federalists prior to his election. Jefferson proposed to eliminate all internal taxes, including the excise, stamps, auctions, licenses, carriages and refined sugars. The President argued that the great revenues being realized by imposts were adequate to meet the obligations of the government and, in fact, to accelerate the payment of the national debt.[18] Hamilton attacked these tax cuts as rash, imprudently considered and with no foresight as to the difficulty with which these taxes could be re-instituted should the need arise. Hamilton questioned whether,

---

16 Chernow, *Alexander Hamilton*, 640 - 642
17 Hamilton, *Intimate Life of Alexander Hamilton*, 213, 218; Syrett, *The Papers of Alexander Hamilton*, Vol. XXV, 437
18 Syrett, *The Papers of Alexander Hamilton*, Vol. XXV, 446 (note)

if reduced taxes could be sustained, it would not be more wise to reduce both the imposts and internal taxes so as to maintain the taxation base and revenue collection systems. Hamilton gave the opinion that Jefferson's actions were intended to pander to popular opinion rather than managing the nation's best interests.[19]

In 1800, by the *Treaty of San Ildefonso,* France regained the Louisiana territory. Following the defeat of the French army on Hispaniola by revolting slaves and an epidemic of yellow fever, Bonaparte abandoned all ambition of French colonialism in the Caribbean and America. President Jefferson sent James Monroe and Robert Livingston to France to negotiate a new treaty giving America rights to the Mississippi and to the port of New Orleans. Napoleon was fearful that, should war breakout between France and Britain, the United States would forcibly take New Orleans and then would be able to defend it against either British or French Naval attacks. Napoleon saw that the Louisiana Territory was then indefensible; so he decided to offer it to America, for a price. When the American emissaries approached him with an offer to purchase a strip of land along the lower Mississippi as a commercial port, he offered them instead the entire Louisiana Territory. His price was $15 million. Of this, $11,250,000 was to go directly to France and the remainder to be used by the United States government to cover the outstanding obligations that France had to American merchant ships for their losses to French privateers.[20]

In Hamilton's legal career he participated in numerous important cases. When Britain evacuated New York in 1783 he persuaded the courts to abide by the Paris Treaty in dealing with Tories, overcoming the bitter and vengeful spirit of many patriots. He frequently argued cases before the United States Supreme Court, establishing a number of legal precedents. His last important law case came early in 1803. Henry Croswell, editor of a small newspaper in Hudson, New York, was charged with seditious libel of President Jefferson. Croswell had charged in his newspaper that Jefferson paid Callender (the publisher of the Reynolds Pamphlet in 1797) for calling Washington a traitor, a robber and a perjurer; for calling Adams a hoary-headed incendiary; and for most grossly slandering the private characters of men he well knew were virtuous.[21] The article repeated the charge of James Callender that twice Thomas Jefferson had sent money to him to support the publication of the pamphlet, *The Prospect Before Us*. Thomas Jefferson had brushed aside the charge of supporting Callender's publications by saying the money payments were meant merely as charity.[22] Prior to his election as President, Thomas Jefferson had strongly supported the idea of a free press. Once in office, however, he thought that a "few wholesome prosecutions" might be effective in silencing his critics.[23]

The court first convened on the Croswell case on July 11, 1803 with Justice Morgan Lewis presiding. William Van Ness and Elisha Williams were attorneys for the defense along with James Scott of New York and Abraham Van Vechten of Albany. Attorney General Ambrose Spenser, aided by Ebenezer Foote, prosecuted the case. Croswell was convicted and the defense team appealed the decision and prepared to argue the case before the New York Supreme Court. The central issue was whether the truth was an acceptable defense in a libel case. Judge Lewis had ruled on the basis of the common-law doctrine that the truth was not a defense. Croswell was to appear before the Supreme Court on the first day of its next sitting for sentencing. The defense counsel made a motion for a new trial on the grounds that: (1) the jury had been misdirected, and (2) the truth might be given in evidence. The court heard the cause for a new trial. The printed appeal was filed at the Supreme Court on February 4, 1804. The Supreme Court heard the arguments on February 13 and 14 while sitting in Albany. Justices sitting included Morgan Lewis, Chief Justice, James Kent, Brockholst Livingston and Smith Thompson. Although Attorney General Spencer had recently been appointed to the Supreme Court, he chose to prosecute the case together with George Caines. Defense counsel included William Van Ness, Richard Harrison and Alexander Hamilton. In his turn, Hamilton took the floor and gave a monumental defense presentation lasting six hours. Many of the New York legislators had left work at the state capitol and had come to hear Hamilton's defense. They had new libel legislation before them and felt confident that Hamilton would give them much food for thought on the subject.[24]

21 Miller, *Alexander Hamilton and the Growth of the New Nation*, 553
22 Fleming, *The Duel*, 167
23 Knott, *Alexander Hamilton and the Persistence of Myth*, 21
24 Goebel, J., *Law Practice of Alexander Hamilton*, Columbia University Press, 1964, 780 - 799

Hamilton argued that, as the truth may profoundly manifest the intent of the action, the jury should be instructed, to this extent, to consider the law and the fact.

> The Liberty of the press consists, in my idea, in publishing the truth, from good motives and for justifiable ends, though it reflect on government, on magistrates, or individuals. If it be not allowed it excludes the privilege of canvassing men, and our rulers. It is in vain to say, you may canvass measures. This is impossible without the right of looking to men.[25]

Hamilton further cited precedence in English law, showing that Lord Holt believed that presentation of the truth in evidence should be allowed. "This then is a decision as we contend, that not only the interest, but the truth is important and constitute the crime, and nothing has been shown against it."[26] He went further to define the proper role of truth in vindicating libel.

> It is evident that if you cannot apply this mitigated document for which I speak, to the cases of libels here, you must for ever remain ignorant of what your rulers do. I never did think this ought to be; I never did think the truth was a crime; I am glad the day is come in which it is to be decided for my soul has ever abhorred the thought, that a free man dared not speak the truth. I have for ever rejoiced when this question has been brought forward.[27]

In summary the following morning, Hamilton presented fifteen points that he proposed be used to define the law of libel. The first of these points is particularly worthy of mention.

> The Liberty of the press consists in the right to publish with impunity Truth with good motives for justifiable ends though reflecting on government, Magistracy or individuals.[28]

At the conclusion of the hearing the justices were split, two for and two against, so the requested new trial was denied. This ruling gave the prosecutor the right to petition for sentencing on the original trial but no petition was requested, and Croswell was never sentenced. Although technically he had lost the appeal, the New York legislature passed new libel laws that incorporated Hamilton's points. Eventually all states adopted the libel laws of New York, based on the arguments given by Alexander Hamilton during the Supreme Court hearing of February 13 and 14, 1804.

---

25 Ibid., 809
26 Ibid., 818
27 Ibid., 822
28 Van Ness, *Speeches at Full Length of Mr. Van Ness,* 62

Much praise was showered on Hamilton's performance at this hearing. Chancellor Kent said of his argument,

> A more able and eloquent argument was perhaps never heard in any court.[29]

Every school child knows the manner in which Alexander Hamilton met his end in the most notorious duel in American history. This duel was occasioned by a notice in a newspaper, written by a Charles D. Cooper, claiming that General Hamilton and Judge Kent said that they looked upon Mr. Burr to be "a dangerous man, one who ought not to be trusted with the reins of government." Near the closing of the article, Mr. Cooper further stated, "I could detail to you a still more despicable opinion which General Hamilton has expressed of Mr. Burr."[30] Burr took exception to these statements and, through his selected second and friend, William Van Ness, challenged Hamilton to explain, retract or to apologize for these affronts to Burr's honor. Repeated letters handed through seconds were able to resolve nothing and finally Burr and Hamilton agreed to settle the matter on the "field on honor." The place agreed upon was at Weehawken, New Jersey, across the Hudson from Manhattan. The morning of July 11, 1804 was set for the "interview."

The men met early on the morning of July 11. Following the conventional rules the two seconds marked off ten paces, identifying the place for each man to stand. They drew lots for which second was to conduct the interview. Hamilton's second, Nathaniel Pendleton, drew this assignment. Pendleton gave the order, "Present," at which time both men raised their pistols. Hamilton fired first, according to the preponderance of evidence. Burr stumbled, as if hit, but recovered, took aim and fired. He later confided that he had turned his ankle on a stone, causing him to stumble. Almost immediately Hamilton slumped to his knee. Dr. David Hosack was the attending surgeon and, when called, went immediately to Hamilton, finding him half sitting on the ground and still conscious. Hamilton told Hosack, "This is a mortal wound, Doctor." Pendleton later returned to the site and, searching, found a tree branch that had been shot off by Hamilton's bullet, twelve feet high and four feet off to the side of the Hamilton-Burr line, proving that Hamilton had, in fact, "thrown away his first shot."[31]

29 Goebel, *Law Practices of Alexander Hamilton*, 848

30 Syrett, *The Papers of Alexander Hamilton*, Vol. XXVI, 243 - 246

31 Chernow, *Alexander Hamilton*, 702-704 Syrett, H., *Papers of Alexander Hamilton*, Vol. XXVI, 293

His final letter to his wife Eliza, to be sent only in the event of his death, reveals his enduring and lively love for her and their family.

> This letter, my very dear Eliza, will not be delivered to you, unless I shall first have terminated my earthly career; to begin, as I humbly hope from redeeming grace and divine mercy, a happy immortality.

> If it had been possible for me to have avoided the interview, my love for you and my precious children would have been alone a decisive motive. But it was not possible, without sacrifices which would have rendered me unworthy of your esteem. I need not tell you of the pangs I feel, from the idea of quitting you and exposing you to the anguish which I know you would feel. Nor could I dwell on the topic lest it should unman me.

> The consolation of Religion, my beloved, can alone support you; and these you have a right to enjoy. Fly to the bosom of your God and be comforted. With my last idea; I shall cherish the sweet hope of meeting you in a better world.

> Adieu best of wives and best of Women. Embrace all my darling Children for me.[32]

> When Aaron Burr shot and killed Alexander Hamilton, the Southern senator Pierce Butler, no friend of Hamilton and his Federalism, intervened to offer Burr asylum in his plantation, *Hampton.*[33]

Alexander Hamilton's funeral was conducted with full military honors on Saturday, July 14. The casket containing Hamilton's remains was conducted to the Trinity Church at 11 o'clock, preceded by the military escort. Gouverneur Morris gave a summation of Hamilton's life and character. The body was taken to the burial ground of Trinity Church, where the Reverend Bishop Moore conducted the funeral service. During the ceremony, minute guns were fired from the Battery, and in the harbor warships of the United States, England and France fired other minute guns in his honor. It was said of the day, "We have no observations to add. The scene was enough to melt a marble monument."[34]

---

32 Syrett, H., *Papers of Alexander Hamilton, Vol. XXVI*, 293
33 Bell, M., *Major Butler's Legacy*, 95
34 Ibid., 329

EPILOGUE

Alexander Hamilton has been presented by history as an important but enigmatic founding father. He first rose to national prominence in the Constitutional Convention, where he spoke strongly for the form of republican government he felt was best suited to America. He spoke for life terms for the Executive and for Senators, just as for Justices, a recommendation the convention did not adopt. They did, however, hear him speak eloquently, encouraging the delegates to consider the importance of the work they were attempting to establish a republican government. He told them that the world was watching their actions to see if it were possible for men to peacefully establish a republican form of government to rule themselves or whether man would forever be ruled by tyrants who take control of populations forcefully. When the work of the convention was completed and the states assembled conventions to decide whether or not to ratify the constitution, Hamilton joined in collaboration with John Jay and James Madison to write *The Federalist Papers*, that collection of treatises explaining and defending the Constitution that helped to sway at least the Virginia and the New York ratifying conventions and that stands today as a reference for the meaning of the Constitution according to the founding fathers. When the new government began under George Washington as its president, Alexander Hamilton was enlisted as Washington's Secretary of the Treasury. Again he drew the sharp attention of the nation when he introduced to Congress his comprehensive and detailed plan for recovering the credit of the nation and for introducing sufficient stable currency into circulation in the country to spur a vigorous economic growth.

Hamilton's economic reform plan included the consolidation of the debts of the nation and the war-related debts of the states into one federal debt. This consolidation had two aspects that were objectionable to many. First, the certificates issued to the war veterans in consideration for their service was to be paid at par value to the holders of the certificates. Since most veterans had chosen (or been obliged to) sell their certificates to speculators for values as low as twenty cents on the dollar, this move of Hamilton's seemed to many to favor the wealthy over the more deserving veterans; but Hamilton justified his view by championing the inviolability of contracts. Likening the manner in which a country handled its contracts to the "virtue" of the country, Hamilton said that the contract that the certificates represented had to take precedence over the sentimental desire to see the veterans fully paid. Second, the plan to consolidate the war debts of the country with those of the various states, along with the federal government assuming the singular right of taxation over the imports into the country, signaled to commercial states that the central government was exercising its dominance over the states and showing that the sovereignty of the states was to be greatly reduced. This triggered a wide and rancorous reaction over states' rights issues that extended even into the economic concern of the Southern States that the institution of slavery would come under attack by the all-powerful federal government. Finally, Hamilton's plan for chartering The Bank of the United States to stabilize the US currency with the backing of the federal government and for providing a means to get more currency in circulation to spur the economy were viewed as measures to enhance the wealth of the "moneymen" at the expense of the common farmer. All of these charges and fears were ill-founded and the proposals eventually were enacted, contributing to the improved economic health of the country and the improved credit rating abroad. The improved credit of the country generated further economic growth by obtaining better interest rates for American purchases abroad and producing readily available foreign loans at reasonable interest rates for the federal government.

During the 1790s, American politics became polarized between the Federalists who, in a word, were proponents of a strong central government, and Republicans, who were strong states' rights advocates. Alexander Hamilton was viewed by the Republicans, and perhaps rightly so, as the embodiment of Federalism. During the administrations of George Washington and John Adams, Federalist policies were assailed by Republicans as taking the country toward a monarchial government with financial policies that only favored the wealthy. These accusations were answered time and again, showing their falsity and demonstrating that they were distortions of the truth intended to gain political advantage for the Republicans.

With the election of Thomas Jefferson in 1800, the Republicans began a dynasty lasting twenty-four years, followed by the Jacksonian Democrats, with the administration of John Quincy Adams sandwiched in between. During that long period of small government and state sovereignty issues there was little appetite among the controlling party to memorialize the man who epitomized their opposition, regardless of his accomplishments.

Any positive reference to Hamiltonian principles became a political anathema that was diligently avoided by the Republican Presidents of Jefferson, Madison and Monroe and the Democrats, including Andrew Jackson, Martin Van Buren, John Tyler and James Polk.[1] The administration of the last Federalist, John Quincy Adams offered a support of Hamiltonian principles that was tempered by the memory of the contentious relationship that existed between Hamilton and the elder John Adams.

When the Civil War came, Hamilton's politics won out over Jefferson's view of a more tenuous and tentative union. It was finally generally conceded that a lasting union required a strong national government with the attendant diminution of the sovereignty of the individual states. While the republican form of the US government protected the rights of minorities, it did not extend to permitting a small group of states to destroy the union that all of the states were dependent upon. The issue of slavery however had to be resolved. It was a cancer destroying the tissue of the Union and was obviously hypocritical, given the national tenet that "all men are created equal." The South was economically dependent on the profits generated by the low labor cost of slavery and its elimination was certain to bring an instant and

---

1 Knott, Stephen, *Alexander Hamilton and the Persistence of Myth*, University Press of Kansas, 2002, 27

deep depression. Neither side was willing or able to expend the funds and efforts to peaceably overcome the burden of emancipation, but they ended up expending 600,000 lives to settle the question. The ensuing economic hardship and political occupation of the South lasted for generations, along with the racial problem that is only beginning to find resolution some one hundred and fifty years after the conflict.

The "Great Emancipator" himself, Abraham Lincoln, embraced and implemented much of Hamiltonian politics but was strangely silent on his assessment of the man.[2] It was as though the pall that had been cast over the memory of Alexander Hamilton by his detractors presented too great a political hazard for Lincoln to risk by openly praising his contributions to the American government.

Even in the light of vindication of Hamilton's politics, however, his fame and achievements were not permitted an unbiased popular assessment. Hamilton's political philosophy had been so badly distorted that opponents continued to slander his memory either by invoking the weary argument that Hamilton was working to install a monarchial government in place of America's representative democracy, or by arguing that Hamilton's Federalism favored the wealthy at the expense of the working masses. The fallacy in this opposition argument is easily seen in the record. Hamilton's writings are abundant where he promoted the benefits of a representative democracy. In his financial plan, created while he was the Secretary of the Treasury, Hamilton gave investment direction to the wealth of the country to restore the public credit, create a stable currency and to power a strong and growing economy. No amount of distortion can alter the record that the objective of Hamilton's public life was to assure that America would realize its potential for greatness in the world and that the American experiment in republican government would succeed.

Alexander Hamilton and the Federalists gave to the nascent republic a Constitution that would provide stability; they formed a strong central government that gave unity, security and permanence to the country; and, they introduced a financial system that regained for the country a high public credit and spurred a robust and growing economy. These three accomplishments of Alexander Hamilton and the Federalists provided the republic with a solid foundation and beginning.

2 Ibid, 53 - 55

From this auspicious start it was the opportunity and responsibility of each succeeding generation to mold and shape the government to best serve its needs and ambitions. In the Constitutional Convention when the extent of powers to be delegated to the federal legislature was being discussed, Pierce Butler of South Carolina requested that a more definitive explanation be given of the terms used in the proposed article. He stated that the vagueness of the wording hampered his ability to decide on the merits of the clause. Nathaniel Gorham of Massachusetts said that it was the vagueness that gave merit to the clause. He explained that the convention was establishing general principles; and suggested that the legislature would, in the course of time and under specific tests, define precisely the extent of their legislative powers. Likewise, the original structure and fiscal policies of the government were consigned to subsequent generations to trim and define to suit the necessities of the era.

For the unity, the soundness and the promise of the beginning of the republic, Alexander Hamilton and the Federalists should be remembered. For the correctness and errors of the decisions of succeeding generations, those generations alone are to be applauded or censured.

ACKNOWLEDGEMENTS

In the preparation of this book, the author recognizes the benefit of having such a wealth of information available in the form of biographies, histories of the era and primary sources. The author is particularly indebted to Harold C. Syrett, editor of *The Papers of Alexander Hamilton*, for making so conveniently available the vast amount of Hamilton's writings that provide unambiguous evidence of his position on so many critical issues of the times. The preparation of this book relied to a large extent on the writings contained in Syrett's volumes.

The author also acknowledges indebtedness to works complementary to Syrett's volumes, including John C. Hamilton's *The Works of Alexander Hamilton*, and Henry Cabot Lodge's compilation of Hamilton's writings under the same title. These works were found in the Library of American Civilization.

The positive endorsement of my manuscript and the constructive suggestions made by Dr. John Wiseman, Professor of History at Frostburg State University, are gratefully recognized. The library at Frostburg State University (FSU), under the direction of Dr. David Gillespie, has provided the lion's share of resources used in this work. Through their collection of the compiled writings of Hamilton, Washington, Jefferson and Madison, in addition to the large amount of data available through their *Library of American Civilization* microfiche, the author was able to use primary sources of information extensively. The Inter Library Loan Department at FSU was most helpful in acquiring reference materials from institutional and other university librar- ies across the country. Special thanks go to Kathy Showalter, Rhonda Hensel and Marje Aylor for their assistance that has been most helpful throughout this effort. The outstanding support provided by Pamela Williams of the Frostburg library in finding and providing library resources, proofreading the manuscript and helpful suggestions too numerous to define have been a major assistance that was gratefully received.

My sister Mabel Murray has also provided important assistance in the form of proof reading and that essential element of writing, encouragement. My good friend, David Shave, through our many discussions and his insight- ful suggestions, has lightened the task of this writing more than he can guess. Finally, and by no means the least helpful, has been the constant presence and support of my wife, JoAnn. She was always available to discuss impor- tant points and to offer constructive suggestions in her characteristically delicate way. My lasting and heartfelt gratitude is extended to all.

Bibliography

Books

Abbott, Wilbur C., *New York in the American Revolution*, C. Scribner's Sons, New York, 1929

Adams, Abigail, *New Letters of Abigail Adams*, Greenwood Press, West Port, Conn., 1973

Adams, Henry, *The Life of Albert Gallatin*, Peter Smith, New York, 1879

Baker, Leonard, *John Marshall, A Life in Law*, Macmillan, New York, 1974

Beeman, Richard P., *Patrick Henry — A Biography*, McGraw-Hill Book Co., New York, 1974

Bell, Malcolm, Jr., *Major Butler's Legacy — Five Generations of a Slaveholding Family*, University of Georgia Press, Athens, 1987

Bemis, Samuel Flagg, *Jay's Treaty*, New Haven, 1962

Bobrick, Benson, *Angel In the Whirlwind*, Simon & Schuster, New York, 1997

Bowen, Catherine Drinker, *Miracle at Philadelphia*, Atlantic Monthly Press Book, Boston, 1966

Boyd, Julian, Oberg, Barbara, (ed.), *The Papers of Thomas Jefferson*, Vol. 1–31, Princeton University Press, Princeton, 1950–2004

Brands, H. W., *The First American*, Anchor Books, 2002

Brandt, Clare, *An American Aristocracy; The Livingstons*, Doubleday Publisher, New York 1986

Burrows, Edwin G., Mike Wallace, *Gotham: A History of New York City to 1898*, Oxford University Press, New York 1999

Champagne, Roger J., *Alexander McDougall and the American Revolution in New York*, Union College Press, Schenectady, 1975

Chernow, Ron, *Alexander Hamilton*, Penguin Press, New York, 2004

Cooke, Jacob E., *Alexander Hamilton — A Biography*, Charles Scribner's Sons, New York, 1982

Cooke, Jacob E., *Tench Coxe and the Early Republic*, University of North Carolina Press, Chapel Hill, 1978

Cooke, Jacob, ed., *The Reports of Alexander Hamilton*, Harper & Row, New York, 1964

Crow, Jeffrey J., Tise, Larry E. (eds.), *The Southern Experience in the American Revolution*, University of North Carolina Press, Chapel Hill, 1978

Cunningham Jr., Noble, E., *The Jeffersonian Republicans, The Formation of Party Organization, 1789-1801*, University of North Carolina Press, Chapel Hill, 1957

Cunningham, Noble E., *Jefferson vs. Hamilton*, St. Martin's Press, Bedford, 2000

DeConde, Alexander, *Entangling Alliance*, Duke University Press, Durham, 1958

Dill, Alonzo T., *George Wythe–Teacher of Liberty*, Virginia Independence Bicentennial Commission, Williamsburg, 1979

Dunn, Richard S., *Sugar and Slaves: The Rise of the Planter Class in the English East Indies, 1624-1713*, University of North Carolina Press, Chapel Hill, 1972

Elkins, Stanley & McKitrick, Eric, *The Age of Federalism, The Early American Republic, 1788–1800*. Oxford University Press, 1993.

Ellis, Joseph J., *Founding Brothers*, Vintage Books, New York, 2000

Farrand, Max, *The Framing of the Constitution of the United States*, Yale University Press, New Haven, 1913

Ferguson, E. James, *The Power of the Purse*, University of North Carolina Press, Chapel Hill, 1961

Fitzpatrick, John C. (ed.), *The Writings of George Washington*, United States Government Printing Office, Washington, D. C., Vol. 1–39, 1932 - 1944

Flexner, James, *The Young Hamilton*, Little, Brown & Co., Boston, 1978

Ford, Paul L. (ed.), *Writings of Thomas Jefferson*, G. P. Putnam, New York, 1896

Ford, W. C. (ed.), *The Writings of George Washington*, Vol. XIV, G. T. Putnam's & Sons, New York, 1893

Grotius, (Campbell, A. C., trans), *The Rights of War and Peace*, M. W. Dunne, Washington, 1901

Hamilton, Alexander, *Papers of Alexander Hamilton*, ed. Harold C Syrett, vols. I-XXVI, Columbia University Press, New York 1961-1976.

Hamilton, Alexander, John Jay and James Madison, *The Federalist Papers*, New American Library, New York, 1961Ed. Robert Scigliano, New York 1910

Hamilton, Allan McLane, *The Intimate Life of Alexander Hamilton*, Charles Scribner's Sons, New York, 1910

Hamilton, John C. (ed.), *The Works of Alexander Hamilton*, 7 Volumes, John Trow, Printer, New York, 1850

Harper, John L., *American Machiavelli: Alexander Hamilton and the Origins of U. S. Foreign Policy*, Cambridge University Press, Cambridge, 2004

Hendrickson, Robert, *Hamilton*, (2 vols.) Mason/Charter, New York 1976

Hume, David, *Essays Moral, Political and Literary*, Liberty Classics, Eugene F. Miller (ed.) (Indianapolis, 1985)

Jefferson, Thomas, *The ANAS of Thomas Jefferson*, Franklin B. Sawvel (ed.), Da Capo Press, New York, 1970

Jones, Thomas, *History of New York During the Revolutionary War*, (2 vols.) New York Times, New York, 1879

Kalm, Peter, *Travels in North America, (1753–1761)*, 2 Vols., Imprint Society, Barre, Mass., 1972

Ketcham, Ralph, *James Madison, A Biography*, University Press of Virginia, Charlottesville, 1992

Knott, Stephen F., *Alexander Hamilton & The Persistence of Myth*, University Press of Kansas, 2002

Larsen, Harold, *Alexander Hamilton: Facts and Fiction of His Early Years*, Wm & Mary Quarterly, 91 (April 1952) 139-51

Latourette, Kenneth S., *A History of Christianity*, Harper & Brothers, New York, 1953

Leckie, Robert, *George Washington's War*, Harper Perennial, New York, 1993

Lee, Robert E. (ed.), *The Revolutionary War Memoirs of General Henry Lee*, Da Capo Press, New York, 1998

Locke, John, (Goldie, Mark, ed.), *Political Essays*, Cambridge University Press, New York, 1997

Lodge, Henry Cabot (ed.), *The Works of Alexander Hamilton*, 12 Volumes, 2nd Edition, G. P. Putnam sons, New York, 1904

Madison, James, *The Papers of James Madison*, Mattern, D. B., et al (ed.), University of Virginia Press, Charlottesville, Vol. 1–17, 1962–1991

Martyn, Charles, *The Life of Artemus Ward*, A. Ward, New York, 1921

McCullough, David, *John Adams*, Simon & Schuster, New York, 2001

McDonald, Forrest, *Alexander Hamilton*, W. W. Norton & Co., New York, 1979

McDonald, Forrest, *The Presidency of Thomas Jefferson*, University of Kansas Press, Lawrence, KA, 1976

Miller, John D., *Alexander Hamilton: Portrait in Paradox*, Harper, New York, 1959

Minot, George Richards, *The History of the Insurrections in Massachusetts*, James W. Burditt & Co. Publishers, Boston, 1810

Mitchell, Broadus, *Alexander Hamilton: Youth to Maturity 1755-1788*, The Macmillan Co., New York, 1957

Mitchell, Broadus, Mitchell, Louise P., *A Biography of the Constitution of the United States*, Oxford University Press, New York, 1964

Morris, Gouverneur, (ed. Beatrix Cary Davenport), *A Diary of the French Revolution*, Vol. I & II, Greenwood Press, Westport, CT, 1972

Morris, Richard B., *Great Presidential Decisions*, Lippincott, Philadelphia, 1969

Oliver, Frederick Scott, *Alexander Hamilton An Essay on American Union*, G. P. Putnam, New York, 1925

Postlethwayt, Malachy, *The Universal Dictionary of Trade and Commerce*, Fourth Edition, London 1774

Ramsing, H. U., *Alexander Hamilton og hansmodrene Slaegt. Tidsbilleder fra Dansk Vest-Indiens Barndom, Personalhistorik Tidsskrift*, 59 de Aargang, 10 Rekke, 6 Bind (1939). Trans. Solvejg Vahl, MS of trans.

Randall, Willard S., *Alexander Hamilton–A Life*, Harper-Collins, New York, 2003

Remini. Robert V., *Andrew Jackson and the Bank War*, W. W. Norton, New York, 1967

Ritcheson, Charles, R., *Aftermath of the Revolution*, Southern Methodist University Press, Dallas, 1969

Rossiter, Clinton, 1787, *The Grand Convention*, The Macmillan Co., New York, 1966

Rutland. Robert Allen, *The Ordeal of the Constitution*, University of Oklahoma Press, Norman Oklahoma, 1966

Slaughter, Thomas P., *The Whiskey Rebellion*, Oxford University Press, New York, 1986

Smith, Richard Norton, *Patriarch: George Washington and the New American Nation*, Houghton Mifflin, Boston, 1993

Spaulding, E. Wilder, *His Excellency George Clinton, - Critic of the Constitution*, Ira Friedman, Inc., Port Washington, L. I., New York, 1938

Stinchcombe, William C., et al, (eds.), *The Papers of John Marshall*, University of North Carolina Press, Chapel Hill, 1979

Stokes, I. N. Phelps, *The Iconography of Manhattan Island*, Arno Press, 1498–1909

Stourzh, Gerald, *Alexander Hamilton and the Idea of Republican Government*, Stanford University Press, Stanford, CA, 1970

Syrett, Harold C., (ed.), *The Papers of Alexander Hamilton*, Vol. I–XXVI, Columbia University Press, New York, 1962

Taylor, Robert L. (ed.), *Papers of John Adams*, Harvard University Press, Cambridge, 1977

Thomas, Charles Marion, *American Neutrality in 1793: A Study in Cabinet Government*, AMS Press, New York, 1967

Van Doren, Carl, *Secret History of the American Revolution*, Viking Press, New York, 1941

Vance, Clarence H. (ed.), *Letters of a Westchester Farmer*, White Plains, 1930

Van Ness, Wm., *Speeches at Full Length of Mr. Van Ness*, G. & R. Waite, New York, 1804

Whittemore, Charles P., *A General of the Revolution: John Sullivan of New Hampshire*, Columbia University Press, New York, 1961

Zahniser, Marvin R., *Charles Cotesworth Pinckney*, University of North Carolina Press, Chapel Hill, 1967

JOURNALS

Smithsonian, Lindsay, Merrill, *Pistols Shed Light on Famed Duel*, November 1976, 94-98.

The Independent Reflector, *The American Magazine*, Livingston, William (ed. Milton Klein), New York, 1752-1753

Wm & Mary Qrtly, Schachner, Nathan, *Alexander Hamilton: Viewed by His Friends: The Narratives of Robert Troup and Hercules Mulligan*, 3 set 4 (1947) 203-25.

Wm & Mary Qrtly, *Alexander Hamilton, Melancton Smith and the Ratification of the Constitution in New York*, July1967, Robin Brooks, 339-358

Wm & Mary Qrtly, Coxe, *Tench Coxe, Hamilton & the Encouragement of American Manufactures* July 1975, Jacob Cooke, 369–92

Wm & Mary Qrtly, *Federal Taxation and the Adoption of the Whiskey Excise*, 3rd Series, Vol. 25, No. 1 (January, 1968)

Wm & Mary Qrtly, 28 (1971) 637. *Cooke, Jacob E., Dinner at Jefferson's, A Note on Jacob E. Cooke's, The Compromise of 1790.*

WEBSITES

1998 Avalon Project, *An Act Imposing Duties on Tonnage*, www.edu/lawweb/avalon/statutes.html

Gateway New Orleans 2004, *Louisiana Purchase*, http://gatewayno.com/history/La-Purchase.html

Jefferson, Thomas, *1801 Inaugural Speech*, Junto Society Presidential Inaugural Speeches, www.juntosociety.com

Madison, *Notes of Debates in the Federal Convention of 1787*, http://www.teachingamericanhistory.org/convention/debates

Richards, Mark David, *Touring Hidden Washington*, www.dcwatch.com/richards/0106.htm, 2001

INDEX